Villains of Yore

By

D. Lawrence-Young

Copyright © D. Lawrence-Young (2020)

The right of D. Lawrence-Young to be identified as author of this work has been asserted by him in accordance with section 77 and 78 of the Copyright, Designs and Patents Act 1988.

All rights reserved. No part of this publication may be reproduced, stored in a retrieval system, or transmitted in any form or by any means, electronic, mechanical, photocopying, recording, or otherwise, without the prior permission of the publishers.

Any person who commits any unauthorised act in relation to this publication may be liable to criminal prosecution and civil claims for damages.

A CIP catalogue record for this title is available from the British Library.

ISBN 978-1-912964-41-3 (Paperback)

www.cranthorpemillner.com

First Published (2020)

Cranthorpe Millner Publishers

Historical Novels by D. Lawrence Young

Fawkes and the Gunpowder Plot

Tolpuddle: A Novel of Heroism

Marlowe: Soul'd to the Devil

Will Shakespeare: Where was He?*

The Man Who Would be Shakespeare

Will the Real William Shakespeare Please Step Forward**

Of Guns and Mules

Of Guns, Revenge and Hope

Arrows Over Agincourt

Sail Away from Botany Bay

Anne of Cleves: Unbeloved

Catherine Howard: Henry's Fifth Failure

Six Million Accusers: Catching Adolf Eichmann

Mary Norton: Soldier Girl

Two Bullets in Sarajevo

King John: Two-Time Loser

*Reissued as: Welcome to London, Mr. Shakespeare

**Reissued as: Who Really Wrote Shakespeare?

Go Spy Out the Land

Entrenched

Emma Hamilton: Mistress of Land and Sea

My Jerusalem Book (Editor)

As: David L. Young

Of Plots and Passions

Communicating in English (Textbook)

The Jewish Emigrant from Britain: 1700-2000 (contrib. chapter)

Website: www.dly-books.weebly.com

Contents

Introduction 1

Chapter 1 5

  Richard of Pudlicott and The Great Crown Jewels Robbery, 1303 5

Chapter 2 43

  Mary 'Moll Cutpurse' Frith (1584–1659) 43

Chapter 3 57

  'Colonel' Thomas Blood (1618–1680) 57

Chapter 4 89

  Mary Carleton (1642–1673) 89

Chapter 5 106

  Jonathan Wilde: 'Thief-Taker General' (1682-1725) ... 106

Chapter 6 126

  Elizabeth 'Moll' Adkins King (1696-1747) 126

Chapter 7 137

  Mary 'Jenny Diver' Young (1700-1741) 137

Chapter 8 170

  Jack Sheppard (1702-1724) 170

Chapter 9 194

  Dick Turpin (1705-1739) 194

  Laurence Shirley, ... 231

  4th Earl Ferrers (1720-1760) 231

Chapter 11 248

William 'Deacon' Brodie (1741-1788) 248

Chapter 12 265

Isaac 'Ikey' Solomon (1787-1850) 265

Chapter 13 285

William Burke (1792-1829) & William Hare (c.1792-after 1829): 285

'The Body Snatchers' 285

Chapter 14 312

Charles Peace (1832-1879) 312

The "Banner Cross Killer" 312

Chapter 15 336

Amelia Dyer: 'The Ogress of Reading' 336

(1837-1896) 336

Chapter 16 349

Adam Worth: 'The Napoleon of the Criminal World' .. 349

(1844-1902) 349

Chapter 17 366

The Forty Elephants (c.1950) 366

About the Author 380

Bibliography 381

Dedicated, and with apologies, to my wife, Beverley, who has had to share our house with some of the most villainous characters she has heard about.

Introduction

Why is there such an ongoing interest in reading about crimes and villainy? What makes a normal law-abiding citizen shell out several pounds or dollars in order to spend many happy hours reading about how a criminal robbed, forged and even murdered in order to obtain their ill-gotten gains? Is it because the above-mentioned reader has a secret empathy with the villain who is trying to fool the authorities? Does reading about 'baddies' provide a vicarious source of excitement in the reader's otherwise hum-drum life?

In this book you will meet all sorts of dubious characters: men and women, robbers and highwaymen, young and old, high class and low, dubious coffee-shop owners and corrupt public officials - in other words, a whole world of people who broke the law. They appear here in chronological order, from Richard Pudlicott who stole King Edward I's treasury in 1303, to the 'Forty Elephants' gang who raided Britain's shops and department stores for several decades until the 1950s.

Most of the villains included in this book were not murderers. Usually, if they killed anyone, it was as a 'by-product' of their thieving and other illegal activities. Several of the villains dealt with here were not at all like the mythical image that developed following their demise – usually at the end of the hangman's rope. Dick Turpin was not a romantic highwayman who galloped over the hills from London to York on his faithful horse, Black Bess. He was a ruthless robber, horse thief and killer. Colonel Blood was not merely a dark curly-haired villain who tried to steal the crown jewels. He was a man who had an obsession about killing the Duke of Ormonde. Mary Carleton did not just like to dress up in fine clothes and pass herself off as European royalty. She deliberately exploited her feminine wiles and her gullible victims' hopes in order to live the high life as she defrauded them of large sums of money.

    The lives and exploits of several of the villains in this book have come down to us today not only through history but also through the pages of literature, films and YouTube. Daniel Defoe based his book *Moll Flanders* on Moll King, a well-known coffee-house owner who played an important role in London's 18th century underworld. Deacon Brodie's nefarious activities in Edinburgh were used by Robert Louis Stevenson in his classic *The Strange Case of Dr Jekyll and Mr Hyde*. The story of Adam Worth, nicknamed 'the Napoleon of the criminal world', was used by Sir Arthur Conan-Doyle to provide Sherlock Holmes with an arch-enemy, Professor Moriarty. In addition, films, long and short, have been made about the exploits of Jonathan Wilde, Colonel Thomas Blood and the murderous body snatchers, Burke and Hare, among others. Even opera has been appropriated to educate us about the wicked ways of the underworld. The story of the infamous 18th century pickpocket, Jenny Diver, was central to John Gay's 1728 musical work, *The Beggar's Opera*.

As for this book, all of the stories here are genuine; that is, the plots and their conclusions stay true to the documented facts. However, since none of the characters featured within these pages recorded their conversations, I have taken the liberty of inventing them. I have done my best however, to keep them in line with the criminal and the tone of the crime that was about to be or was indeed committed.

Finally, for the source material of this book, please refer to the bibliography at the end. A word must be said here, however, about one of the sources used – *The Newgate Calendar*. This collection of stories, allegedly based on the truth, was subtitled *The Malefactors' Bloody Register* and first appeared in the early 18th century. It was reissued by different publishers who wished to cash in on the public's bloodlust and love of criminal sensationalism for over a century. While the *Calendar* contained stories about many of the villains mentioned in these pages, some of its goriest details have to be read with a pinch of salt. This dramatically written collection even contained a section, 'The Innocent Wrongly Accused', which refers to thirty unfortunate souls, one-third of whom were indeed wrongly accused and punished. Like their guilty counterparts they were hanged on the infamous Tyburn Tree, the site where many villains were sent to meet their Maker over several hundred years. Today this grim relic of the past is no longer visible, but it has been commemorated by a plaque set in the ground near London's busy Marble Arch.

David Lawrence-Young
Jerusalem, April 2020

Chapter 1

Richard of Pudlicott and The Great Crown Jewels Robbery, 1303

King Edward I

In August 1963 a gang of fifteen men took half-an-hour to rob a Royal Mail train near Mentmore, Buckinghamshire, on its way from Glasgow to London. Apart from assaulting the train driver and his 'secondman', the gang resorted to no other violence or use of firearms. Eventually most of the gang were arrested and convicted, but most of the stolen money was never recovered. In all, the gang stole over two-

and-a-half million pounds, worth about forty-one million seven hundred and fifty thousand pounds today.

Dramatic as the above robbery may seem, it did not compare with the Great Crown Jewel Robbery which took place at Westminster Abbey in April 1303. There, a merchant turned criminal, Richard Pudlicott and his handpicked gang of four, took THREE DAYS to steal jewels, plate, gold and silver worth, at that time, about a hundred thousand pounds from the treasury of King Edward. Today this loot would be worth well over several hundred million pounds! This is how it happened.

*

Knock! Knock!

"Go away!"

Knock! Knock!

"Go away, I said."

"But I've got a message from the king!" a muffled voice came through the heavy oak door.

"Well, come back in an hour. He's sleeping now," the guard called back.

"But it's urgent! I've just arrived from London," the voice shouted. "I was told to tell him as soon as I arrived."

"Christ and all His Saints," the guard swore as he lifted his fat body out of his chair and walked towards the door. "This had better be good," he said to the mud-spattered man standing by the now open door, "or you'll have me to deal with. Anyway, who are you?"

The messenger ignored his question. "Where is he?" he asked, puffing slightly. "Where's the king?"

"You answer my question first. Who are you?"

"A messenger from the King's court in London. Now where is the King?"

The guard hearing the words 'the King's court in London' was somewhat surprised, and stepped aside as the messenger again demanded to know where his royal master was.

"At the end of the corridor," the guard pointed quickly. "But make sure you knock first and wait for permission to enter, or you'll find yourself swinging off the nearest tree."

The messenger did not look impressed by this threat and immediately set off down the dark corridor. He stopped at a door where two sconces holding barely glowing torches smoked away on each side, their fumes adding to the thick and gloomy atmosphere. The messenger knocked on the door and waited impatiently. He had just ridden nearly four-hundred-and-fifty miles. His arse, thighs, and in fact his whole body, was sore and he felt in need of a good soak in a tub. But now he had to face his King and tell him some terrible news.

There was no answer from his knocking. He knocked again. Again, no answer. For his third attempt he used the heavy hilt of his sword. The sound echoed down the corridor. He heard the guard inside swear and then the sound of a heavy chair being pushed back. This was followed by a rough scraping, and as the door opened, he found himself facing another similarly overweight guard. But this one had his sword in hand.

"Who are you and what do you want?" he asked, thrusting out his chin.

"I'm Thomas of Aylesbury," the still sweating messenger replied, "and I've just arrived from London. I've been told…"

"Thomas of Aylesbury? One of the King's chief advisors? Well, why didn't you say so? And you've just come from London? What have you got to say to the king?"

"I cannot tell you," Aylesbury replied. "I must speak to the King personally."

The guard stepped aside, and Thomas stepped into the torch-lit chamber. He could see that his King was lying in a wide bed. He was not alone. Thomas could make out another, shorter shape parallel to the King under the maroon counterpane.

He was not looking forward to passing on his message to King Edward. His Majesty had a short temper and did not suffer fools gladly. Only last month the King had had a scribe soundly whipped for accidentally setting fire to an important document. The long piece of parchment had caught fire while the man had been holding it near a flickering candle. Half was destroyed before the King in his fury had thrown a flask of wine over it and doused most of the flames. That scribe had been Thomas's half-brother.

Just as the guard was about to ask Thomas what his message was, the messenger noticed the smaller shape in the bed start moving. Suddenly a tousled mass of fair hair and a plump face appeared above the bedcovers. He saw her pull herself up a little, and then noticing the two men standing there looking at her, she quickly pulled the maroon counterpane up to cover her naked breasts before sliding back down into the bed. Her movements woke the King up, and from where he was waiting, Thomas could see the other long ridge move about in the bed. Then the King's head appeared out of the covers in a similar way to that of his mistress a minute earlier. He blinked, ran his fingers through his long hair as he tried to concentrate his gaze on his messenger.

"Thomas? Thomas of Aylesbury?" he asked as he squinted at the messenger still standing at the far end of the chamber.

"Yes, Sire."

"What are you doing here?" the King asked as he sat up. He shivered for a moment. "Here," he said to the guard. "Give me a jacket. It's always cold in this damned country. I don't know how those Scottish bastards can live here all the time."

Pulling the jacket over his shoulders he turned to face the faithful Aylesbury. "Yes, Thomas. What is it? It had better be good news for which you have woken me up in the middle of the night. Now, come on, man. Out with it."

Thomas approached the bed. But not too close. He had heard how the King had punched a palace servant who had crossed his path.

"Sire," he began quietly, "there's been a robbery in London. A big one and…"

"And that's why you have woken me up? To tell me about a robbery in London? And have you ridden all the way up here just for that? There're always robberies in London. And elsewhere," he added as an afterthought.

"Yes, Sire. No, Sire. It wasn't just an ordinary robbery, Sire. Your… your crown jewels have been stolen," Thomas continued quietly.

"*My crown jewels?*" King Edward, the Hammer of the Scots, shouted. "*Are you mad?*"

"No, Sire. It's true, Sire. They were stolen a few days ago. As soon as it was discovered, my fellow advisors suggested that seeing how much was stolen, I was to rush up to you here in Scotland and tell you about it and…"

"My jewels in the Abbey? Westminster Abbey?"

Thomas nodded.

"All of them?"

Thomas nodded again. And as he did so, the first King Edward of England since the invasion of 1066 let out a great cry. As he did so the tousled head of his mistress, or at least, the one for this night, reappeared from among the bedclothes. Taking care to pull the thick counterpane up to her neck, she turned to face her royal master.

"Did I hear correctly, Sire? Have they stolen your jewellery?" she asked.

"Yes, yes, Goddammit!" the King roared. "According to Thomas, here, all of it."

"But, Sire…" she began, but was not allowed to continue.

"Go on, get out of here," the King shouted at her and pushed her out of the bed, slapping her smooth rump as she tumbled to the floor. She picked herself up and rushed naked to the far end of the chamber, her arms wrapped tightly round her pale plump body. Thomas and the guard watched as she wriggled naked into a heavy robe and ran off to a small side chamber. She disappeared from sight, slamming the door behind her, but as she did so, her robe caught on the door handle. As she opened the door again to pull her robe around her, the three men were treated to the sight of the now less than seductive body of Mistress Jane. Grabbing her robe, she whirled around and again slammed the door after her, this time even more loudly than before.

"Well, Thomas of Aylesbury, now that you have feasted your eyes on the flesh of that whore," the King said, "tell me about this robbery."

"Sire, it was like this," the messenger began now facing the King and doing his utmost to speak quietly and calmly. "It appears that some men – we don't know who and how many yet, Sire – broke into the crypt in Westminster Abbey. It seems, Sire, that they smashed one of the windows above where the jewels were kept and then somehow slid down into the crypt, where they proceeded to ransack your royal treasury."

"And nobody saw or heard them?"

"No, Sire, or if they did, they are not admitting to it."

"But the Abbey is full of monks. Did not *they* see or hear anything?"

Thomas shook his head. "No, Sire. The robbers must have worked very quietly or managed to distract everyone's attention away from that part of the Abbey. I don't know how, Sire. For surely they must have made quite a noise as they broke open all the coffers and chests that are stored there."

"And they took all the cups and goblets and relics? All of them?" the incredulous King asked quietly.

"Yes, Sire. All the precious jewels, gold and silver coins and gold and silver plate. Everything."

"And nothing was left behind?"

Thomas shook his head. "No, Sire. Well, that's not exactly true, Sire. They did drop a few of the smaller jewels and pearls when they left, but nothing of great value." Thomas lowered his head and waited for his master's calm to once again break into a storm. He had seen this happen more than once before and he was ready for it. But it never happened. King Edward of England and Wales was too stunned for rage. He fell back onto his pillow and lay without moving.

Thomas thought that his news may have killed his royal master, he was lying there so still. Thomas looked at the bed and wondered what he should do next. He then looked at the guard in the corner, but he stood there motionless as if he were one of the carvings on the palace walls. Then Thomas saw his King's long body suddenly jerk under the decorated counterpane.

Now what? he thought. *Do I leave now or not?* He looked at the guard again, but the man just remained standing there impassively.

For want of something to do, Thomas walked over to the window and opened one of the shutters. They grey dawn of Linlithgow seeped into the room as if reluctant to whisk away the torch-lit gloom of the King's chamber.

Suddenly Thomas's attention was distracted from the castle courtyard. Out of the corner of his eye, he saw his royal master sit up in bed and pull his jacket even tighter around him.

"This is what we are going to do," the King said in a harsh, determined voice. "I must remain here in this accursed country to finish grinding down these infernal Scots. You, Thomas, will return to London and see about catching these thieves and having them punished. That is," he added, "if you haven't started already."

"Yes, Sire, and we have started looking for them," Thomas said, happy to think he would not have to remain in the presence of his violent and revengeful king.

"However, before you go, I will give you a letter to take back to London with you. Come back and see me later this morning."

Thomas nodded, bowed and left the room. He was looking forward to washing himself after his long ride before tucking into a good meal and a long drink.

At least, when you work for the King you dine well, he thought, and walked off in the direction of the castle's stables. There he would find his saddlebags which contained a fresh set of clothes and a dry pair of boots.

At the same time that Thomas of Aylesbury was wondering what he would have for breakfast and how good the ale was in this godforsaken part of Scotland, his royal master was wondering how it had happened that robbers had broken into his supposedly well-guarded crypt and escaped with all of his precious treasury. One of his first thoughts was, *how am I going to pay my army here if I don't have the money?*

This is how the robbery had happened.

1302. It was a raw and grey late October afternoon in the centre of London. A strong wind was blowing in from the west and with it came patches of squally rain. Very few people were out in the streets; just those who had urgent business, and of course, the city's ever-present gangs of villains, the homeless and the unfortunates down on their luck.

That morning, one of those unfortunates, Richard of Pudlicott, had also been wandering around the streets of the capital, but now he was now sitting in a dark corner in the Black Bull nursing a tankard of warm ale. His gnarled hands were wrapped around the tankard, and stared at it, as if hoping that somehow the action would warm his whole body, not just his hands. And as he sat there on a wooden stool hunched over the table, he kept asking himself how he had fallen so low.

After I left Oxford, I was a prosperous wool merchant, he thought. *Me, Richard of Pudlicott, or Dick Pudlecote as my friends, who no longer want to know me, had called me. I had been a respectable wool merchant and on good terms with all the other wool merchants in London, Calais and Flanders. They couldn't buy enough wool from me. Fine English wool. The best that there was. But now look at me. Sitting here in this rotten tavern escaping from the wind and the rain.*

He smiled to himself for a split second. *Well, at least it's warmer and dryer here than that miserable hovel off Eastcheap near St. Swithin's Church that I now call my home. And at least I don't have to listen to the whining voice of my wife and the screams of my three brats.* He wrapped his hands even tighter around his now almost empty tankard. And just as he was feeling thus, he felt a friendly clap on the back. He looked up and found himself looking at the fleshy face and the sharp, restless eyes of his friend, William Palmer.

"Ho! Master Pudlicott. What are you looking so miserable for? Don't you know you are not allowed to look like this in a tavern, especially with a tankard of ale in front of you?"

Richard pushed his tankard over to where William was now sitting. "Look at it," he said. "It's nearly empty and I've barely got enough money left to buy another."

"Fear not, my friend. Let me buy you one, and one for myself."

"No, Will, I can't. You bought me a drink last time we met. I want to…"

"Hush yourself, man. I'll get you one now, and when your luck changes, you'll buy one for me. And there's the end of it."

Five minutes later, the ragged wool merchant and the shrewd deputy keeper of the Fleet prison were tucking into large bowls of bean and onion pottage together with large chunks of dark brown rye bread, and enjoying a finer ale than the former had previously been drinking.

"And now, my friend," William said, wiping the back of his hand over his mouth. "Why were you looking so low when I came in?"

"Looking so low? Because I feel that way. That's why. You see that poor sod sitting over there?"

Richard asked, jerking his head over to the far table by the window where a heavily bewhiskered man in a torn brown coat sat picking over a plate of bread and cheese. "Well, William, *he* is probably better off than me. At least he can afford some bread and cheese without waiting for his friends to come along."

"Och, Richard. Stop feeling so sorry for yourself. You know…"

"Sorry for myself? Just look at me, man. Look at my clothes. Look at my hair. Once I wore the latest fashion and my hair and beard were as well-trimmed as the King's. Now I walk down the street and everyone steps out of my way or even crosses the road as if I'm about to rob them."

"Yes, but Richard, you…"

"And once, William, I was a successful wool merchant here in the city. Remember? Successful, man – and respected. Everyone came to trade with me. Not only here, but in France and Flanders as well. I had a fine house, a carriage and a pair of horses and my family wore clothes of the finest cloth."

"So what went wrong?"

Richard shook his head. "I don't know, William. I really don't. It's like everyone suddenly stopped wanting to wear wool. One minute I was up there and now I'm down here. That's what happened."

"Ah, that's what the scriptures say, man," William said. "The Lord giveth and the Lord taketh away. Blessed be the name of the Lord."

"Aye," Richard nodded. "You are right, there. And He has certainly taken it away from me. All of it. But you know, William," he added, a sudden light in his eyes. "I'm going to get it back. All of it. And more."

"What do you mean?"

Richard looked around him carefully and leaned over the table. He then signalled for his friend to do the same. With their heads just about touching, Richard whispered, "Robbery, man. Robbery."

Doing his best to keep his voice down, William whispered back, "Robbery? What? Who? How?"

"Come outside, man. Around the back and I'll tell you," Richard replied as he stood up, finished the last of his ale and, grabbing his hat off the table, he walked out of the tavern. William followed him, and in a couple of minutes the two men were leaning against a wall in a narrow passage behind the disused stables facing the rear of St. Catherine's Church.

Richard looked around and then pulled William closer. "Listen, my friend, this is my plan. I am desperate. I need money and lots of it. I've got debts up to the top of the spire of yon church. D'you understand? Now where am I going to get it?"

"From wool, like before," William said.

"No man. I can't from wool anymore. No-one will trade with me. It's like I've got the pox. No-one will touch me. No, William, there's only one way for me to get a lot of money quickly, and that's by stealing it."

"From the Jews? Those Christ-killers and moneybags. They always have lots of it."

"No, William. I want more. Even those Jews don't have enough for me. The only one who has enough is the king."

"*The king!*" William guffawed.

"Ssh, man! D'you want everyone to hear us?" Richard looked around again. There was no-one in sight.

"And how are you going to do that?" William asked. "Walk up to him and say, 'Excuse me, Sire, I am a poor subject who once paid a lot of taxes and now I need my money back?'"

"No, my friend, of course not. I've worked out a plan to rob his treasury."

"*The King's treasury!* Are you mad?"

Richard shook his head. "No, William. I am not mad. Just desperate. Desperate and tired of being poor, cold and hungry. D'you know what it's like to live in a hovel with a wife screaming at you all day for food, and children who—"

"So how are you going to carry out this robbery? And where?" William interrupted.

"Westminster Abbey," Richard replied quietly. "The crypt under the chapterhouse. That's where the King stores all of his treasure, isn't it? At least while he's away campaigning in Scotland."

William looked hard at his friend and shook his head. "Now I know you're mad. Who would dream of breaking into Westminster Abbey? Do you think the monks would let you just walk in, take a few sacks of gold coins, a silver chalice or two and walk out?"

Richard nodded. "That's right, William. Just like that. Or nearly so. I've been talking to some of the people who work there and if I pay them something, they'll help me."

William looked closely again at his friend's face. "You're serious, aren't you? You really *are* planning to rob the royal treasury."

Richard nodded. "I have no choice. If I want to regain my honour and have people respect me again, I must have money. And lots of it." He shrugged. "William, it's as simple as that. Now, are you with me or not? Will you support me? Will you help me?"

William looked at his friend, thought for a minute, then held out his hand and nodded. "Aye, Richard, I'm with you. But if we get caught, the King will show us no mercy. Hanging will be the least of our sorrows."

Richard clapped him on the back. "Fear not, my friend. We'll not get caught. I have thought out all the details. Soon, you and me are going to be so rich that the King will come to *us* to pay for his Scottish wars."

"Aye, and his English whores," William grinned. "Now tell me your plan. It's clear that you have given much thought to this crazy idea."

Richard put a reassuring hand on his friend's shoulder. "Listen, Will. It will take too long to tell you now, and anyway, I'd prefer to tell you somewhere more private where the walls are less likely to have ears."

That night, in one of dark rooms leading to the cellars below the Fleet prison, Richard of Pudlicott, now washed, shaved and wearing a new suit of clothes that William had given him, told his friend about how he was planning to relieve his King of all or most of his treasure.

Once the merchant-turned-robber had William fully on his side, he set out to put his plans into action. First, he recruited four friends and acquaintances. By odd coincidence all four where named John. They were: John of St. Albans, a stonemason; John of Newmarket, a London goldsmith, a man with a reputation for knowing how to buy and sell stolen property; John de Lenton, one of Richard's closest friends and one who possibly had a key to the Abbey, and John Rippinghale. This last John was another one of Richard's closest friends and would be especially useful as his specialised skills with a hammer and chisel, which he used for breaking into churches, were known far and wide. Ironically, he was also known as 'the Chaplain'.

In addition, Richard recruited several high-ranking church officials who would help him overcome the problems of security. He also rounded up some monks working in the Abbey to help him.

Now, owing to William's generosity and self-interest, Richard's outward appearance changed for the better. The ex-wool merchant renewed his connections with a few of London's goldsmiths and jewellers and they expressed their willingness to do business with him in the future. They would be useful as potential buyers of his new-found riches.

"How did you get these people to help you?" William asked one evening.

Richard tapped the side of his nose. "Promises and bribery," he smiled. "I told them that the Lord will give – and in a very generous way. Their devotion to the Church and Mammon…"

"The god of riches?"

"Aye, will be very well paid for."

During the late spring of 1303, while the King was still many miles far away to the north and with very little ecclesiastical action taking place in his Abbey, Richard of Pudlicott, aided by his stonemason friend, John of St. Albans, spent their nights quietly working away on the building's stonework. In the area near the chapterhouse they picked and chiselled, picked and chiselled, weakening the masonry - though none of this began before the quick-growing hempen seeds that Richard had planted months earlier by the Abbey's walls had flourished into entangled bushes thick enough to hide their nefarious activities. As they pried the stones loose around the window of the chapterhouse, John of St. Albans told Richard that he was not sure if their plan would work.

"Don't you recall, Dick, that someone, or some people, tried to break into the crypt three years ago?"

Richard nodded. "Yes, John, but they failed. I don't know why. It was probably because they weren't as determined as we are. All I know," he added, "is that the abbot found out and reported it to the king."

"And what did he do about it?"

"Surprisingly, nothing, my friend. A wool merchant I know who was at court at the time told me that the King just hushed the matter up. I suppose he didn't want to give ideas to anyone else."

"Like us," John grinned.

Night after night, hidden from view by the thick hempen bushes, Richard, John of St. Albans and three others chipped away at one of the chapterhouse windows, frame and sill. They carried the loose stones away or buried them in the Abbey grounds. They certainly did not want to leave any visible evidence in the vicinity.

No-one saw them. Not the passers-by who wished to use the Abbey's latrines, and not the local farmers who grazed their cattle on the grassy area surrounding the Abbey. The setting up of a few strategically placed barriers and fences also kept any prying eyes far away.

Even from within the confines of the Abbey, no-one apart from a few select souls had any idea what was happening just a few thick stone walls away. The monks, bribed or not, continued with their time-honoured daily routine: Vigils, Matins and Vespers, as well as the less spiritual rounds of study and confession, feeding the poor and working in the Abbey's gardens. No-one heard, or at least commented on or reported the sounds of muffled mallets and chisels.

And then the night arrived, in the last week of April 1303, when Richard and his friendly stonemason decided that the time had come when they could force the bars protecting the chapterhouse's windows apart.

"Are you sure we have loosened the stones up enough?" Richard asked.

John nodded and took up a thick iron crowbar. "Fear not, my friend. If these bars won't budge now, they never will. Tell me," he added, as he wrenched another piece of stone away from the frame, "haven't I been a master mason for these past twelve years? Haven't I learned something of my craft during that time?" He laid a supportive hand on Richard's shoulder. "If you are right about where the King keeps his treasure, we are going to be very rich men very soon." And with that, he nodded to Richard to pass him another large chisel.

Several hours of hard but almost silent work passed before John the mason smiled at his fellow-robbers and told them that the time had come to break into the Abbey. Helping them to quietly remove the thick protective window bars, they forced open the window and climbed in over the sill.

Now they were in the poorly lit chapterhouse. From there, entering the crypt holding the King's treasure would be as easy as "farting after a good meal," as John de Lenton had crudely put it.

Using the early morning light to help them see their way around, they slid down into the crypt. Here, separated from the outside world by thick stone walls, they lit their torches and were immediately stunned to see so much treasure lying there just waiting to be taken.

"Well, look at that!" John de Lenton said in wonder, as he thrust his fingers into a sack of silver coins. "I knew the King was rich, but I never thought that he would be as rich as this."

"Forget those silver coins, John," William said. "Just look at these sacks of gold ones. There must be at least a dozen," he added as he moved his flickering torch around and started to count.

"And here," John Rippinghale added. "In all my years of breaking into churches, I've never seen so many chalices and pieces of fine plate stored together. Just look at it." And he picked up a glistening ruby encrusted gold chalice, his face a picture of pure joy. "It must be worth a fortune. A veritable fortune."

"Come, you fellows," Richard said somewhat sharply. "Stop gawping at all of this and start packing it up into the sacks. We haven't got all day. We'll take the chalices, goblet and jewellery first. Then we'll take the coins. They're already in sacks so they are all ready to move. Come, let's get started now, and don't forget to keep the noise down."

"Fear not, Dick," William said, patting his friend on the shoulder. "No-one will hear us down here."

"Aye, and if they do, those monks will be paid to be deaf," John de Lenton chuckled. "They will certainly be rewarded for their prayers."

As the men bent to the task of filling their sacks with the King's treasure, William Palmer looked at Richard. "Dick, how much do you think this is all worth?" he asked.

Richard shrugged. He had never seen so much gold, silver and other riches stored together before. "I don't know. But I guess that all of this must be worth at least one hundred thousand pounds."

"If not more," John the stonemason added, as he hauled a sack full of shining goblets over to a small doorway in preparation to taking it out of the Abbey that night.

The men worked hard through the day, only taking short breaks to grab a chunk of bread and cheese or an apple before carrying on with their criminal activities. From time to time they changed places as each one of them took turns to be on guard to see if an inquisitive monk was coming their way. Fortunately for the gang, this never happened. And as they packed the royal treasure into the sacks and bags they had brought with them, every so often one would stop, hold up a chalice or a string of jewels and wonder at its beauty. "Just look at this. It's so beautiful. It's perfect."

"Aye, and it's worth a fortune," one of the others would reply.

"That's right. And our fortune, to boot."

At the end of the day, as a weak sun was going down behind grey clouds, Richard told the men to stop their work. "I don't want to chance the monks hearing us at night," he said. "We'll come back tomorrow at dawn and continue then. In the day, any noises outside will drown out any sounds that we might make."

And with a backward glance at the loot they had already packed, and an appreciative look at that which still remained to be made ready on the morrow, the five men, after looking around carefully, climbed out of the chapterhouse window. Then they were quickly swallowed up by the crowds of Londoners making their way back to the city.

The following morning just as the sun was breaking through the clouds to give London another typically mixed sunny and showery day, the robbers pulled aside the loosened bars and slid their way back into the crypt. As before, they lighted their torches and spent the day packing their King's treasure into large sacks. As they had done so on the previous day, every so often one of them would straighten up and comment on the beauty, the workmanship of the goblet, chalice or other fine piece of King Edward's treasure.

"Just look at the hilt of this sword," John the stonemason said, holding up the weapon and its bejewelled scabbard.

"Aye," William said. "I think it must be the Sword of Neath. I've heard about it before. And the one next to it was made by Wayland the Smith. A very fine piece of work, I might add. If it's the one I think it is, then it was made during the reign of the second King Henry."

"So that means it must be well over one hundred years old. It must be worth a fortune."

"Yes, ours," Richard and John de Lenton said in unison.

And as Richard had told them to stop working on the first evening, so he did on the second. Straightening his aching back, he stood up and told them that they would finish on the morrow. "Remember, my friends," he said. "We don't want to risk anything by having a sharp-eared monk wonder what's going on down here, do we?"

And with that, the five men eased their way out of the crypt thinking, that by that time tomorrow they would all be richer than they had ever dreamed about.

The third day of the 1303 Great Crown Jewels Robbery passed for the most part like the two previous days. The men met at dawn behind the tangling bushes hiding their entrance to the chapterhouse and quickly descended into the octagonal crypt. They saw the sacks they had filled and prepared leaning against the wall or stacked around the crypt's thick central column. It did not take them long to get back into their routine of packing the various treasures into sacks and adding them to the previous days' work.

By late afternoon, they were able to ease up and think of the next stage – taking all their plunder over the rough pastureland surrounding the Abbey down to the river. There they would load it onto barges and sail up the Thames for the mile or so that separated Westminster Abbey from the city.

But here, the men began to grow careless. After months of planning and three days of hard work, the three Johns repaired to a nearby tavern that night where they began drinking strong ale. It was their way of easing their physical and mental tension, but with drink came loose tongues. *In vino veritas.* And with loose tongues came paying for their drinks with the small jewels and pearls that they had stuffed into their pouches.

For by now, the King's stolen treasure reached London. Here it was soon spread around through the city's various goldsmiths or stored in the vaults of William Palmer's Fleet prison. The remainder, being too heavy or too bulky to carry far without arousing suspicion, was buried in or near the cemetery of St. Margaret's Church. This last cache was later accidentally discovered by an old woman called Margaret or Isabella Lovit (or Lovett). Her discovery would prove a link in the chain connecting the robbery to Richard Pudlicott and his merry men. Another link was supplied by the robbers themselves. This happened when, under the cover of darkness, they dropped quite a few loose jewels in the wasteland bordering the riverbank. Other loose jewels were used to bribe some of the monks who, not being used to such a situation, had a tendency to talk too much.

But while the robbers and their helpers, ecclesiastical or not, were celebrating their newly acquired wealth, the noose was beginning to tighten around their necks.

As soon as King Edward had dismissed his messenger, Thomas of Aylesbury, he called for his scribe and wrote the following letter, which was to be taken to London as quickly as possible. He began with the traditional regal opening:

> *'Edward, by grace of God, King of England, Lord of Ireland and Duke of Aquitaine, to his well-beloved and faithful Ralph de Sandwich, Walter of Gloucester, John Bakewell and Roger de Southcote, greetings.'*

He went on to state that he had been informed about the robbery that *'malefactors and disturbers of our peace have, by force of arms, broken into our treasury within the Abbey at Westminster'*. He then insisted that the above officials and others find answers to the following questions:

'Who are the malefactors?
Who knew about the robbery?
Who offered and gave the robbers help, counsel and assistance?
Who knowingly received the said treasure?
How was the said treasure taken and how much?
In whose hands is the treasure now, as well as all the other circumstances surrounding the said robbery?

He then enjoined them to *'do whatever is necessary to elucidate the full truth of this matter'.*

The King's last paragraph ordered his officials to make a full enquiry, arrest the robbers without delay and have them kept safe and secure in prison pending their trial. The treasure, when it was found, was to be stored in a safe place, while the King's knights, sheriffs and other 'upright men' were to discover what had really happened.

As His Majesty had instructed, copies of this letter were taken by Thomas of Aylesbury to London as fast as he and his horses could manage. Two of its most important recipients were Sir Ralph de Sandwich, Constable of the Tower of London, and John de Drokensford, the official in charge of the King's treasure in Westminster Abbey. No doubt this last-named official had been extremely shocked on learning about the robbery, and presumably receiving this letter from his royal master did nothing to help him feel any better. All he could do now was to make sure that he caught the culprits – the sooner the better. John de Drokensford knew that it did not pay to have a vengeful King breathing down his neck.

Luckily for the king, Drokensford was no fool. He had received a good education (probably at Oxford or Cambridge) and he was well-versed in the law. He was exceptional in understanding finance and from his early start as a humble clerk in the King's exchequer he swiftly rose in the ranks. In 1295, after nine years hard work, Drokensford had been appointed to the top job, the King's Keeper of the Exchequer. Now all he needed to do, together with Ralph de Manton, his good friend and assistant, was to catch the robbers. They needed to operate quickly and quietly, and hope that they would start receiving some valuable information soon.

The first step that Drokensford took was to meet with John le Blund, the Mayor of London, then issue a public proclamation in the King's name. Among its various clauses, the proclamation stated:

> *'We do command you, on behalf of our Lord the King, upon forfeiture of life and of limb and lands and chattels and whatsoever else you*

> *may forfeit, that all those who found any of the treasure of our Lord the King, be it gold or silver or precious stone or anything whatsoever, whether within the city or without, in whatsoever place it may be coming from the treasury at Westminster, which has been broken into, such a person shall come into the Guildhall before the Mayor and the Sheriffs and restore what they have found between this and Sunday next by the hours of Vespers.'*

This was followed by another command which stated:

> *'All those who have sold or bought any of the said treasure, or know any persons have found any part of the said treasure, or have the same in their keeping, in any manner whatsoever shall come into the Guildhall and report this. If they do not do so, the proclamation concluded, the King will hold them as felons against him.'*

In other words, King Edward was taking the robbery personally. The use of the word *felon* meant that if any of the robbers or their helpers were caught, they could expect the death penalty.

Next, Drokensford and the Royal Justices began a search of the Abbey and its environs.

"This is how I want this search organised," Drokensford began. "I want the King's soldiers to completely surround the Abbey. Then we will go through every nook and cranny as well as look over the nearby grounds from the Abbey to the river as carefully as possible. Surely, these robbers must have left some evidence behind."

"Sir, what if the monks protest that we are violating their domain?" the captain of the guard asked.

"You are to ignore their protests and continue with your search. Remember that you are on the King's business and that that is more important than anything else."

"Does that include searching the Sanctuary, sir?"

"Yes, captain. Everywhere is to be searched. Everywhere."

Soon after Drokensford's men had dispersed, one of the justices came hurrying back to him. "Sir," Walter of Gloucester panted, "we have found some precious stones in the long grass near the cemetery."

"And, sir," another official added as he joined John de Drokensford. "While we were investigating the

Sanctuary, we found a man who looked like a priest, but who was behaving in a most ungodly way. All he will tell us is that his name is John."

"Where is he now? Have you detained him?"

"Yes, sir. We are holding him in the Abbey prison above the gatehouse. My men are interrogating him now."

Later enquiries were to show that this ungodly and unfrocked priest was none other than the so-called 'Chaplain,' John de Rippinghale. For some reason, probably the hope of retrieving some of dropped jewels, he had returned to the scene of the crime.

During the next few days, Drokensford made a detailed list of all the treasure that had been found or left behind in the crypt. He also recorded that Adam de Warfeld, the sacristan or sexton, had known about the robbery, and that he had hidden some of the loot from the King's ministers.

It was at this point that the whole fabric of the robbery started to unravel. Drokensford and his officials began interrogating the monks and other members of the Abbey's staff. It did not take them long to find out what had happened. Fortunately for the royal investigators, these allegedly holy men, who were not used to this kind of treatment, broke down and began divulging names and other relevant information.

With this newly acquired knowledge, Drokensford, knowing that he had to act fast, immediately located and arrested Richard Pudlicott together with his chief 'fence,' the London goldsmith, John of Newmarket. This happened in mid-June, some six weeks after the robbery.

The stonemason, John of St. Albans, was arrested soon after. In order to show how his investigation was progressing, Drokensford then took several important officials to see the crypt and the damage that the robbers had caused to the Abbey's masonry. One of the minor officials complained about having to leave his house in Holborn and make his way by boat down the river to Westminster.

"Sir," he asked the King's Keeper. "Is it necessary to come all this way? Do we not have enough evidence already to charge these evil men?"

"Young man," Drokensford replied, looking at his questioner in the eye, "you should know that the King, your royal master and mine, does not tolerate fools gladly. I assume you know what happened to his official, Adam of Stratton, who acted in an unseemly manner?"

The young man lowered his head. "Yes, sir," he muttered. "His property was immediately seized and the man was banished."

"That's right, but not before he was disgraced, fined and imprisoned. Do you want that to happen to me? Or even to yourself?"

"No, sir."

"Therefore, we will carry out our appointed task as thoroughly as we can. Is that understood?"

"Yes, sir."

Two weeks after Drokensford had inspected the damage done to the Abbey he, together with John de Bakewell, the Deputy Royal Warden of the City of London, proceeded with the trial of Richard Pudlicott, William Palmer as well as Adam de Warfeld, whom the authorities regarded as one of the chief receivers. The trial took place at the Bishop of London's Palace near St. Paul's on 3 July 1303. In addition to Richard Pudlicott, William Palmer, Adam de Warfeld being accused, two goldsmiths, William Torel and John de Bridgeford were also put on trial. As part of their defence, the latter claimed that they did not know that a felony had taken place or that they were buying stolen goods.

Later, three other goldsmiths were named: Geoffrey de Bradley, Thomas Frowick and Adam le Orfevre. The court declared that Richard Pudlicott was guilty of breaking into the treasury and that William Palmer and Adam de Warfeld had 'consented to and helped him'.

If this part of the proceedings was predictable, the next part was not.

"Sir," a justice official announced to John de Drokensford. "I have just learned that the accused, Richard Pudlicott, has escaped!"

"*Escaped!* From where? Wasn't he being held in the house of Hugh Pourte, Sheriff of London?"

"Yes, sir, but after five days there, he was found to have fled."

"And has anyone seen or heard from him since?"

"Yes, sir. He has claimed sanctuary in the Church of St. Michael Candlewick."

"Did anybody connive in this escape?"

"Yes, sir. A Master Richard, the valet of Gaucelyn le Servient."

"Then he must be removed from there immediately and I will interrogate Sheriff Pourte."

Despite the laws of sanctuary, Richard Pudlicott was recaptured by Drokensford's men, who ignored the age-old traditions and dragged him out of the Sanctuary. At the same time the sheriff called on several men to swear that he had taken no part in the robber's escape.

From here on the trial continued as expected. Its progress was helped when it was proved that when Richard and John of Newmarket, his fence, had been initially arrested, much of the stolen loot had been found in their house. From this point it did not take long for Drokensford to speed up the trial. He did so because in October 1303, while the King was still absent, immersed in his campaign in Scotland, he had sent a message to London saying that an inquiry *Oyer et Terminer* – to listen and determine – should be conducted, providing a long list of suspects he thought should be investigated. Many on this list of accused were monks serving at Westminster Abbey.

Three who made confessions, Richard Pudlicott, John de Rippinghale and William Palmer were of particular interest to the authorities. In an effort to save his friends and fellow-accomplices, Richard Pudlicott claimed that he had carried out the robbery on his own. He also claimed that he had stolen what he had because of his earlier losses in Flanders, and that the King was responsible for this. Drokensford and his officials did not believe Pudlicott, as it was clear that it would have been impossible for a single man to have removed such a vast quantity of loot.

Rippinghale turned King's approver, the medieval equivalent of state's witness. By claiming he was a monk from Peterborough he tried to hide his shady past. This did not work as his criminal reputation, as well as the fact that he was a defrocked priest, went against him. During his interrogation he tried to bluff his way out of trouble by mixing a few facts with a lot of lies, but in the end this did not help his cause.

William Palmer, the Deputy Keeper of the Fleet prison had to face twenty indictments. In order to try and clear his name he said that John of St. Albans had organised the tools used for the break-in. He also claimed ignorance about the operational details of the robbery and argued that he had no idea what was in the sacks that were loaded onto the barges. As with Richard Pudlicott and John de Rippinghale, his testimony did not save him.

Due to the many people who were interrogated and also because the wheels of justice have a tendency to grind slowly, it was only on 13 January 1304, eight months after the robbery, that the King's justices began their summing-up. Six weeks were to pass before the final verdict was pronounced on 5 March 1304 – nearly one year after the robbery had been committed.

In the spring of 1304 the King's instructions, *Ad audiendum et terminandum negocium* – to hear and finish the business – were heard. William Palmer, alias William of the Palace, together with 'four others' – John de Rippinghale, John de Lenton, John of St. Albans and John of Newmarket – were to be dragged through the city on hurdles and to be hanged on the elm trees at Smithfield.

In addition to being hanged, in accordance with medieval ideas of retribution – that justice must be seen to be carried out - they were also publicly humiliated. First, the Town Chaplain heard their confessions. Then they were stripped down to their tunics and bound to horse-drawn hurdles *usque elmes* – to the elms. This meant being dragged over the bumpy roads accompanied by guards and other figures wearing masks. The final stage was for them to be strung up at Smithfield surrounded by huge cheering and jeering crowds.

Richard Pudlicott suffered the same fate. But this happened some eighteen months later. As the *Annales Londonienses* records:

'In that year on the fourth kalends of November, John de Putticot [Pudlicott] 'Clerk' was led in a certain hand cart 'careta' from the Tower of Westminster to Westminster and there judged on the account of his violation of the King's Treasury.'

King Edward wanted to exact the maximum humiliation for the instigator of the Great Crown Jewel robbery. Therefore, he ordered that instead of using the standard wicker hurdles to transport the guilty man to the scaffold, he was to be sat in some sort of wheelbarrow and pushed along through the city streets to the site of his execution.

And now for the final twist in this criminal tale. The vengeful King decreed that Richard Pudlicott's body was to be skinned and that his skin was to be dried and cured. This was to be hung on the south door of Westminster Abbey as a warning to the monks who had helped him, as by claiming clerical immunity in a civil court many of them were able to evade the King's retribution.

In 1861, over five hundred and fifty years later, the Victorian antiquarian, G.G. Scott, wrote in his book, *Gleanings from Westminster Abbey,* that he had found pieces of white leather hanging from the south door's hinges. After consulting with a Mr Queckett of the

Royal College of Surgeons, he was told that the leather was in fact skin taken from a human body. Scott assumed that the skin-turned-leather of Richard Pudlicott, merchant-turned-robber, had been later used as a medieval draught excluder!

Chapter 2

Mary 'Moll Cutpurse' Frith (1584–1659)

Moll (or Mal) Cutpurse was one of the most colourful characters and incorrigible villains of Jacobean London. Apart from being a renowned pickpocket (which is what cutpurse means) and fence in the capital's underworld, she was perhaps one of the country's first and most famous cross-dressers.

Cutpurse was a standard description for pickpockets, and even Shakespeare in King Lear *referred to them. He linked Moll and the like to other disreputable figures such as bawds and whores. Moll Cutpurse's real name was Mary Frith, but she was also referred to as a 'Roaring Girl', a nickname derived from the 'Roaring Boys' - gangs of riotous lower-class young men who copied the fashions of the upper classes. Much of what is known, or thought to be known about her, is based on* The Life of Mrs Mary Frith, *an incredibly exaggerated account of her life written three years after her death.*

Finally, it may be said that Mary Frith's reputation was influenced more by her being a woman rather than a pickpocket, fence and procurer, because in those activities she was just one of many. Although fewer women were involved in the underworld, their involvement was usually connected with sex and prostitution. In the first half of the 17th century, only Mary Frith seemed to have been able to cross the line and lead her criminal life in predominantly masculine dominated areas of endeavour.

*

"Mummy," the small boy said as he pointed across the crowded street. "Who's that strange looking man over there? He looks as if he could be a woman. And he's smoking a pipe and carrying a sword."

"Ssh, child and don't point. It's very rude."

"But who is it?" the boy persisted. "And why are you hurrying me along? I want to have another look at him or her."

"That is Moll Cutpurse, son, and she's a very wicked woman," the mother replied, as she pushed young William through the crowds looking at the stalls in the Strand. "She likes to dress like a man and steal people's money. Now let's get on home and make some dinner for your father."

"But mummy, why does she dress up? Doesn't she like being a woman?" the boy asked, as he turned his head around to catch yet another glimpse of this fascinating creature.

"I don't know, son. Now let's go."

And not many other people knew why Mary Frith, later to be known as Moll Cutpurse, enjoyed dressing up as a man, either. Even though she was born in Aldersgate Street near St. Paul's Cathedral in the mid-1580s to a respectable couple – her father was a shoemaker and her mother was a housewife – it was recorded in the 18th and 19th century *Newgate Calendar* that:

> *'She was a very tomrig or hoyden (boisterous girl), delighting in boys' play or pastime... she could not enjoy that sedentary life of sewing or stitching... and on her needle, bodkin*

> *and thimble she could not think quietly, wishing them changed into sword and dagger for a bout at cudgels... She would fight with boys, and courageously beat them; run, jump, leap or hop with any of her contrary sex...'*

By the time Mary was sixteen she had had her first brush with the law. She was accused in a Middlesex court of stealing nearly three shillings (seventeen pounds today). However, in this particular case she was lucky. Her uncle, who was a minister, managed to have her set free and her family thought it would be best if the high-spirited Mary were sent away from the temptations of London across the Atlantic Ocean to New England. It was hoped that as young women were much in demand in the new country, she would soon be married, settle down and raise a family. But this was not to be. Before the ship set sail, she jumped overboard and resolved never to have anything to do with her uncle again.

She decided to improve her financial situation by perfecting her pickpocketing skills by joining a gang of pickpockets who operated in the area of St. Paul's Cathedral. Mary's role was to be the whipster.

"What's that?" she asked the gang's leader.

"Oh, you'll be the one who actually dips their fingers into the person's pocket, and I'll be the bulk," her new friend, a red-faced man with a large wart on his equally large nose explained.

"What's a 'bulk'?" she asked.

"Don't you know anything?" the bulk asked. "A bulk, me, will be the one who'll distract the person while you're dipping him. Is that clear now?"

Mary nodded and asked what would happen to the stolen goods.

"We share 'em, don't we? I sell 'em to a fence and then we share the money what 'e gives us."

Mary nodded again and it was from this period in her life that the successful whipster became known as Moll Cutpurse.

However, two years after jumping ship, Mary was arrested again for theft. Over the next few years she was 'burned on her hand' four times as a criminal – a judicial punishment designed to prevent convicted felons from pleading 'the benefit of the clergy' – the right to quote the Biblical sentence, "O Lord have mercy on me and forgive me my transgressions."

It seems that Moll did not need any spiritual help. Although she may not have liked doing so, she would appear in court in female clothing and this seemed to have saved her from any harsher punishments. She began appearing in public smoking a long-stemmed clay pipe while wearing a doublet and loosely worn breeches. If this shocked any conservative Londoners, then her swearing and blasphemy shocked them even more.

The authorities tried to curb her extreme behaviour and sentenced her at least once to undergo a public penance. This meant that after being arrested on Christmas day 1611 she was sent to Bridewell prison, where two months later she had to stand up in public at St. Paul's Cross wearing a white sheet. While she was doing so, a clergyman gave a sermon inspired by her crimes in front of the assembled crowd. A spectator, John Chamberlain, described this scene in a letter to a friend, writing, *She wept bitterly and seemed very penitent [but] it is since doubted as she was maudlin drunk, being discovered to have tippled off three quarts of sack before she came to her penance.*

Apart from her crimes against property, cross-dressing in public during the early years of the 17th century was much frowned upon by the establishment, both civil and clerical. To do as she did with such effrontery was certainly a way to clash head to head with the various heads of authority, especially those of the Puritan variety.

However, it was not only her public penance and choice of attire that caused Mary to become a celebrity. During this period, her exploits became even more widely known through the play, *The Madde Pranckes of Mery Mall of the Bankside*. This entertainment was written by John Day, a known villain of the time who may have been arrested for murder. Although this play does not exist today, another, *The Roaring Girl* by Thomas Dekker and Thomas Middleton still survives.

"Have you seen the play about Moll Cutpurse? It's on at the Fortune Playhouse."

"Which one? The one by Day or by the other one?"

"The last one. It's all about a young man who knows that the mad woman who he loves and wishes to make her his wife won't be accepted by his father. Moll's lover plays a trick on the father and makes him think that his son is going to elope with her."

"And does he?"

"No, and in the end the old man is so happy that they don't elope, he agrees to his son marrying her. And not only that, but then Moll comes up on the stage wearing her men's clothing and tells stories to the audience while she plays the lute. And yes, she also wore a sword and danced a jig just like they did at the end of that comedy we saw last week by that Shakespeare fellow. I'm telling you, my friend, it was a wonderful show and I'm glad I went. I hope she does it again."

And like the plot in *The Roaring Girl,* in 1617 Moll did get married. Her husband was Lewknor Markham, the son of Gervase Markham, a playwright. We do not know anything about their marriage, as we never hear any more about him. It is possible that it was just a marriage of convenience, a way of making Moll look a little more respectable.

In addition to Moll appearing on the stage, she also set herself up as a pawnbroker. This was probably a cover for her activities as an underworld fence. As she was now a celebrity with links to the criminal world, people would approach her and ask her to see if she could retrieve property that had been stolen from them. Many of these requests were about sentimental items – watches and jewellery. Moll was often able to locate these goods and return them to their happy owner – at a price. However, not everything turned out according to Moll's plans. One day a man asked her to find his watch, and when she returned it he arrested her for dealing in stolen goods. The man was a constable who had been tasked to catch her. She was brought to trial but was saved when a fellow pickpocket stole the watch in question. Since the evidence was missing the authorities had no choice but to release her.

On another occasion, a young gentleman called Henry Killingrew asked Moll if she could retrieve his watch and gold seal ring from a prostitute he had met the night before. Moll found out that the young lady in question was called Mary Dell. When Moll and Killingrew went to her house and demanded that she return the stolen goods, Mary's husband appeared and laid a complaint with the authorities. He claimed that Moll and Killingrew had burst into his house and threatened them with no evidence. It is not recorded what happened as a result of this somewhat murky accusation.

However, one of her most profitable side-lines was to act as a panderer – a procurer. She would find mistresses for rich men, but then this was a 'normal' way of doing business. What was different was how Moll also worked to find older women who wanted to consort with young men, bringing excitement and challenge into the amorous lives of both parties. This was the most profitable aspect of Moll's pandering or pimping activities as she was paid both by the grateful women and the appreciative men, whom she described as 'the sprucest fellows the town afforded'.

Moll also made contacts with people in the upper levels of society – contacts that would prove useful to her later when she had more problems with the law. It was during this period at the height of her dubious fame that showman William Banks made her an offer she could not refuse.

"Mary Frith, I bet you twenty pounds that you wouldn't ride from Charing Cross to Shoreditch dressed as a man."

"But that's about two miles!"

"You see. I said you wouldn't."

Mary puffed out her chest and poked the showman in his shoulder. "Who wouldn't? I'll take you on and show everyone that what they think doesn't bother me."

And showed them she did. In front of a large crowd and dressed in her manly jacket and breeches, she mounted Banks' horse with a flourish and set off. And to prove that she was indifferent to what the people thought, she flew a large banner and blew a trumpet as she rode.

It was not only Mary who was in the public eye. It was her horse as well. To win the bet, worth three thousand four hundred pounds today, she rode Banks' famous horse, Morocco. This horse was well-known throughout the city as the best performing animal ever. It could count money with its hooves, dance and play dice. Its best-known trick was to climb the hundreds of narrow steps of St. Paul's Cathedral and then dance on the roof. In other words, if Mary Frith was going to win a bet, she was going to do so in style.

For the twenty years after 1624, Mary Frith hardly appears in any official records. It is not known whether she had calmed down and taken to wearing regular women's apparel or not. But what is known is that when the Civil War broke out in 1642, unlike any of the other villains mentioned in this book, Mary showed an active interest in national politics. According to *The Life and Death of Mrs Mary Frith, Commonly Called Moll Cutpurse,* she was a keen supporter of King Charles I. It is said that she showed her sympathy for the Royalist side by becoming a highwaywoman and robbing Parliamentarian travellers.

The above-mentioned book, published soon after Mary's death, states that one of the most famous criminal activities during the Civil War was robbing Sir Thomas Fairfax, the Parliamentary Commander-in-Chief. This took place west of London on Hounslow

Heath, near where London Airport is situated today. Forcing his carriage to come to a stop, she stole 250 'jacobuses' – gold coins worth twenty-five shillings – and shot the unfortunate general in the arm. The story also says that she then killed his horses so that he would not be able to chase her when she galloped off with her loot.

However, not everything went according to plan. As she was returning to London, her horse became lame west of London at Turnham Green, where she was caught, tried and found guilty. She received the death sentence and it was thought that this would be the end of her colourful career. But as criminals and others have known throughout the ages, money talks. Mary Frith paid an enormous bribe of two thousand pounds (nearly half a million pounds today) and on 21 June 1644 walked out of the Bethlehem Hospital (Bedlam), the authorities declaring that she had been cured of her insanity.

For the next fifteen years until her death in 1659 we do not find her name much recorded. The *Newgate Calendar* says that after paying the huge bribe, she settled down, more or less, in Fleet Street and spent her time dispensing justice among 'wrangling tankard bearers by often exchanging their burden of water for a burden of beer'. She died of dropsy (today known as oedema – the abnormal accumulation of fluid in the body) at her home on 26 July 1659. She was buried in St. Bride's churchyard, Fleet Street and, to quote her will, she was buried, 'with her breech upwards that she might be preposterous in her death as she had been all along in her infamous life'.

As part of her literary legacy, it has been claimed that Daniel Defoe, the writer of *Robinson Crusoe*, was so fascinated by her story that he based part of his play *Moll Flanders* on it. In addition, John Milton, the author of *Paradise Lost* and *Paradise Regained* composed the following epitaph for her gravestone. Unfortunately, the stone, but not the epitaph, was destroyed in the Great Fire of London that broke out seven years later in 1666:

> *Here lies, under this same marble,*
> *Dust, for Time's last sieve to garble;*
> *Dust, to perplex a Sadducee,*
> *Whether it rise a He or She,*
> *Or two in one, a single pair,*
> *Nature's sport, and now her care.*
> *For how she'll clothe it at last day,*
> *Unless she sighs it all away;*
> *Or where she'll place it, none can tell:*
> *Some middle place 'twixt Heaven and Hell*
> *And well 'tis Purgatory's found,*
> *Else she must hide her underground.*
> *These reliques do deserve the doom,*
> *Of that cheat Mahomet's fine tomb*
> *For no communion she had,*

Nor sorted with the good or bad;
That when the world shall be calcin'd,
And the mix'd mass of human kind
Shall sep'rate by that meeting fire,
She'll stand alone, and none come nigh her.
Reader, here she lies till then,
When, truly you'll see her again.

Mary Frith was as much a criminal – a robber, a pickpocket and procurer – as many of the other villains mentioned in this book. She probably died richer than most of them, and if she was able to pay a two thousand pound fine or bribe to buy her freedom, we may conclude that at least on a financial level she had made a success of her life.

However, where she shines most in the annals of English criminality is that the way she challenged the social standards and moral codes of her day. She loved to attract attention by her cross-dressing, despite the fact that those who did so were considered 'sexually riotous and uncontrolled'. Today we do not give much thought to such behaviour, but it should be remembered that two hundred years before Mary Frith swanned around London in men's clothes, doing so was one of the major crimes for which Joan of Arc was burned at the stake.

The iconic picture we have on record of Mary Frith is of her defiantly facing the viewer as she wears a man's hat, jacket and breeches. At the same time, she is holding a sword in her left hand while smoking a pipe with her right (see illustration p.43). Nothing in Jacobean London could be more outlandish than that. And to be a villainous thief, pickpocket and procurer, well, that was really too much.

Chapter 3

'Colonel' Thomas Blood (1618–1680)

Over three-hundred-and-fifty years after Richard of Pudlicott had broken into the royal treasury at Westminster Abbey to steal vast amounts of gold and silver, jewels and plate, 'Colonel' Thomas Blood tried to pull off a similar stunt. In 1671 he and his gang broke into the Tower of London with the aim of stealing the Crown Jewels. But although he is remembered today mainly because of this venture, he was also a spy, a

favourite of King Charles II, the instigator of several Irish revolutionary and other plots, as well as the would-be kidnapper of an English lord. And if all this was not enough, he was also involved in an ambush with the King's men in order to rescue one of his friends from the gallows.

And now, please meet the self-styled Colonel Thomas Blood (1618 -1680) who was described in the New American Cyclopedia (1859) *as a 'noted bravado and desperado'.*

*

Thomas Blood was born in 1618 in Sarney, Ireland, the son of a successful dealer in iron. Using his influence, Blood's father was able to have his handsome and dashing son made a Justice of the Peace. In 1642, soon after the Civil War had broken out, the twenty-four-year-old Blood crossed 'o'er the water' to England to become an officer in King Charles I's Royalist army.

However, as the war progressed, Blood changed sides and became a lieutenant in Oliver Cromwell's Parliamentary army. He profited well out of the war by selling off large quantities of captured Royalist loot. When the war ended with Cromwell ruling England and Ireland as the Lord Protector, Blood continued to benefit by amassing more lands and money. One year after Charles I was executed on a cold morning at the end of January 1649, Thomas Blood promoted himself to become Colonel Thomas Blood. But here his run of good luck ran out.

Cromwell died in 1658 and his son, Richard 'Tumbledown Dick' Cromwell was not the man to inherit his father's position. After nine months trying to follow in his father's footsteps, he resigned. Parliament then asked the exiled Prince Charles to return to England, restore the monarchy and reign as King Charles II. On 29 May 1660, on Charles' thirtieth birthday, the exiled monarch returned to England from France. After being crowned in Westminster Abbey, he set out to punish those responsible for his father's execution.

In addition, in order to recoup the Royalist losses, the new King charged his men with finding those who had financially benefitted from the war. As a result, Blood had to forfeit his profits and land. To make matters worse, his wife, Mary, abandoned him, returning to England from Ireland.

A now much poorer and embittered Blood was evicted from his house. He joined a group of Irish republicans and ex-parliamentarians who plotted to start a major Irish uprising and drive the hated English out of their land. Using his charm, his military experience and native cunning, Colonel Thomas Blood naturally became one of the group's leaders. A major part of their plot was to capture Dublin Castle, take James Butler, the Duke of Ormonde, hostage and use him as a bargaining chip when it came to dealing with the Crown. In addition, Blood had a personal axe to grind. It was the Duke of Ormonde who, as the King's representative in Ireland, had been responsible for seeing that Blood lost all his financial gains after the Restoration.

One evening, Blood, William Leckie, his brother-in-law, Lieutenant Richard Thompson and James Tanner, a past Cromwellian official, that is, men who had suffered as a result of the King's new laws, met at the White Hart in Dublin to finalise their plans for a coup. They were later joined by Colonel Alexander Jephson, Sir Richard Ford, Captain Lawrence and Philip Alden.

Blood opened the proceedings, "Gentlemen, what we must do is get rid of that damned Duke of Ormonde, once and for all."

"D'you mean kill him?"

Blood looked at Leckie straight in the eyes and replied, "Yes, man. I do. Anything else would be a waste of time."

"What about just taking him hostage instead?" Thompson asked.

Jephson nodded. "Aye, he is Lord Lieutenant, after all and…"

"Aye," Tanner agreed. "And he is one of us, a Protestant."

Blood banged his fist down on the table. *"Ormonde must die!* Anything else is a waste of time."

"I agree with the Colonel, here," Ford said, raising his hand. "If the duke is spared assassination, then he may prevail upon *us* one day."

After more heated discussion and argument, it was decided that the Lord Lieutenant of Ireland, James Butler, the Duke of Ormonde was to be killed while he was at Dublin Castle.

"So before we leave here tonight," Blood concluded, "here is our plan. We will use six simple men, including Jenkins the baker. They will enter the castle tomorrow morning through the Great Gate."

"What just like that?"

'No, no," Blood replied. "They'll be dressed up as petitioners who are exercising their legal rights to see the Lord Lieutenant about some wrongs that have been done to them. They'll walk right through the castle grounds inside and then give us a signal to rush in and take the castle and kill the duke."

"Who is 'us'?" Philip Alden asked.

"Me and a hundred officers who I have already rounded up and who fought with me and Cromwell," Blood replied with pride. "We'll sweep in when Ormonde is least expecting any trouble, capture the castle and grab the Duke."

"And that's it?" Alden persisted. "Just like that?"

Blood shook his head. "No, no. One of the officers, Crawford's his name, will lure Lord

Dungannon's men away, so we'll not have any one to oppose us when we rush in."

"And then?"

"Then, once we have secured the castle and its arsenal, we'll raise the flag so that our men outside will know. Their job will be to put down any insurrection in the town. After that," Blood added, with growing enthusiasm, "together with the men who'll join us, we'll head north to Ulster and with our supporters there, we'll sweep the Catholics out of the way."

But it was not to be as simple as that. The two landladies in the tavern overheard the seditious plans and told Blood and his men to leave their premises immediately as they did not want to become involved. The men realised that as their coup may have been compromised, they decided to postpone it for a week. At this point they expected a further five hundred men would be ready to join them.

Blood's plot and the subsequent uprising failed. Unknown to the plotters, Philip Alden was a government agent and he immediately informed the authorities. Many of the revolutionaries, including Blood's brother-in-law, were arrested, tried and hanged, but Blood escaped. He spent the next few years on the run in Ireland, England and even in Holland. Back in England in 1667, where for some time he had pretended to be a Dr Ayliff, Blood planned again to have his final revenge on the Duke of Ormonde, the man responsible for his great financial losses.

This was in 1670. Blood, now living in London, noted that the duke followed the same routine every day. One evening as Ormonde's coach was driving along Pall Mall, it was stopped by a man shouting that there was a dead man lying in the way. The coach-driver halted the coach, which was then attacked by Blood and his men. They dragged the duke out, mounted him on one of their horses and tied him to the rider so that he would not escape. However, Ormonde, despite his sixty years, managed to struggle free and disarm his fellow horseman. In the meanwhile, Blood, not knowing that his plan had failed, had raced off in the direction of the 'Tyburn Tree' to make sure that the rope with which he intended to hang his sworn enemy was in place.

This failed operation had three results: the first two were that the duke managed to escape from Blood and that Blood managed to escape from the law. The last was that Blood was left feeling even more vengeful, especially as there was now a reward of one thousand (over a hundred and fifty thousand pounds today) for anyone who could accurately describe the would-be kidnappers.

Six months later, Blood was still smarting over what had happened. The result of this was that one evening at the end of April 1671 he was to be found plotting with his son, Edmund, now known as Hunt, and two of his closest friends, Captains Robert Perrot and Richard Halliwell. To his son's and his friends' surprise, Blood greeted them wearing a long black clerical robe.

The four men, sitting around a table in Halliwell's parlour, looked at him, said nothing and assumed that he would tell them later why he was so dressed. Meanwhile, they continued studying a map of the Tower of London that Blood had brought with him. A few cheap candles cast a flickering light on the map, causing shadows to flit around the buildings and paths that made up London's central fortress. Suddenly a draught from a half-open window blew all of the candles out bar one, plunging the plotters into a shadowy gloom. Then the still burning candle fell over and rolled dangerously close to the edge of the map.

"For Jesus' sake!" Blood shouted. "Someone move that candle away and shut the window!"

Hunt did so as Blood asked, "Now, where were we?"

"In the Tower, Colonel," Perrot smiled as he winked at the others to break the tension.

"Very funny," Blood muttered. "But my friends, that's where we'll end up if my plan doesn't work. Now look here at this map. Here is the Martin Tower between the Brick Tower and the Constable Tower. Here, on the far corner opposite the Traitors' Gate."

"And that's where Edwards the Keeper keeps the Crown Jewels?" Halliwell asked.

Blood nodded. "Aye."

"And do Edwards and his folks live upstairs?"

Blood nodded again.

"So what's your plan?" Perrot asked. "I mean, you can't just walk in there and steal them just like that."

"Gentlemen," Blood began, "listen carefully for this is my plan. It is simplicity itself. And yes, it will also explain why I am dressed up tonight in this priestly garb. So, listen and take note of the details and which parts you will play."

The three men leaned forward eagerly.

Blood began. "First, I will go to see the Edwards family dressed as I am now, as a priest. And you, Master Halliwell, as the smoothest face among us, will come with me disguised as my wife."

Halliwell looked shocked. He had not been expecting anything like this. "What me dress up as a woman? Not me! Anyway, Perrot is just as smooth as me," He added as he ran his hand over Perrot's cheek.

Blood nodded. "Aye, he may well be that, but he is a little taller than me and if you've noticed, husbands are usually taller than their wives."

"Yes, I suppose you're right," Halliwell conceded. "But tell me, what do I have to do as your beloved wife, the wife of a parson? Bless everyone and tell them they must go to church?"

"No," Blood replied. "Suddenly you will come over feeling faint and I will ask if there is anywhere in their house where you can lie down and rest."

"Why?"

"Because in that way we will gain their friendship and trust. Then a few days later, we return to the Edwards, again dressed up as before, but this time we'll say that we have a handsome nephew who will be a very suitable match for their daughter, the comely Mistress Elizabeth."

Hunt smiled. "Father, this is beginning to sound like one of those Shakespeare comedies."

"No, son," Blood replied. "This is much more serious. Now let me continue. We and the Edwards will become the best of friends and—"

"And then we'll have free access to the Crown Jewels!"

And that is exactly what happened. Blood and Halliwell presented themselves to Talbot Edwards and his wife as tourists who wanted to see the Tower. Then Halliwell 'fainted' and Edwards and his wife unwittingly played their parts by allowing the parson's 'wife' to lie down for a while and recover her strength.

A few days later, Blood and Halliwell returned disguised as before and cemented their friendship by bringing several pairs of fine white gloves as a thank you present. They then brought up the subject of their nephew and how he "who had an income of two or three hundred a year in land" would be a most suitable match for the Edwards' daughter – a pretty gentlewoman.

Then Edwards took his honoured guests, soon to be family, on a tour around the Martin Tower. There, Blood persuaded his host, in addition to showing him the Crown Jewels, to sell him a 'handsome case of pistols' that he had noticed. The Colonel explained that he wished to give them to one of his neighbours who was also a lord. The gullible Edwards agreed without realising that by selling these weapons, he had no means of defending himself in the future.

Soon after, on 9 May 1671, Blood returned with four others. They came early in the morning so that they would catch Edwards and his family unprepared and this time the robbers were all armed with swordsticks - rapiers hidden in their canes. Three of the men went to see Edwards and his wife while the fourth man waited outside with their horses, ready for their escape. Blood then asked Edwards if he would show them the Imperial Crown and the Crown jewels. The Keeper was delighted to take them to where they were stored.

As soon as Edwards, Blood and his men were in the room with the Crown Jewels, Blood threw a cloak over the old man and stuffed a rag into his mouth to gag him. The unfortunate Edwards was then told that if he stopped struggling they would spare his life. This threat did not silence the Keeper. He started to shout for help and was knocked to the floor by 'several unkind blows' with a wooden mallet. Blood had brought this with him in order to flatten the crown, so it would be easier to hide after they had stolen it.

"Now be quiet, old man," Blood threatened the still writhing Edwards, but the Keeper wouldn't listen to him.

Blood hit him again with the mallet while his men drew their swords and daggers to show that they meant business. At this point, Edwards, lying on the floor, pretended to be unconscious.

"Is he dead?" Hunt asked. "Did you kill him?"

Blood looked up. "Yes, he's dead. It's hard to see in this light but I don't think that he's breathing at all."

"Good. Now we can grab the jewels and get out of here."

"Right," Blood said, pointing at Perrot. "You flatten the crown, the big one, and I'll do the same with these things."

Hunt then asked his father, "Shall I flatten this orb as well? It'll be worth more if I don't."

"Well, see if you can stuff it into your cloak as it is. If not, use the mallet on it."

"Give it to me," Perrot said. "I've still got some room in my breeches." And saying that, the three men began to make their preparations to flee the chamber.

"We're leaving him here?" Hunt asked.

"Of course we are, son. What did you expect? We'd take him with us?" Blood replied before adding, "No, it'll be some time before they find him here and by then we'll be far away. Now pick up that sword and let's be having you."

But now their plans began to unravel. Edward's son, Wythe, suddenly appeared on the scene. He was a sailor and after having been away from home for ten years now happened to return just at this very moment. Halliwell, who was on guard outside with the horses, saw this stranger approach the Martin Tower and asked him what he wanted. Wythe pushed him away and told him to mind his own business. Wythe then ran upstairs to his parents' apartment and was happily welcomed home by his mother and sister.

In the meanwhile, Halliwell rushed over to where the rest of the gang was 'modifying' their loot in order to warn them. Thinking that Edwards was dead, they ran off without tying him up. Despite his severe wounds, the Keeper struggled to his feet and shouted out, "Murder! Treason!" His daughter, Elizabeth, heard him and then she too ran outside shouting, "Treason! Treason! Murder! Treason!"

As she was doing this, and then discovering what had happened to her father, Blood and his men escaped over the open area in the Tower's grounds. They reached the Bloody Tower, where the guards had been alerted by Wythe Edwards.

Meanwhile a man called Beckman shouted for Blood and the others to stop. Naturally they did not obey, and although Blood fired at Beckman twice, he missed his target and the latter kept chasing him. Unfortunately for the organiser of this reckless plot, Beckman was not encumbered with heavy crowns and swords. He quickly caught up with Blood, wrestled him to the ground and grabbed the battered crown. By now other guards had arrived and there on Tower Wharf, Blood was surrounded and forced to surrender. His first words were, "It was a gallant attempt, however unsuccessful."

Several of the jewels had become loose and had fallen along the escape route. Most of them were found and returned, including a large pearl that was later found by a poor cinder-woman.

Blood was not the only one to have been captured. Perrot was also caught with the orb hidden in his breeches together with a ruby found in his pockets. The other would-be robbers decided to flee the scene as quickly as possible. However, in the same way his father had suffered bad luck, so too did Hunt. As Blood's son was making good his escape, he bumped into an empty cart on Gravel Lane which caused him to fall off his horse. The other two members of the gang did not waste any time trying to help their fallen comrade in crime but just kept galloping away.

Hunt was arrested by a constable who almost believed the young man's denials that he was involved in the robbery. However, on hearing shouts of, "The crown is taken out of the Tower," Hunt was held in custody and returned to the Tower. There he joined his father and they were locked up and manacled in the dungeons to await the King's justice. While there, they heard that Perrot had also been captured.

The King's justice took some time in coming. So much so that Blood's wife, Mary, petitioned one of the King's favourites, Lord Arlington, 'for access to her husband and eldest son who have been now near eight weeks so closely confined in the Tower that she could neither hear of their health nor receive any direction from them'.

Despite London being the country's largest city with a population of nearly half-a-million, it did not take long for everyone to hear about the failed robbery. Typical of the anti-Blood feeling was this poem written by the well-known poet, Andrew Marvell:

> *When daring Blood his rent to have regained*
> *Upon the Royal Diadem distrained*
> *He chose the cassock, surcingle (*clerical belt*) and gown*
> *The fittest mask for those who rob the Crown*
> *But his lay pity (*humanity*) underneath prevailed,*
> *And while he sav'd the Keeper's life, he failed:*
> *With the priest's vestment had he but put on*
> *The prelate's cruelty, the crown had gone.*

It was also during this period that even though Blood was interrogated by Sir Gilbert Talbot, the Provost-Marshal, and various other important officials, he refused to answer their questions. He said that he would only confess to the King himself. This was seen as pure chutzpa, considering that Blood was the man who not only had been involved in several anti-Royalist plots, but had abandoned the Royalist side during the Civil War ending his military career fighting for Cromwell and the Parliamentary army. Now, after attempting to steal His Majesty's most important jewels and symbols of state, he demanded an audience with the king.

Even though public opinion was heavily weighted against Blood and his attempted robbery, His Majesty, to everyone's surprise, agreed to question him. As a result, the Bloods, father and son, both heavily chained, were taken in an armed carriage to the Palace of Whitehall to be questioned by King Charles II himself.

The question that has intrigued researchers ever since is *why* the King agreed to Blood's strange and impertinent demand. Some, such as historian Robert Hutchinson, have stated that this may simply have been a regal whim, an irresistible curiosity to meet the 'notorious traitor and incendiary'. At the same time Hutchinson and others also suggest that the King's accession to Blood's demand was motivated by the vested interests of King and several of his chief ministers.

It seems that Blood had several important friends, or at least influential acquaintances, at court and that he could embarrass them by disclosing some secrets that these high and mighty men would prefer to remain just that – secret. One of these men was Lord Arlington himself. He had probably used Blood as a spy five years earlier when the former was in Holland, employing him to trap the regicide, Edmund Ludlow, before catching him in Paris. There was also, George Villiers, 2nd Duke of Buckingham, who was perhaps working in cahoots with the King's mistress, the alluring Barbara Palmer, Duchess of Cleveland, and who had good reason for Blood to restrain himself by not divulging any embarrassing secrets to which he was privy.

In addition, Sir Joseph Williamson, a prominent politician and the King's spymaster, said that Blood was better alive than dead, that there was nothing to gain turning Blood into another nonconformist martyr. Even the Duke of Ormonde, a man who had great reason to despise and perhaps even fear Blood, prophesied, "Surely no King should wish to see a malefactor, but with intention to pardon him." The Duke was right.

Blood now found himself in a small room at the rear of the palace. It was clearly not used very often and was decorated with only a few medium-sized portraits of past generals and aristocrats in heavy gilded frames. When Blood and his son were hauled in to face the king, they found him sitting in a large maroon padded chair in the centre of a line of smaller chairs behind a long highly polished table. Two bottles of wine, some glasses and a few documents lay on the table in no apparent order.

Blood looked at his royal master sitting there slowly drinking from a silver beaker. What he saw was a tall man with a mass of long blackish curly hair surrounding a well-tanned face which was lined in the lower half. He had sharp dark eyes which sparkled, a thin moustache over a thin-lipped mouth and a strong chin. He was a wearing a white cravat and a royal blue coat over a white shirt. His gold chain of office shone over the top of his coat and the small jewels in it flashed when they caught the light.

"Your Majesty," Blood began, trying to bow despite the shackles binding him. "I am honoured that you have agreed to talk to me and..."

"Tell me, Blood," the King interrupted. "I won't call you Colonel Blood, because I've been informed that colonel is not your true rank. However, tell me, was it you who was involved in the attack on the Duke of Ormonde six months ago, while he was driving along in his carriage in Pall Mall?"

"Yes, Your Majesty," Blood answered immediately, without any sign of regret. "The duke had caused me to lose much money and land in the past and I wished to have revenge on him."

"I see, so please tell me more about what made you make so bold an assault on one of my lords."

"Sire," Blood continued as he looked around and noted the King's brother, James, his younger nephew,

Prince Rupert, Sir Joseph Williamson and two or three other officials listening very carefully. "Sire, well, not only did the Duke of Ormonde take my money and strip me of my lands, but he also had several of my closest friends and supporters executed. It was after this that I and several others swore that we would have revenge on him."

"And who were these friends, or may I call them accomplices?" Prince James, Duke of York asked, looking down his long nose.

"I regret, Sire, but that I cannot tell you. You see, I would never betray a friend's life, nor deny any guilt in defence of my own."

Prince James leaned over, whispered something to his brother who nodded in agreement. Blood noticed that although there was a certain family likeness between the two brothers, the King looked as though he had a stronger personality. His brother's face was longer and paler, and his eyes were less sharp. The way he stood, as he did to face Blood, gave the impression that the prince looked down on everyone surrounding him.

"Tell me, Blood," he asked languidly, "why did you then try and steal the Crown Jewels? Did you really think that you would be able to sell them just like that?"

Blood nodded. "Sire, I was hoping to make up the wrongs, injuries and losses I had made earlier in Ireland…"

"But that was eight years ago," Sir Joseph Williamson interrupted.

"I know that, sir, but I was so angry when I thought about the losses I had sustained – the disgraces and disappointments that I had met with."

"And how much did you think my crown, orb and sceptre were worth?" the King asked. "Enough to solve your financial difficulties?"

Blood straightened himself up and looked at his King straight in the eye. "I believe they are worth at least a hundred thousand pounds, Sire."

This reply was received with a loud guffaw. "Blood, you're a fool," His Majesty said at last after he had stopped laughing. "They are worth nothing like that. Tell him, James, how much they were worth."

His brother stopped smiling. "Blood, the crown, orb and sceptre were worth about six thousand."

"Aye, that was what they were worth before you and your gang rudely battered them with your mallets," the Earl of Arlington couldn't help himself from adding. "But I doubt they'll be worth anything like that now."

Blood stood there. His face crestfallen. All that work for six thousand pounds. A sum that would not make up his losses – yet a crime that would most probably send him to the hanging tree at Tyburn.

"Oh, the mistakes we make in life, eh, Blood?" Prince Rupert said. "And I remember you during that accursed war when you were a very stout and bold fellow fighting for His Majesty's father. Now look at you. Standing here in front of my uncle, His Majesty, hoping against hope that he won't have you hanged like a common criminal."

Blood looked along the line of his interrogators and said nothing. Then suddenly he raised his head and looked straight at the king. "Sire, I have a confession to make, but one that is nothing to do with this business of my taking the Crown Jewels."

"What, taking?" Sir Williamson exploded. *"Stealing, man. Stealing!"*

Blood ignored this outburst and continued in a flat even tone. "Some time ago, Sire, I cannot remember exactly when, but I restrained myself from shooting your Majesty."

All of the King's men leaned forward – this was new.

"You were bathing in the river at Vauxhall, Sire, and you were there completely defenceless. If I may say so, you were swimming there as clothed as on the day you came into this world. I was standing there in the nearby reeds holding a carbine and I could have shot you as easily as that." Blood tried to click his fingers, but his shackles prevented him from doing so.

"And?"

"And then, Your Majesty, I stopped myself. I realised that you were not responsible for my losses and that if I had killed you, you might have been replaced by someone far worse."

At this point Blood caught the expression on the King's brother's face, and he thought that he had been too free with his tongue. For someone facing the gallows it did not pay to denigrate the King's successor, his brother – and in front of his most senior advisors.

The King looked at Blood and Blood looked back at him. This time he did not bow his head. He had said his piece.

"Is that all, Blood?"

Blood nodded. Then he opened his mouth. "Sire, I have just one other thing to add, and it is this – to have me executed would be a serious mistake."

"Oh, why is that?" the King asked.

"Because, Sire," Blood continued in the same flat, even tone. "If you were to have me hanged, I have hundreds of friends and supporters who have sworn to take revenge. This of course would cause a very dangerous situation in your realm, Sire, and I have no wish for that."

James looked at him in that superior way of his. "Oh, that's very noble of you, Blood."

Blood ignored him. "And, Your Majesty, if you will be so Christian and generous to spare my life and that of my son, who did nothing more than to be obedient and follow his father's instructions, then you will find that you will have no more loyal subjects than us in the whole of your kingdom. That I can promise with my hand on my heart."

The King said nothing. He merely bent forward and scribbled something on a piece of paper and passed it over to his brother. James read it, nodded and passed it on to Sir Joseph Williamson and the King's nephew.

Charles then stood up. "Take Blood and his son back to the Tower. We will resolve with this matter later."

Clanking their way out of the room, Blood and his son were escorted back to the carriage and returned to their damp, dank dungeon in the Tower. They were to wait there for two months before they heard the King's decision.

As Blood and his son sat on their low stools or lay in the smelly hay that was their bedding, they endlessly debated what their fate would be as, in more comfortable surroundings, the Earl of Arlington and Sir Joseph Williamson addressed the same concerns. Williamson considered that Blood acting as a spy in the future would be 'ten times his value' to the Crown than him being hanged. Arlington agreed, especially as he thought that a possible war with Holland would break out soon and that the King could use another spy. When they spoke to Blood in his cell, they were somewhat surprised to hear the prisoner say that if he were to be released, His Majesty should appoint him as a governor of one of the new colonies in America.

"That will never be," he was told, and was informed that if he and his son were freed then one of the conditions would be that he would write a letter of apology to the Duke of Ormonde for all the past violent acts that he, Blood, had carried out against him. Blood was not pleased about this, but after weighing the cost of his freedom against the writing of a letter, he penned a long-winded apology, signing it 'Your Grace's most humble servant'.

Blood was released in mid-July 1671, and soon after so were his son and Perrot. Then two weeks later, at the beginning of August, Blood received an official document beginning:

> *'Pardon to Thomas Blood the father of all treasons, misprisons* [failure to report a treasonable offence] *of treason, murders, homicides, felonies, assaults, batteries and other offences whatsoever at any time since 25 May 1660,* [the date he returned to England from his exile in Europe] *committed by himself alone or together with any other person or persons...'*

If this royal pardon shocked many of His Majesty's court and other citizens, they were to be further shocked when the King granted Blood a pension of five hundred pounds (more than seventy thousand today) from lands in County Kildare, Ireland, and the return of Blood's English and Irish properties. This was not a case of Charles being particularly forgiving or generous; there was a price to pay. The king, despite his manner of external nonchalance, had a sharp eye on what was happening in his kingdom. He needed experienced men to report to him concerning any possible acts of sedition and conspiracy. Blood was such a man.

Influential courtiers and men of letters were horrified to see Blood in Whitehall Palace, now dressed, as a Mr T. Henshaw noted, 'in a new suit and periwig'. John Evelyn, the diarist, wrote that Blood, 'that impudent bold fellow… How he came to be pardoned, and even received into favour…I could never come to understand'.

But pardoned he was, and he was even seen in the royal apartments, where he 'affected particularly to be in the same room where the Duke of Ormonde was'. The witty satirist, John Wilmot, the Earl of Rochester, wrote:

> *Blood that wears treason in his face*
> *Villain complete in parson's gown*
> *How much he is at court in grace*
> *For stealing Ormonde and the crown!*
> *Since loyalty does no man good,*
> *Let's steal the King and outdo Blood!*

One month after Blood's release, Talbot Edwards was awarded two hundred pounds, while

Edward's son, Wythe and Captain Beckman, the man who had wrestled the escaping Blood to the ground and arrested him, each received one hundred pounds.

As for Blood, he was as good as his word. He became a loyal citizen and spent the next ten years acting as a spy for the government. The king, who had spent the nine years of Cromwell's reign in exile, was now concerned about the possible outbreak of a war with the Netherlands. In addition, he was well aware of potential Catholic and Nonconformist religious strife in the country. Therefore, he had good reason to be suspicious when it came to the people surrounding him at court, each with their own agenda.

Blood was in regular contact with both Arlington and Williamson, although the latter did not trust him very much. However, to stay in the authorities' good graces, Blood turned on those he had supported in the past and, in October 1677, informed Williamson that a group of Fifth Monarchists, extreme Puritans, were plotting to kill the king.

Blood was also involved for some time with Titus Oates, an Anglican priest. This disreputable cleric deliberately perjured himself and instigated what was known as the 'Popish Plot.' This plot claimed that the Catholics were planning to assassinate the king. Eighty-one people were accused, of whom thirty-five were executed. Blood later tried to plant some evidence to show that Oates was not as patriotic as he had claimed to be.

However, it was Blood's involvement with George Villiers, the Duke of Buckingham, that finished off the 'Colonel's' career. Towards the end of a very up-and-down career, in 1680, Buckingham, one of the several rakish aristocrats who was close to Charles II, was accused of sodomising a gentlewoman called Sarah Harwood. The accusation claimed that, afterwards, Buckingham paid for her to go to France in order to keep the matter a secret. However, he was known as a violent man and several witnesses were prepared to testify against him. Of course, the powerful Buckingham denied the charges, no doubt being aware of the fact that sodomy was a capital crime. It was said that one of the witnesses, Philip Le Mar, had been paid three hundred pounds to accuse the duke by the Countess of Danby, one of Buckingham's worst enemies.

In January 1680, Blood was called to in a secret meeting in a tavern in Westminster by the magistrate, Sir William Waller. He was questioned about the affairs of the duke, his past friend and soon after a warrant was issued stating:

> *'Oath has been made by two witnesses* [Samuel Ryther and Philemon Coddan] *that Colonel Thomas Blood has been a confederate in a late conspiracy of falsely accusing and charging his grace the Duke of Buckingham of*

> *sodomy and has refused to give bail for his appearance at the next general sessions to be held for the city and liberty of Westminster.*
>
> *These are therefore to will and require that you seize and apprehend the said Colonel Thomas Blood and if he shall refuse to give in bail, to carry him and to deliver him into the hand of Mr Church, keeper of the Gatehouse in Westminster, according to the tenor of the* mittimus [court warrant] *in your hands.'*

Blood refused to put up bail and demanded to see the warrant for his arrest. In the meanwhile, the duke was cleared of all charges and proceeded to bring a legal action for defamation of character against Blood, his past employee. The charge was for *scandalum magnatum* – defamatory speech or writing against an aristocrat, judge or high officer – a civil suit in which Buckingham claimed and was awarded ten thousand pounds in damages. There was no way that Blood could pay this amount, so he sent his other son, Charles, to the King's brother, James, to intercede on his behalf. Nothing came of this and so the unfortunate 'Colonel' contacted various other influential people, but none would come to his rescue. As a result, Blood found himself confined within the Westminster gatehouse, though he was not to remain there long. In July 1680 he was released after an unknown person paid the fine.

By now Blood was sixty-two years old, and he returned home to his house in Bowling Alley, Westminster. He was a sick man, having contracted gaol fever in the meanwhile. He became depressed and lethargic and, two weeks after leaving prison, he died on 24 August 1680. He was buried two days later near the grave of his wife, Mary, in the New Chapel cemetery, Tothill Fields, Westminster.

This should have been the end of the story, but it was not. It was rumoured that Blood had not really died, but that his alleged death was merely one more of the many tricks this devious man had played throughout his life. So much public noise was generated by this rumour that his grave was opened one week later. A jury and a coroner together with twenty-three people who had known Blood gathered around the graveside to witness the exhumation.

By now, owing to the warm summer weather, the face of the corpse was 'so altered and swollen' that it was impossible to identify the corpse. The final decision that it was indeed Blood resting there was made when an army captain who had known the 'Colonel' swore under oath that he recognised Blood's left thumb, which was enlarged. Not everyone was prepared to accept this but, in the end, it was decided that the body was that of Thomas Blood and he was then peacefully reinterred.

However, even though he had died, his spirit and reputation lived on. Various broadsheets were soon making the rounds about Blood, and a certain J. Shorter wrote a long poem about the villain who among his many nefarious activities would always be remembered as the man who tried to steal the Crown Jewels. The poem began:

> *Thanks, ye kind fates for your last favour shown*
> *Of stealing BLOOD who lately stole the Crown*
> *We'll not exclaim so much against you since*
> *As well as BEDLOE* you have fetched him hence,*
> *He who has been a plague to all mankind*
> *And never was to anyone a friend...*

The poem finished with this suggestion:

> *Here lies the man who has boldly run through*
> *More villainies than ever England knew*

And nere to any friend he had was true
Here let him then by all unpitied lie
And let's rejoice his time was come to die.

*Bedloe, a Popish Plot informer and crook who had died four days before Blood.

As for the other *dramatis personae* of this story, Blood's wife, Mary, had seven children and probably died in Lancashire in 1671. Blood's fifth son, Charles, became a lawyer and defended his older brother, Holcroft, against accusations of assault by his estranged wife.

Charles also warned King James II about 'dangerous conspiracies against him'. Blood's eldest son, Thomas, alias Thomas Hunt, died aged twenty-four in c.1675. After helping his father to pretend he was a doctor, he had become an unsuccessful highwayman. He was captured, fined and jailed, before helping his father again, this time taking part in the unsuccessful attack on the Duke of Ormonde. The young man never learned to steer clear of his father's plots and went on to help him try and steal the Crown Jewels. Like his father, Thomas 'Hunt' was pardoned, before marrying and then sailing off to New York State where he became a captain in the British army.

Of Blood's friends and fellow conspirators, Captain Richard Halliwell managed to escape arrest for his part in the failed attempt to steal the Crown Jewels. It is thought that he was 'R.H.', the author of a contemporary biography of 'Colonel' Blood and that, as a Fifth Monarchist, he was involved in other conspiracies against Charles II.

Halliwell's fellow Fifth Monarchist and Crown Jewels thief, Robert Perrot, was pardoned and later took sides against King James II. He joined Charles II's illegitimate son, the Duke of Monmouth, in his unsuccessful rising against King James II at the Battle of Sedgemoor in July 1685. He fought as a major and was wounded, captured and soon after executed for treason. Blood's perennial enemy, James Butler, the Duke of Ormonde, served as the Lord Lieutenant of Ireland for two terms, (1662-1669 and 1677-1685) and died in Dorset in 1687 leaving behind debts of well over a hundred thousand pounds.

Chapter 4

Mary Carleton (1642–1673)

Some of the villains in this book, such as Richard of Pudlicott, gained their infamous reputations by robbery; others, such as Jack Sheppard, became known for being a Houdini-type thief who was able to escape from all sorts of imprisonment. Moll Cutpurse and Jenny Diver were well-known pickpockets, and Adam Worth and Ikey Solomon made their fortunes by robbery and dealing in stolen goods. 'Colonel' Thomas Blood

tried to steal the Crown Jewels and highwayman Dick Turpin achieved legendary status through his alleged ride from London to York on his faithful horse, Black Bess.

The crimes of the 'heroine' of this chapter, Mary Carleton, were of a completely different nature. She too was a villain who broke the law, but the way she obtained her ill-gotten gains was by acting as an imposter. This young lady from Kent is remembered for pretending on more than one occasion that she was a German princess. In this way she fooled several rich and gullible victims into parting with their money. She was fortunate that she was attractive, but in the end her beauty, skills and deviousness did not save her from meeting her Maker at the Fatal Tree at Tyburn.

*

Traditionally, after getting married, women have taken their husband's surnames as their own. As such, Mary Carleton could have easily been called Mary Stedman, Mary van Wolway, or one of several other names. However, she has gone down in the history of English villains and imposters as Mary Carleton.

She was born Mary Moders in Canterbury, Kent on 11 January 1642. Little is known about her early life, though it is thought that her father was either a chorister in Canterbury Cathedral or that he was some sort of trader in the city. Some say that she loved to read, especially romantic works and stories about princesses and high-born ladies, and this may explain why she later behaved as she did. The first definite thing we know about her is that she married Thomas Stedman, a shoemaker, and had two children by him. Unfortunately, they died in infancy and this too may have influenced how she led her life from then on. As her husband was not able to keep her in the manner she desired, she left him and moved to Dover. There, she married again, this time to a wealthy surgeon.

Unfortunately for this female villain, Dover is less than twenty miles south of Canterbury, and it did not take long for the news of Mary's bigamous marriage to become known to the authorities in Dover. She was arrested and indicted at Maidstone, Kent, but using her ready charm and wit, she managed to have herself acquitted.

At this point, she decided to leave England and try her luck abroad. She went to Cologne, Germany and had an affair with an older German nobleman. He was very generous and showered her with valuable jewellery, large sums of money and gold chains. However, when he was about to propose to her, she fled Cologne after breaking open and ransacking his jewellery chest to steal even more money and trinkets. She then fled to Amsterdam, sold some of her stolen jewels and gold chains before continuing to Rotterdam. At nearby Brill she took a ship to England and landed in Billingsgate, in the City of London.

In 1663, now aged twenty-one, she made out she was Princess van Wolway, an orphaned German aristocrat. When asked about her past and why she had come to London, Mary claimed that she was the daughter of Henry van Wolway, Lord of Holmstein, and had fled to England to escape from a possessive lover. Mr King, the landlord of the Exchange tavern where she was staying, heard this tale of woe. He told his brother-in-law, a surgeon who, after seeing her jewellery and the forged letters in her possession, fell in love with her and married her. His name was John Carleton. It was his surname that she was to take with her into posterity.

One day soon after their wedding, John Carleton accosted his wife. "Mary, what's this letter about that my brother-in-law has just given me?"

"Why, my dear? What does it say?"

"It says you are a fraud. An imposter. You are no more a German princess than I am a cousin to the king."

Mary stood up, hands on her hips. "That's rubbish. Here, read it out."

And John Carleton did:

> *'Sir, I am an entire stranger to your person, yet common justice and humanity oblige me to give you notice that the pretended princess, who has passed herself upon your brother, Mr John Carleton, is a cheat*

> *and an imposter. If I tell you, sir, that she has already married several men in our county of Kent, and afterwards made off with all the money she could get into her hands, I say no more than could be proved were she brought in the face of justice. That you may be certain I am not mistaken in the woman, please to observe that she has high breasts, a very graceful appearance and speaks several languages fluently. Yours unknown. T.B.'*

Once again Mary found herself in court being charged with bigamy. Attack being a good form of defence, she attacked John Carleton, claiming that he too had lied and said that he was a lord. And not only that, she claimed, but that he had married her for her money as his first wife had not brought any money to their marriage. This complicated case attracted much attention, especially as both sides had pamphlets published stating how the other partner was lying and inventing all manner of salacious tales. As a result, Mary managed, for the second time, to get herself exonerated from charges of bigamy.

Mary, not being one to waste an opportunity for making money, then wrote an account of her past, *The Case of Madame Mary Carleton*. In addition, she acted in a play, *A Witty Combat* or *The Female Victor,* which fictionalised her career and was seen by Samuel Pepys. This drama must have been quite a tear-jerker, as soon after, she attracted more admirers who were happy to give 'the poor lady' valuable presents. Of course, it did not take long for her to marry one of these unsuspecting dupes, a fifty-year-old man who made her large presents of rings and other jewels. He became so enamoured with her that he gave her more and more. Then feeling that she had exploited the situation well enough, she either got him drunk or waited for him to fall asleep, and as before, she ran away. But not before she had stolen even more money and valuables, as well as the keys to his trunks and *escritoires*. Part of her loot included a bill for a hundred pounds from a goldsmith in the city.

According to the *Newgate Calendar,* Mary now began to play a new game. She presented herself as an unfortunate but rich virgin. She claimed that she had fled an undesirable suitor whose father insisted that she marry his son. To make this story appear genuine, she had friends send her letters which reinforced her story by including news of the family from whom she had escaped. She left these letters lying around in her room for her landlady to find and read, persuading the landlady to make a match between the rich virgin and her nephew. This plan succeeded. The nephew gave Mary an expensive watch and soon was hoping to marry the lovely creature.

One evening, while Mary and the nephew were in an intimate romantic situation, they were disturbed by a knock on the door. It was a porter.

"Sorry, ma'am, for bothering you at this hour," he mumbled, acting out the scene as he had been instructed, "but I have been told to give you this letter."

She took it, broke the seal, opened the letter and began to read. Just as she reached the end of it, she threw the letter aside and shrieked, "Oh, I am undone! I am undone!" and fell to the floor in a faint.

The gallant nephew grabbed some smelling salts, revived her and asked, "What was in the letter, my love, to have caused you to faint away?"

"Read it," Mary replied, picking up the letter and thrusting it into his hands.

What he read was that Mary's brother had died, and that he had left all his estate of two hundred pounds per annum to her.

"But surely that is both good and bad news," the surprised nephew said. "It is truly sad that your brother has died, but you are now a rich lady indeed."

"That's true," Mary replied, sobbing quietly, "but read the rest of the letter, to the very end."

The nephew did so, and saw that Mary's father and the lover she had escaped from were planning to come to London.

"I see," the nephew concluded, looking up from the letter. "But as your father says, you will not receive this money unless you marry your past and hated lover."

"Yes, and the writer of this letter advises me that if I won't marry him, then I should flee and change my habitation, my address."

"And who, my love, is the writer of this letter? He has just signed himself as S.E."

Mary shrugged. "I don't know. But is that relevant now? All I know is that I must disappear, and as quickly as possible."

Hearing this, the infatuated nephew made arrangements for Mary and her female servant to move into his rooms. Of course, what he did not know was that he was unknowingly acting out his part in a plot that Mary and her servant had planned to the last detail. They moved in the following day, and that night Mary and her villainous servant broke open the nephew's trunk, stole a hundred pounds and some clothes, and fled.

From here she continued on her merry way, fooling unsuspecting people with fake stories, tears and light fingers. According to the *Newgate Calendar,* she tricked a trader in Cheapside, London where, together with a female accomplice, she bought six pounds worth of silk, but when it came to paying for it Mary found there was no money in her purse apart from a few gold pieces, which she claimed had great sentimental value for her. The trader, not willing to believe that he was about to be duped by this well-dressed lady, sent one of his men to accompany Mary to her lodgings to collect the money there. He arranged a coach for the journey but, on the way, Mary and her maid got off at the Royal

Exchange saying that she needed to purchase some ribbons for the silk she had just bought. Telling the trader's man to wait a few minutes, the two women disappeared into the busy London streets leaving the trader to wait there until he realised that one should not believe every alleged lady of quality that one meets.

The *Newgate Calendar* records that Mary pulled a similar ruse later in Spitalfields, London. There she ordered forty pounds worth of silk from a French master weaver, saw that she did not have enough money in her purse and asked him whether he would come back with her to her lodgings. There she would pay him, and all would be well.

When they arrived, she told him that she wished to divide the silk into two parcels, one for her and the other for her kinswoman in the next room. Naturally, he agreed, for after all, who would not want to do business with this high-born lady? Mary then went next door, ostensibly to show the silk to her niece, leaving the weaver drinking some wine.

After waiting for some time and hoping that he was not disturbing the young ladies, he knocked on the door and opened it to find that there was no-one there. When he asked around, he was told that Mary and her maid had left and were not due to return. He must have been an unhappy weaver that day when not only had he been deceived, but that he had lost a considerable quantity of silk as well.

Soon after this Mary fooled her landlord, a tailor by trade. She asked him to make up some clothes for her from the material she had tricked out of her previous victims, requesting that he make the dresses as quickly as possible. Being charmed by his lovely tenant, he agreed, and hired a few people to help him finish the job quickly.

When the time came for him to deliver the dresses and receive his pay, he found that Mary was due to receive quite a few visitors that day. She gave her landlord's wife twenty shillings and asked her to use this to buy food for her guests. The result was that Mary organised a large party during which the landlord became drunk. While his wife was busy looking after him and putting him to bed, Mary and her guests stripped the house of anything of value and then they all went their various ways. None of them was caught.

On another occasion, Mary decided to exploit the 17th century fashions of mourning. Telling a shopkeeper in the Strand that her father had died, she ordered a wide range of mourning accoutrements. Then in a similar manner to that in which she had behaved on the previous two occasions, she made some excuse that she could not pay immediately and that she would pay the unsuspecting shopkeeper later in the day. The lady shopkeeper agreed and was later informed that her customer had disappeared and that not only had she had taken the various accoutrements with her, but she had also stolen many valuable pieces of furniture.

One day, while living in Holborn, Mary asked a young lawyer to come to her lodgings for an important meeting. After he had sat down and drank a small glass of wine, she began.

"Mr Justinian," Mary began, looking both as attractive and serious as she could. "I wish to discuss with you a major problem I have about writing my will."

Hearing the words 'a major problem', the lawyer leaned forward to hear all the details. From his little experience he understood that much money was involved, which would mean a significant fee for him.

"It is like this, sir. I am now an heir to a large amount of money and property that has been left to me by my late father." At this point she made the sign of the cross and continued. "However, as you may know, I am married but I do not live with my husband as he is such an extravagant fellow."

The lawyer nodded sympathetically. "Yes, ma'am, I quite understand."

"Therefore, what I want is to secure this estate in such a manner that my husband, profligate man that he is, will not benefit from my will in any shape or form. Is that clear?"

Mr Justinian nodded again and then handed a handkerchief over to his client as tears began to well up in her eyes. Just as he was about to ask her a question, a woman burst into the room.

"O Lord, madam," she screamed." We are all undone! Your master is below! He has been asking after you, and he swears that he will come up to your chamber. I am afraid the neighbours will not be able to stop him. He seems so resolute."

Mary put her hands to her face. "O heavens! What shall I do?"

The lawyer stood up, trying to look as if he were in command. "Why?"

"Why?" Mary repeated. "I mean for you, sir, as a lawyer. What excuse shall I make for your being here? I dare not tell him your quality and business. If I did, that would endanger us all. He is such a jealous fellow."

Mr Justinian looked troubled. He had never had to cope with such a situation before. Just as he was about to say something, Mary crossed the room and opened a large closet door.

"Sir, step into here and then I will send my husband away. If he sees you here, there is no telling what may transpire."

The lawyer, not wishing to be part of a violent scene, promptly stepped into the closet. Mary locked the door, drew a curtain across it as her counterfeit husband stormed into the room.

"O, Mrs Devil," he cried. "I understand you have a man in this room! A man who is not your husband. Tell me, where is this son of a whore? I shall sacrifice him this moment. Tell me," he shouted at his alleged wife, "Is this your modesty, madam? Is this how you behave when I am not present? This is your virtue?"

"But, husband, I…"

"But, husband me nothing! Let me see your gallant immediately, or, by the light, you shall be my next victim instead." And saying that, the 'husband' strode across the room, swept the maroon curtain aside, and yanked open the door of the closet. "You, you rabbit in there! Come out here and show yourself."

The lawyer stepped out, trembling like the rabbit he had just been called. The counterfeit husband whipped out his sword and Mr Justinian stepped back smartly into the cupboard. Just then, Mary pushed her way forward between the 'husband' and the shaking lawyer.

"Husband, desist!" she cried. "He means nothing to me. He is only a…" And just then, a man announcing himself to be a friend of her husband charged into the room and wrested the sword from the 'husband'.

"He is up to no good," the husband insisted. "He wanted to have his way with my wife."

"No, no. It's not true," the lawyer said from the depths of the closet. "All I wanted was to…"

"I know what we should do," the 'husband's' friend said, laying a restraining hand on the 'husband's' arm. Either we sort this out through a duel or that lawyer pays five hundred pounds to satisfy your honour."

The 'husband' appeared to think about this and in the end agreed to accept the five hundred.

"But I don't have that sort of money," the lawyer said, nervously stepping out of the closet. "Will a hundred suffice as a first payment?"

A nodding of heads showed that this was an acceptable solution and the matter came to an end. This show of threatened domestic violence had netted Mary and her accomplices one hundred pounds (eleven thousand four hundred pounds today); a goodly sum for less than one hour's work.

It was through tricks like this that Mary Carleton kept herself for the next ten years, living a life with gold, jewellery and other property, as well as fawning lovers.

Once these unfortunate dupes found out they had been taken for a fool, they were not willing to expose her for the fraud she was. This would have meant that not only would they too have been shown up as naïve dolts, but that their wives would have heard about their extra-marital escapades. Therefore, it was no surprise that Mary soon earned the nickname 'The Grey Widow' – one of her favourite ploys being to pretend that her dear husband had recently departed this world.

However, all good things come to an end, and in 1671 Mary Carleton found herself behind bars in Newgate Prison. She had been arrested for stealing a silver tankard in Covent Garden. She was tried, found guilty and sentenced to be hanged. But again, she was fortunate. The judge reprieved her and ordered her to be transported to Jamaica instead. There, he assumed, she would find herself working hard in the sugar cane fields.

The judge was wrong. Mary became a prostitute, and a year later either tricked a sea captain into taking her back to England or that she simply sneaked aboard a London-bound ship.

Back in England she returned to her old tricks. She married a rich apothecary in Westminster, stole three hundred pounds from him and disappeared. Later she moved into a lodging house which she shared with her accomplice-maid, the landlady and a watchmaker. One evening Mary invited these two ladies to come with her to see a play. While they were there, Mary's maid, who had been left behind, stole two hundred pounds and about thirty watches. This haul netted Mary about six hundred pounds (over ninety thousand pounds today).

The end of Mary Carleton's bigamous and thieving career came from an unexpected direction. One day, a Southwark brewer called Mr Freeman was robbed of two hundred pounds. He went to Marshalsea prison and demanded that Mr Lowman, the Keeper, allow him to search various places. He particularly suspected a man called Lancaster and went to his premises. While there, they saw a lady dressed in a nightgown. This seemed very suspicious and the lady's story somehow did not ring true. Mr Lowman entered the room and found three letters. The lady was offended by this action and promptly made a fuss. It did not help. She was arrested with the letters and taken to prison. She was tried at the Old Bailey where, under questioning, she admitted that she was Mary Carleton.

"As you are Mary Carleton and you have returned early and illegally from your transportation to Jamaica," the judge decreed, "I have no alternative but to sentence you to death. Do you have anything to say?"

Mary smiled as sweetly and demurely as she could. "Yes, Your Honour. You cannot hang me as I am with child."

"I see. Then I will have some matrons examine you. Next case."

The matrons examined Mary, found that she was not pregnant and she was returned to Newgate. While there she had many visitors, some who came out of curiosity and others, probably including those she had fooled in the past, to gloat.

One week after her conviction, on 22 January 1673, Mary was taken to the 'Fatal Tree' at Tyburn. It is said that she was in good spirits and even wore a picture of John Carleton, her third husband, on her sleeve. Her last words at the gallows were to admit that she had been a vain woman but that she hoped that God would forgive her as she forgave her own enemies.

Later, her body was cut down and she was buried, aged thirty-one, in St. Martin's Churchyard. Soon after someone wrote the following on her grave:

> *The German princess here, against her will,*
> *Lies underneath, and yet oh, strange!*
> *Lies still.*

Although Mary Carleton's name is less well-known today in comparison to other English villains such as Dick Turpin, Colonel Blood or Moll Cutpurse, she was the subject of several publications which appeared during the next eighty years. Daniel Defoe, the author of *Robinson Crusoe,* referred to her in his novel, *Roxana: The Unfortunate Mistress* (1724), and the exploits of Mary Carleton also appeared in the satirical *Poor Robin's Almanack* from 1675 until 1707. In this popular book Mary, as an imposter, was compared to Sancho Panza, Doctor Faustus, Pope Joan and the Whore of Babylon.

Chapter 5

Jonathan Wilde: 'Thief-Taker General' (1682-1725)

Of all the villainous characters in this book, one of the most disgusting is Jonathan Wilde (c.1682-1725). Not only was he an accomplished thief, fence, blackmailer and ruler of a vast underworld empire with tentacles reaching into all levels of society, but he was also responsible for sending tens of his fellow thieves to the infamous Tyburn Tree to be hanged. By the time he was in his mid-thirties, in 1718, this devious underworld

figure who worked both sides of the law had himself called the 'Thief-Taker General'. He acted as a prototype Mafia-style criminal godfather who controlled many of the thousands of criminals who were a major aspect of life in Georgian London. His story is one of insatiable and selfish greed and power, and if other criminals had to pay for his importance and success with their necks, then that was how he wanted it to be.

In addition to being one of the major icons of the capital's eighteenth-century crime scene, he is also remembered in literature. He appears as Peachum, the powerful betrayer of criminals and prostitutes in The Beggar's Opera *by John Gay (1728) as well as featuring in many other Georgian satires. Over 150 years later, Sir Arthur Conan Doyle said that he based his arch-villain, Professor Moriarty, on Jonathan Wilde, as well as on Adam Worth, another villain who appears later in this book.*

*

"Hello, what are you doing here?" Jonathan Wilde asked the young lady with straggly blonde hair and smuts on her pretty face. "Not the old game, is it?"

She was standing in a murky alley one evening when Wilde noticed her among the grimy brick walls half-covered with grubby notices. All manner of litter and broken bottles were lying in the gutter.

She stuck her pert nose up in the air. "No, of course not," she replied. "I'm off to give some Bible lessons to a young man, aren't I?"

"I see. Well, d'you want to give me a lesson as well? I can pay you. No favours."

She smiled, put out her hand for some money, stuffed it into a small pouch and then pulled him into a dark passageway where she gave him his 'Bible lesson' on an old disused wooden bench. Afterwards they just sat there, neither of them having anything else to do. Just two lone souls in the dingiest part of London looking for some company. He took out a bottle of ale from his bag and shared it with her.

"So this is what you do every night?" he asked.

She nodded. "Yes, most evenings I suppose. After all, it pays more than being in service, doesn't it? And," she smiled, "I don't have any fat cow of a mistress telling me that the pots aren't shiny enough or that I have to go out to bring in some more coal for the fire. By the way, what's your name and where are you from? You're no Londoner, are you? That I can tell from the way you talk."

"No, I'm not from here. I'm from Wolverhampton."

"Where's that?"

"Near Birmingham, and if you must know, my name is Jonathan Wilde. What's your name?" he asked, finishing off the bottle and throwing it down the alley.

"Mary. Mary Milliner, but I think it may have been Mollineaux in the past. But anyways, I call myself Mary Milliner now. So what are you doing here in London? You don't look like a country boy."

"I'm not. They've given me the liberty of the gate. Y'know, they let me out of Newgate at night to help them arrest thieves and the like. So far, until I met you, I hadn't had a good night."

Mary slid along the bench nearer to him. "Here, put your arm around me. I'm a bit cold."

Wilde didn't have to be asked twice. As he pulled her closer to him and slipped his hand down inside her warm blouse, she asked him what he had done to be spending time in Newgate.

"Well, Mary, it's like this. My father was a carpenter and my mother sold fruit and stuff in the local market. I didn't want to do any of that and so I left home, more like running away, and became a servant to this rich gent in London. But then I had to run away from him as well – he thought I'd pinched some of his money and a silver tray."

"And had you?"

"Only the money. I didn't want no trouble in fencing off a tray. And anyway, I only pinched twenty guineas. He could afford that easy without any problems. And then I thought it best to go back home to Wolverhampton."

"And did you pinch any stuff there?"

"Yes, Mary, but not much. There wasn't much to pinch apart from horses and the bums of the wenches in the Red Lion."

"So that's why you're back in London, I suppose."

"That's right, lass, and because I wanted to get away from my wife and son and..."

"Ah, so you're married then. So am I, but my husband, if you can call him that, ran off with some slut. Called Jenny, I think. Skinny bitch. No tits at all," she added, pushing out her own full bosom. "Dunno what he saw in her."

"Yes, well my wife started off all right, but then she began nagging me for more money and stuff like that. And then, when I found out she was whoring it to make some on the side, I came back to London leaving her with a black eye."

"And what are you doing in Newgate?"

"They got me for debt. I owed this other gent twenty guineas and he had me thrown in Newgate, but it's not so bad there if you know what to do."

"What d'you mean? I've heard it's horrible in there. Just like being in Hell. I've never been in there myself. At least, not yet."

"I do favours for the gaolers. Running errands and the like. They're a lazy lot of bastards and don't like to shift their arses at all. The other prisoners bribe 'em for better food, more visitors and stuff like that and then I get paid from their bribe money. And in fact, but don't you tell no-one this, I've made enough money to lend some to the others, which they then have to pay me back with interest."

"And if not?"

"I give some of the bigger prisoners money to beat them up. Simple, isn't it?"

"And now you're out on this 'liberty of the gate' thing? If you want, I can tell you where a couple of thieves are hiding, and in that way you'll be all right, no?"

From there on Mary helped Wilde out, and soon after his release, despite their previous marriages, they married and moved into her squalid rooms in Macklin Street, Holborn. This worked out to be mutually beneficial. While Mary was prowling the streets at night looking for clients, Wilde would be hiding nearby making sure that she was paid in full and that she wasn't beaten up by any dissatisfied customers. Sometimes he would rob an unfortunate man while he was rendered immobile, his breeches down, wrapped around his ankles.

They combined their ill-gotten gains and took over a drinking-house – a 'flash-house' – where strong drink was sold and where thieves and fences exchanged professional information and made deals. Wilde and Mary did not stop there. They also operated a scam called 'Buttock and Twang'. By lowering her neckline and raising her well-shaped leg, Mary would lure a customer into a dark alley where Wilde would hit him with a cudgel and knock him out. They would then go through his pockets and disappear with the takings. In this way they made enough money to buy the King's Head pub, a drinking establishment which soon became popular with many of the members of London's underworld.

At the same time, Mary also introduced her husband to some useful contacts among their customers and they taught him how they operated. Their financial situation improved even further when Mary became a madam for other prostitutes. Having Wilde around meant that no-one ever quibbled about paying for services rendered. For his part, Wilde contributed to the domestic economy. He used his new-found contacts to fence stolen goods while he continued lending money to thieves and the like to bribe their way out of prison or make their lives easier 'inside'.

Life was going well for the pair when cracks began to appear in their partnership. Mary accused him of drinking too much with their customers and Wilde blamed her for becoming too 'high and mighty' and for not accepting all the young men he brought her. Accusations became louder and nastier and soon the occasional push and shove turned into more frequent blows. Black eyes and bruises became the norm. Finally, in a particularly drunken fight, Wilde grabbed a kitchen knife and sliced off her ear. "There," he gloated as she tried to staunch the blood flowing down the side of her head. "Now you really look like what you are. A whore." And with that, he walked out of their marriage.

From there, Wilde moved on to the next stage in his nasty career - that is, he became a thief-taker. This profession was more or less created by Parliament in 1692. In that year, it passed the Act for Encouraging the Apprehending of Highwayman. In those days there was no professional police force and so the authorities relied upon private enterprise. This meant that the authorities rewarded thief-takers with forty pounds (six thousand pounds today) for the arrest and prosecution of any highwayman who was caught. The thief-taker could also claim possession of the highwayman's horse, saddle, weapons and any other property the unfortunate victim had.

As time passed, the so-called 'Highwayman Act' was expanded to include other crimes and a sliding scale of rewards was brought in, the payment being dependent on the seriousness of the offence. But however much they were paid, thief-takers were never popular. The law-abiding public saw them as scum and exploiters, while villains hated them and were always out for revenge.

In 1713, when Wilde was in his early thirties, Charles Hitchen, one of the first thief-takers and now City Marshal, asked Wilde to become one of his assistants. He would be known as a 'Mathematician' and be paid forty pounds per villain that he caught. These included such characters as the well-loved Jack

Sheppard, as well as members of high-class gangs including the Mohocks, who robbed and pillaged for fun. Wilde took up Hitchen's offer, called himself Hitchen's Deputy and began wearing a sword to show he was now an official representative of the law.

Ruthless and intelligent, Wilde was just the right man for the job. He became London's first 'crime-boss' and he knew how to exploit his power. He was generous and loyal to those who helped him, but he was just as merciless and vicious to those who tried to out-do him. His power and the scope of his work became so well known that when Sir William Thompson, the Recorder of London. became Solicitor General in 1717, he had a law passed – 'Jonathan Wilde's Act' – making it a capital offence to receive a reward under the pretence of helping the owner to recover stolen goods. And this of course was how Wilde was making a fortune on the side.

It did not take long for the new and keen Solicitor General to find out how Wilde worked. "This Wilde character – he has a gang of villains working for him, no?" he asked one of his more knowledgeable lawyers.

"Yes, sir. They keep stolen goods and then sit back and wait for the crime to be announced in the papers."

"And then Wilde, or one of his men contact the person whose goods were stolen and inform them that they have them and that they would be delighted to return them for a fee?"

"That's correct, sir," the lawyer smiled. "And also, if Wilde is able to blackmail the unfortunate victim earlier, he doesn't wait for the robbery to be announced in the papers. Instead, he will 'help' us – the authorities, that is – in finding the goods in question and then make some more money that way."

"I see. And the thieves that Wilde would find would either be members of his own gang…"

"Or those of a rival gang who Wilde wants to be rid of."

"Exactly, sir."

"Hmm," the Solicitor General nodded. "I think we had better keep our eyes open on this fellow. He may be ridding the city of some of its worst elements, but he's not doing it out of public-spirited altruism."

"That's right, sir," the lawyer agreed. "And did you know that he now has the effrontery to call himself 'Thief-taker General of Great Britain and Ireland'?"

Despite the public revulsion for Jonathan Wilde and his devious *modus operandi,* he carried out his operations for seven years. He ran an efficient empire; an early prototype of a model such as the Kray Brothers ran in London in the 1960s. He had his men quietly steal property and then have it returned very publicly. He became known as such an expert on crime that, in 1720, the Privy Council consulted him about how to put down London's growing crime-wave. He was also successful enough in having the forty-pound fee raised to one hundred and forty (twenty-one thousand pounds today).

In addition, he was also very good at glorifying himself and his thief-taking exploits in the press. Wilde made sure everyone knew about it when he had the large Carrick Gang arrested. For this he received an eight hundred-pound (over one hundred and twenty thousand pounds today) reward.

But eventually he overreached himself, and his murky world began to unravel. For a six-year period he had been living in a grand style, but it was not enough for him. He wanted even more, and in 1723 he petitioned the Lord Mayor of London that he be given the formal Freedom of the City. He justified this request saying that the streets of London were safer since he had begun his work, and that he had sent tens of villains to the gallows. Through his self-serving publicity, he convinced many of the capital's influential 'movers and shakers' that the level of crime had dropped. However, the public were no longer listening so uncritically to what he and the authorities were telling them.

In 1720 the financial crisis known as the South Sea Bubble had burst, and not only had many people lost their fortunes but they had also lost their faith in a government which had encouraged them to speculate in this foolhardy investment. At the same time, Wilde's men had caught one of London's most popular villains – Jack Sheppard (see Chapter 8) – who had decided to dispose of his loot through fences who were not part of Wilde's organisation. After having made four daring escapes from prison, including from Newgate, Sheppard was hanged, and so too was Joseph 'Blueskin' Blake, who was Sheppard's and one of Wilde's sometime past accomplices.

While Wilde was present, Blueskin pleaded in court that his death sentence be commuted to transportation. Wilde would have none of it, and in an attempt to kill Wilde in court, Blueskin slashed the Thief-taker's throat. One month later, when Sheppard and Blueskin were hung at Tyburn, Wilde was unable to witness the event as he was still lying in bed, nursing his injured throat.

From here on, it was downhill all the way for Jonathan 'Thief-taker' Wilde. Malicious rumours and whispers began to reach the ears of government officials, including the information that Wilde owned a warehouse stuffed full of stolen goods.

On 15 February 1725, the high constable of Holborn, together with two of his officers, arrested Wilde on Wood Street and took him to a sponging-house – a debtors' prison – where a magistrate had him bound over. From here Wilde was sent to Newgate, from where he continued to run his far-flung operation.

He was brought to trial in May 1725, and several of his men who had resented his heavy-handed treatment of them now came forward and presented evidence against Wilde. They were probably motivated by a combination of revenge and the knowledge that if they spilled the beans about their former leader, the law would deal more kindly with them.

"'Ave you heard wha' he's been charged wiv?" a criminal hanging around the Old Bailey asked.

"Pinching stuff, I suppose. Lots of it."

"No, mate. You're wrong there. 'E's bein' charged wiv filching fifty yards of lace from this ol' lady, Catherine Statham, in 'olborn. Forty pounds it was worth."

"That's it? Are you sure? For fifty yards of lace?"

"Yes, mate. An' 'e's goin' to swing for it as well. Jus' you wait. Once that thief-taker is up before the beak, 'e'll 'ave 'im down in no time. You mark my words."

The man was right, but the case was not as straight-forward as the villain had predicted. The 'beak' in this case was Lord Raymond, a stickler for judicial precision. Although, as the *Newgate Calendar* reported:

> *...the guilt of the prisoner was a point beyond all dispute; but that as a similar case was not to be found in the law-books, it became his duty to act with great caution: he was not perfectly satisfied that the construction urged by the counsel for the crown could be put upon the indictment; and as the life of a fellow-creature was at stake, recommended the prisoner to the*

mercy of the jury, who brought in their verdict Not Guilty.'

No doubt Wilde was delighted to hear this, but then he was indicted again for an offence committed while he was remanded in Newgate. This time the judge claimed that Wilde had been in secret contact with other prisoners and had received money for restoring stolen goods to their owners, the money then being divided between Wilde and his fellow prisoners. This was a capital crime and the jury returned a verdict of Guilty. To many people's joy, criminal and not, he was condemned to hang at Tyburn on 24 May 1725.

This time Wilde pleaded, in Shakespeare's tongue, for 'the quality of mercy' – the same mercy that he had denied over sixty villains he had had sent to the gallows at the west end of Tyburn Street. He pleaded for a reprieve, saying that he had swept the streets of London of many villains and that many influential people who had had their stolen goods returned because of him would no doubt speak on his behalf. None of this did him any good. The verdict stood, and its fatal sentence was not cancelled.

When he was sent back to Newgate to await his final day, he refused to be comforted by the prison chaplain. He said that there were many other prisoners who were present due to his duties as thief-taker and that they would not allow him to pray in peace. When he then asked the chaplain the meaning of 'Cursed is everyone that hangeth on a tree', he was told to repent of his sins and not concern himself with other spiritual matters.

On the morning of 24 May 1725, Wilde, afraid of being hanged, tried to poison himself by drinking a large dose of laudanum – a strong opiate used as a painkiller. However, since he had been fasting beforehand, his weakened body made him vomit, after which he sank into a coma.

When Wilde reached the gallows, the writer Daniel Defoe reported that the crowd was the largest there that he had ever seen. The condemned man was one of London's most hated figures, hated for his merciless bullying and for his hypocritical and two-faced attitudes towards the capital's underworld.

Another reason for the vast crowd was that the event had been so well publicised beforehand. Tickets for the execution bore a picture of Wilde's face above a scroll, gallows, pillory, stocks and manacles, flanked on one side by Father Time with his scythe and hourglass while Death with his spade was on the other. On the tickets was written:

> *'Jonathan Wilde, Thief-taker General of Great Britain & Ireland. To all Thieves, Whores, Pickpockets, Family Fellowes, etc. in Great Britain and Ireland. Gentlemen and ladies you are hereby desir'd to*

> *accompany ye pious Mr J___ W___ from his Seat at Whittington's Colledge to ye Triple Tree, where he's to make his last Exit on_____; and his Corps to be carry'd from thence to be decently interred amongst his Ancestors. Please bring this ticket with you.'*

This time, unlike when criminals were usually driven along Tyburn Street to be hanged, the crowds cheered for the event instead of shouting abuse at the authorities. In addition to hurling insults at the Thief-taker, the crowds, many of them who had previously visited the nearby taverns, alehouses and brandy-shops, also hurled any missile at Wilde that came to hand. This included corpses of dead cats and dogs, excrement and stones. One of these stones hit Wilde in the face, causing him to bleed considerably.

At last the procession, including soldiers, guards and the cart containing Wilde and the three other men who were to hang that day, arrived at the site of the gallows, the infamous Tyburn Tree. This structure, which was near where Marble Arch stands today, was formed by three horizontal crossbars mounted on three vertical posts. Among its many names it was often referred to as the 'Fatal Tree', the 'Three-legged Mare' and the 'Triple Tree'. Nearby was a wooden grandstand called 'Mother Proctor's Pews', where for the price of one penny one could buy a good view of the hangings.

These executions were carried out by tying a noose around the unfortunate victim's neck as he stood in the back of a horse-drawn cart. The other end of the rope was thrown over and attached to the crossbar above, and then the horse was then given a smart smack on its rump. This naturally made the horse move forward, with the consequence that the criminal was whisked off the back of the cart and left swinging in the air, dancing the 'Tyburn jig'.

If the condemned man was fat and heavy, the chances were that he would die quickly. However, if he were small and light, he could hang and swing for well over fifteen minutes before he 'shuffled off this mortal coil.' In order to save themselves from dying such a slow and ghastly death, some criminals arranged for their friends to be stationed near the gallows so that they could pull on their feet and so lessen their final agonies.

Once the criminals were declared dead (they were usually hanged in batches on special days) they were cut down and the bodies were taken to various educational institutions. There they would be dissected to show the students the anatomy of the human body. For the underworld, this was the final humiliating act the authorities could mete out to those who had fallen foul of the law.

On that day in May 1725, four men were to hang: Wilde and three others. As Wilde was still in a semi-coma, he was the last one to die. Six months earlier, the hangman, Richard Arnet, had aroused the noisy antagonism of the crowd when he had hanged the popular robber and escape-artist, Jack Sheppard. Now the executioner, who had attended Wilde's wedding, was cheered on by the raucous crowd for what he was about to do.

Meanwhile, even in his last moments, Wilde disappointed the crowd, which was estimated to be as large as two hundred thousand people - many of whom had paid good money to buy a seat for the festive occasion. Unlike Robert Harpham, who was hanged before him, Wilde gave no speech telling the crowd he repented his life of sin. Neither did he kick and yell as the hangman slipped the noose around his neck – he was still suffering the after-effects of the laudanum and his fasting.

And so, Jonathan Wilde, the hated and despised self-styled Thief-taker General, went the way that many of his victims had gone. The 'soul-driver' – the priest – persuaded him to say a last-minute prayer, and Wilde was seen in his drugged state automatically mouthing the words without understanding anything of what he was really saying. Then the horse started moving and Wilde was yanked off the back of the cart. His last conscious action was to try and get hold of the hanging body next to him, but as his life drained away the hempen noose tightened around his neck and his body began to twitch. In the eyes of the hundreds and thousands who followed this grim scene he then began to dance the much anticipated 'Tyburn jig'.

Afterwards, his body was buried in the churchyard of St. Pancras Old Church next to the body of his third wife, Elizabeth Man. Later, his body was exhumed and, in accordance with the tradition of dealing with the bodies of hanged criminals, it was put in a hearse and taken to be sold to the Royal College of Surgeons for dissection. Today you can see Wilde's skeleton in the college's Hunterian Museum in Lincoln's Inn Fields.

One of the interested people who missed his hanging was Wilde's nineteen-year-old son. This young man was thought to be so ungovernable that it was considered best for him to be kept away. Later, the son left England and was paid off to go and work in a plantation in one of the British colonies in North America. In addition, Wilde left five wives behind. The first was Mary Milliner, the prostitute whose ear he had slashed off. She was followed by Judith Nun, by whom he had a daughter, who was followed by Sarah Grigson and Elizabeth Man, a woman he lived with for five years. We do not know the name of his last wife.

As with many of the criminals dealt with in this book, Jonathan Wilde's life was used as raw material by many writers and so his villainous soul lived on in literature. *Mist's Weekly Journal*, a Tory publication, compared Wilde to Robert Walpole, the leading opposition Whig politician of the day.

Three years later in 1728, John Gay featured Wilde as Peachum in his popular opera, *Beggar's Opera,* and in 1743, Henry Fielding, the author of *Tom Jones* and founder of the first proper London police force, the Bow Street Runners, wrote *The Life and Death of Jonathan Wilde, the Great.* Over one hundred and seventy years later, in 1914, Conan Doyle based much of the character of his villain Moriarty on Wilde in his last Sherlock Holmes novel, *The Valley of Fear.*

Fifty-five years later, Stanley Baker played the role of Wilde in the film, *Where's Jack,* in which the famous popstar and entertainer of the 'Swinging Sixties', Tommy Steele, played Jack Sheppard. Finally, Jonathan Wilde and Jack Sheppard came together again in Jake Arnott's novel, *The Fatal Tree* (2017). Here Jack and his lover, the whore and pickpocket, Edgworth Bess, defy the Thief-taker's power to rouse the underworld mob in order to bring down the evil villain who played both sides of the law off against each other.

Chapter 6

Elizabeth 'Moll' Adkins King (1696-1747)

Among the most popular institutions in Stuart and Georgian London were the coffee houses. These places came about after travellers brought coffee back to England in the mid-17th century from the Islamic world.

Coffee houses were places where men met to discuss current affairs or make to financial deals. Although women were not allowed entrance as customers, they did serve as waitresses and worked behind the counter. It was said at the time that women were against drinking coffee – in pamphlets such as Women's Petition Against Coffee *it was claimed that the drink caused men to be sterile and impotent.*

A cup of coffee cost one penny, and you could also buy tea and hot chocolate. Coffee houses served light meals and patrons could read the latest newspapers and political pamphlets while they relaxed.

The first coffee house, The Angel, was opened by a Jewish entrepreneur called Jacob in Oxford in 1650, and soon the idea spread to London. By 1663 there were over eighty coffee houses in the capital and, because ideas were often discussed in them, they were nicknamed 'penny universities'.

Many of them had their own specific character. For example, Lloyd's coffee house in Tower Street in the centre of London was frequented by sailors and merchants. From their commercial deals and exchanges of news and ideas, the shipping insurance company, Lloyd's of London, evolved. Similarly, stockbrokers would meet and make deals, especially in Jonathan's or Garraway's coffee house.

However, some of these places, such as Tom King's in Covent Garden, earned themselves a somewhat dubious reputation. While outwardly a coffee house, its real business was to act as a meeting place for prostitutes and their clients. It became known as a rowdy place and later, after Tom died, it was renamed Moll King's Coffee House.

In addition to being a partner in this venture, Moll King allegedly supported herself by pickpocketing, while some claim that she was a sex worker herself. If you study the iconic picture of her (on p.126) – she is facing you, squat, ugly and scowling, dressed in a headscarf and shawl - this may be hard to believe. It is certainly easier to accept that she gained her infamous reputation through her criminal activities.

*

Nothing concerning the life of the infamous Moll King seems to be straight-forward. She was born c.1696 in poverty in Vine Street in St Giles-in-the-Fields, London, where she was christened Elizabeth Adkins. A publication entitled *The Life and Character of Moll King* says that her father was a cobbler and that her mother sold fruit and vegetables in Covent Garden. She first started working as a low-level servant but found this work so boring that she began selling nuts and fruit on the street instead. Some books claim that it was at about this time that she started her sex-connected career. It was probably while she was working in Covent Garden that she met her future husband, Tom King. Assuming that she was born in 1696, she would have been nineteen at the time.

"Here, you're a nice looking feller, tell me something about yourself," Moll said in her usual forthright manner. "And you talk nice, too. Bit like a lord or something like that."

"Well, that's not surprising," he replied. "My father, Thomas King, is a squire and my mother, Elizabeth, is Sir John Cordell's daughter. And if you must know, I was educated at Eton and King's College, Cambridge."

Moll Elizabeth Adkins stuck her nose up in the air. "Oooh, aren't we high class! I'm surprised you're even talking to me."

"Well, I am, but I'm busy now. I've got to repair a fishmonger's stall at the other end of the market. So, good day to you." And with that he walked off.

Despite this rather unromantic beginning, Tom and Elizabeth, now Moll, became friends and married in 1717. The marriage did not succeed, and soon afterwards Tom had an affair. He neglected his wife and, when he did see her again, he began beating her up.

Left on her own, Moll King began her own affair with a man called Murray. While she was living with him, she began making connections with fashionable people about town. These connections would later serve her in good stead when she went into business as the part owner of a coffee house.

In 1718, Moll was arrested for stealing a gold watch from a gentleman and sentenced to seven years' transportation to America. It is not known what she did there exactly, but she probably acted as a servant to a rich colonial landowner, or else broke her back working in the cotton, rice or tobacco plantations.

Before long she managed to get back into England, but was caught. She was sentenced to death for her early return, but then won a reprieve. This meant that she was sent to Newgate Prison, from where she gained an early release. It seemed that she was a reformed character, or at least, she was not caught again.

Three years after separating from her husband, she bumped into him again.

"Hello, Tom," she began carefully. "You're looking good."

"Well, so I should be," he said straightening his maroon velvet jacket. "I've made quite a lot of money since I last saw you and I'm thinking of making even more."

"How? By repairing fishmonger's stalls?"

Tom was not going to be baited like that. "No, I worked as a waiter and put away what I earned. Now I want to open up my own coffee house in Covent Garden. In fact, I'm on my way to see a fellow who works for the Duke of Bedford about renting a place."

Moll sounded interested. "How about you and me put the past behind us and start again? You run the shop and I'll work in it, serving the customers and things like that."

Tom stopped to consider her proposal. It would reunite him with his wife and if he employed her, he wouldn't have to pay another woman to help run the new business.

"I agree," he said and held out his hand.

She shook it and added, "And besides, I've become friendly with all sorts of fashionable people over the past couple of years. I'm sure they'll come to our shop once it's started."

Moll was right. Tom King's Coffee House, as it was known, was an instant success. The customers included Moll's rich contacts, as well as the important connections that Tom had made during past few years.

They both invested everything they had in their new venture, even keeping it open all night. This, together with the fact that several of Moll's female contacts were courtesans and prostitutes, gave their coffee house a dubious reputation. However, it did not stop their business from succeeding and soon Tom and Moll were able to buy up other sites and establish more coffee houses. To help them serve their customers better, they took on an attractive black barmaid named 'Black Betty', alias 'Tawny Betty'. In addition, two of London's most popular prostitutes and procurers, Mother Whyburn and Elizabeth Needham, could be contacted at Tom King's Coffee House.

Perhaps one of the factors that helped them succeed so well was that their coffee houses were situated in the shady parts of London. This certainly helped the notables and other customers who went in order to drink coffee and meet 'ladies of easy virtue', *filles de joie* and 'women of the town'. However, Tom and Moll were very clever about this aspect of their business. Apart from their own domestic sleeping arrangements, they had no other beds in their coffee houses. This meant that Tom and Moll could not be prosecuted for brothel-keeping – a crime which was punishable by whipping and prison. This was because the final stages of their customers' assignations were not held on the premises in their coffee houses, but elsewhere. Moll also earned extra money on the side from a loan sharking business that she ran in parallel with her other affairs.

In addition to procuring young ladies, Tom contributed to the friendly atmosphere of their coffee houses by often drinking alcoholic beverages with his customers. This might have been good for trade, but it was not good for him as he died aged 45 in 1739 from alcoholism. This left Moll as the sole owner of their coffee gold mine.

However, not everything went smoothly. Moll was arrested for keeping a disorderly house and after her release she became more and more involved in criminal activities. She also followed in her dead husband's footsteps by taking to drink, which led her to become more quarrelsome. Her reputation and that of her coffee houses suffered, and to keep her head above financial water she began to resort to cheap tricks to extort more money from her customers.

"Excuse me, sir, but look at those broken plates on your table," Moll said to the young man wearing a dark blue jacket and bright red waistcoat. "You are going to have to pay for them."

"But I didn't break them," the customer protested. "They were already like that on the table when I sat down."

"Are you calling me a liar?" Moll asked, advancing on him, arms akimbo.

"No, but I'm telling you that…"

"Yes, I know. You young men always say the same thing when you break any of my plates and cups - 'It wasn't me,'" she mimicked her latest victim.

"Yes, but…"

"Yes, but nothing," Moll said. "Are you going to pay for the damage or am I going to have to send my husband out to find a constable?"

"All right," the young man muttered. "I'll pay even though I didn't break them. How much do you want?"

Moll named her price.

"But that's impossible!" the young man said. "Plates don't cost that much."

"Mine do. Now are you going to pay, or shall I send for the law? Which is it to be?"

"I'll pay," he replied and reluctantly handed over the requested sum.

Moll's stern face relaxed for a moment. She had caught another victim. The broken plates had earned their cost many times over.

In an effort to prevent the rowdy atmosphere from becoming too excessive, Moll hired bouncers, but even they could not always stop all the fighting that happened inside and outside her establishments. In one particularly violent fracas, four of the men who had been drinking in her coffee house burst into the nearby chapel of the Sardinian ambassador and continued their fight there. Two of them were later charged with assault.

Despite such behaviour, Moll's coffee houses did continue to attract the patronage of fashionable society, and even King George II himself paid a visit. However, the visit did not go according to plan as the King's equerry, Viscount Page, began to pay too much attention to the lady friend of one of his neighbours and soon found himself challenged to a duel. Fortunately, the affair was quickly hushed up and the King and his party left immediately afterwards.

The bad reputation that Moll's coffee houses gained came to a head in June 1739 when a riot erupted in one of them. The situation grew out of hand and the rioting spread to the street outside. Moll was arrested charged for running a riotous establishment, tried and found guilty. She was ordered to pay two hundred pounds (twenty-three thousand, five hundred pounds today) and sentenced to three months in prison. She was also asked to supply guarantees for her good behaviour for three years after her release.

"I'm sorry, Your Honour," Moll said, trying to look as contrite as possible, "but I think that for me to pay two hundred pounds is much too much. I simply don't have it. And Your Honour," she continued, "I think that this is not fair. After all, it wasn't me who was fighting, was it? It was the gentlemen outside who were causing the disturbance. While they were doing so, I was in the back of my coffee house attending to my accounts."

The judge looked at her as she leaned forward and nonchalantly lowered her neckline a little. "Well, yes," he decided. "Perhaps I was a trifle harsh. I'll reduce your fine from two hundred to fifty pounds."

Moll breathed a sigh of relief.

"But you will still have to spend three months in Newgate. There is a limit to my generosity, you know."

Moll's nephew, William King, ran her business while she was 'inside', and even while she was mixing with the dregs of London's society she managed to have a better time than she would have had otherwise as, following the standard practice of the time, she bribed the guards so that her food, cell and other services were improved.

Moll King, nicknamed 'the Virago' continued running her very profitable business until about 1745. Then she retired to her villa at Haverstock Hill, north-west London, and unlike several of the other villains in this book, died of natural causes. She passed away two years later, on 17 September 1747, leaving a fortune large enough for her son to be educated at Eton College.

Chapter 7

Mary 'Jenny Diver' Young (1700-1741)

Jenny Diver was not born with a silver spoon in her mouth. Far from it. But by using her native intelligence, cunning and good looks she became the very successful leader of a gang of pickpockets in London during the 1720s and 1730s. By exploiting her attractive face, sexy figure and her elegant wardrobe, she managed to fool

many a rich man and woman, causing them to part unknowingly with their purses, watches and other valuables. But her luck and professional tricks couldn't save her forever and one day, as with many of the other villains in this book, her luck ran out.

In addition to leading a life of crime, Jenny Diver's exploits made her immortal when John Gay used her name for one of his female pickpocket characters who played a part in 1728 in The Beggar's Opera.

*

"Harriet! Harriet Jones! I've just received a message from our mistress," Brigit, the second lady's maid, called out across the yard. "You are to go up to her room now. She wants to talk to you."

"About my being expectant?" Harriet asked, as she smoothed her apron down and wiped a couple of sooty marks off her cheeks.

"I don't know. All I was told is that you are to go up and see her now. And by the way," she added quietly, "that mean ol' bitch wasn't smiling when she told me to tell you."

Knowing her employer and fearing the worst, Harriet made her way upstairs and knocked on the dark brown wooden door.

"Come in."

She stepped into the brightly lit room and immediately walked over to a high-backed chair. She put her hands on it for support. As her pregnancy had progressed, she had felt less and less stable. Now she tried to avoid standing as much as possible while carrying out her household tasks.

"Stand up straight, girl."

"Yes, ma'am," and Harriet let her hands fall to her sides.

"Now what is this that I hear that you are with child?" her mistress asked, looking down her nose at her miserable servant.

Harriet gazed down at the rich maroon and cream carpet. "It's true, ma'am, but it hasn't interfered with my duties here. Why, yesterday while I was…"

"Enough of that," her aristocratic employer snapped. "And do you know who the father is? Is he a local man? Will he help you?"

Harriet shrugged. "I don't know ma'am. He was certainly a local man a few months ago, but now he's run off. I haven't seen him since St. Patrick's Day. The last thing I heard about him was that he was seen in Belfast two weeks ago, ma'am."

"Well, that is a shame," came the unfeeling reply, "because as I think you know, I'm going to have to dismiss you. But to show you that I'm not really as hard-hearted as you may think, I'll give you a half-pound to help you on your way. That is, of course, if you are out of here by Monday. If not, then you'll get nothing. Is that understood?"

Harriet nodded quickly and scuttled out of the room. She went downstairs to the basement and told the other two maids what had happened.

"I said she was a mean ol' bitch, didn't I?" Brigit said. "You're lucky she's going to give you any money at all. She didn't give anything to the last girl she threw out when she was expecting."

Two days later, carrying some clothes the other two maids had given her, Harriet left the large house and set off for the centre of town. Stuffed inside her blouse were two small silver trays that she had stolen, partly for revenge and partly to sell later to a man who had known the baby's father.

Later that day she found lodgings in a brothel where she agreed to work as a cleaner. This would provide her with a minimum wage as well as food and shelter. The baby was born in the middle of the night a month later.

"Oh, she's so pretty," a young cleaning lady cooed as she looked down at the new-born pink-faced baby, now wrapped in an almost clean blanket. "Just look at those beautiful eyes. She won't have any problems finding a husband sixteen years on. You mark my words."

Harriet tried to smile back, but she was not really in much of a mood for it.

"What are you going to call her?"

"Mary. After the Virgin. I hope that will help her in the future."

But as she said this, Harriet Jones was less than happy thinking about her own future. She knew that the north of Ireland was not a forgiving place for unwed mothers and their children. This was so much so, that late one night Harriet packed baby Mary into a small box, wrapped her up in the warmest blanket she could find together with an old wool jacket and left her on the steps of the nunnery next door to St. Catherine's Church. Fortunately for the baby, her mewling caught the attention of Sister Evangeline on her way to Matins. She was brought into the nunnery, washed, dressed in clean clothes and fed. From that day on, Mary was dependent on Christian kindness and charity.

After spending several years in the nunnery, the nuns passed Mary onto a foster home run by a kindly widow known to Sister Evangeline. However, Mary was not to spend more than several months there, as the widow died and she was sent to another foster home. From here she continued in several more foster homes, kindly and less so, until she was ten years old. Then she was taken in by an elderly and lonely gentlewoman looking for company and someone to love. Mary's new 'mam' was a widow who sorely missed her sons serving far overseas as grenadiers in the army of King George III.

"Now, Mary," the widow said one day as she placed a bowl of creamy porridge in front of the girl, "I think the time has come for you to learn some skills."

"What's skills?"

"Things like needlework and reading and writing and numbers."

"Who's going to teach me?"

"I will teach you needlework and sewing, and the school around the corner will teach you your numbers and letters."

And that is what happened. The widow was as good as her word. During the day Mary studied at the small school five minutes' walk away, while in the evenings the widow taught her the traditional skills associated with needle and thread. She noticed that Mary caught on very quickly, and soon the widow was using Mary to make some money by taking in clothes to be repaired. She was even skilled enough to make new blouses and other garments for the local population.

Mary was equally successful at school. She found that she had an aptitude for numbers and was easily the best pupil in her class for 'doing her sums'. Similarly, she learned to read and write quickly, and within three months was reading almost anything that came her way without any problems.

The years passed. Mary helped the widow by earning money and in turn the widow showered love and affection on her pretty adopted daughter. But this wasn't enough for Mary. She knew that there was a bigger and brighter world outside her Northern Irish village. One day she told the widow that she had decided to go to London.

"Whatever for?"

"I want to become a seamstress there and earn a lot of money. I've seen how easy it is for me here, so why not go to London and earn even more?"

The widow, who was sad to hear this, had to agree. "But where will you find the money to pay for the boat fare?" she asked. "London is a long way away."

Mary tossed her chestnut-coloured hair back. "That's no problem," she smiled. "You know Mickey O'Toole who lives down the street? Well, he has agreed that if I marry him, he will pay for my ticket. We will take ship from Belfast to Liverpool and then take a carriage all the way to London. Now isn't that grand?"

"Are you sure that he has the money?" the widow asked. "I've heard that he's a bit of a dubious fellow."

"Fear not," Mary interrupted. "He promised me that by the time we get to Belfast he will have enough money for the fare, and some left over for our first weeks in London. That is, until I start earning enough from my sewing."

The widow said that this sounded like a good plan, although in her heart of hearts she was somewhat doubtful about Mickey O'Toole's honesty. As it turned out, she was right to have had such doubts. O'Toole did indeed come up with the money, but it was not earned by hard work and the sweat of his brow. Rather it came by robbing his master of eighty guineas and a gold watch.

The crossing of the Irish Sea took two days. Two days of continuous seasickness that caused Mary to sit on the deck much of the time retching and holding her stomach. After landing in Liverpool, they took lodgings and spent a short while living together as man and wife. Then the time came to travel on to London. As they were about to step into the stagecoach, they were stopped by two navy-blue-coated officials.

"Are you Master Mickey O'Toole?"

"Aye."

"And did you arrive here in Liverpool from Belfast two weeks ago?" the taller official asked.

"Aye. Why? I…"

"Then I am arresting you for the theft of one gold watch and eighty guineas. Come with us."

"But I'm about to…"

"You are about to do nothing. Hold out your hands."

The last thing Mary saw of Mickey O'Toole was him being escorted away between the two burly officials. She sent him some clothes and money and heard that he was going to be returned to Ireland to stand trial. Later she learnt that he had been sentenced to death, but as often happened then, since it was his first offence, the sentence was commuted and he was transported to one of the colonies in America or to the Caribbean.

Mary arrived in London a week later and immediately found herself lodgings in the centre of the city. After putting up a notice in the window of her room that she took in clothes for repair, she set out to explore her new environment.

Having spent most of her life in a small Irish village, London, with its population of six hundred thousand, was indeed a bewildering place. However, she did not take long to become familiar with her bustling surroundings. After spending much of the day sewing and repairing other people's clothes, she would put on her own finest clothes (or some of the even finer garments that she had restored but not yet returned) and go for a walk in the city. One day, just as she was about to enter her lodgings, a young woman approached her.

"You're Irish, aren't you?"

"Yes. And so are you, though your accent isn't as strong."

"Ah, that's because I've been living here in London for quite some time," Anne Murphy, a woman of Mary's age, replied. "And you're the one who repairs clothes?"

Mary looked at the slim, pleasant woman facing her, nodded and wondered what the connection was between her being Irish and repairing clothes.

"So can you repair this blouse for me this evening? I need it in a hurry."

Mary ushered her into her room and while they were talking about Ireland, clothes and the cost of living in London, she looked at her carefully. Anne was of the same height, had curly ginger hair and sharp blue eyes. Her jacket and skirt were dark brown, and she wore a white blouse which really needed washing. Mary's new customer asked her how much she was paying for rent.

Not seeing any reason to keep it a secret, Mary told her.

"So much! You are being robbed!" Anne exclaimed. "I tell you, they're always trying to take advantage of us Irish girls. They think that because we come from far away and because we are girls living on our own, we don't know anything."

Mary nodded. She had already experienced one or two occasions when she felt that she had been fleeced while shopping in the city. "But what can we do about it?" she asked, as Anne watched Mary's fingers, needle and thread rapidly repair the tear in her blouse. "I don't have a man to look after me."

Anne was clearly impressed by Mary's dexterity. "Fear not, love. I've got an idea. Why not come and live next door to me in Long Acre? It will cost you half the price."

"Long Acre? Near Covent Garden?"

"Aye. Well, you do learn quickly, don't you? A few days in London and you already know your way around. My, I *am* impressed."

And so it was that three days later, Mary moved to her new lodgings and became Anne Murphy's neighbour. And not only did she change her address, she was about to change her profession. For what she did not know was, her new fellow Irish girlfriend was the leader of a bunch of pickpockets. Seeing how nimbly Mary's fingers had worked repairing her blouse, Anne had decided on the spot to recruit her as the latest member of her gang. That night she approached Mary about changing her way of life.

"How much do you earn a week?" Anne asked.

"About ten to fifteen shillings if I'm lucky. And that's good. Back home in Ireland I was earning half of that."

"Huh! That's nothing," Anne guffawed. "Would you like to earn ten to twelve guineas a week? Perhaps more?" she asked as she made a neat stack of gold guinea coins on the table.

Mary looked at the coins. Her eyes were wide open. She had never seen so much money in her life. "Wait a minute. Do you want me to make my money by whoring? Because that I won't do."

"No, no, lass. Nothing like that. By 'cheving the froe' – cutting people's pockets off."

"Cutting off their pockets? Whatever for?"

"For the money in them, lass. For that and their watches and other fine things."

"But don't they feel it?"

"Not if you're good, they don't. There's that," Anne added, "or diving."

"Diving?"

"Picking pockets, Mary. Diving in and becoming rich. How does that sound?"

"It sounds good, but tell me more. Are there any risks and how does this diving thing work?"

Anne answered these questions and several more before Mary said, "Let me think about. This is all new to me. I'll tell you tomorrow."

And so she did. Mary decided to join Anne's gang, and two days later accompanied them when they joined a crowd at the entrance to a church at the junction of Fetter Lane and Fleet Street. There she watched as several members of the gang mixed in with the crowd as they listened to an impassioned sermon given by a particularly handsome young cleric.

As the priest's words elevated his listeners' souls, the gang members' fingers quickly dived down into the congregation's pockets to retrieve coins, purses and watches. One member of the gang even found three gold rings that its owner had just had repaired at a local jeweller's shop.

As Anne saw that Mary was a willing pupil, she gave her ten guineas to help her with her living expenses while she started her 'apprenticeship' in the capital's bustling streets. In the same way Mary had been a good pupil at school and had learned to use a needle and thread professionally, it did not take her long to perfect her pickpocketing skills. Soon Anne saw that her investment was worthwhile.

Before long Mary was doing so well that the gang decided that she should become their leader instead of Anne. Fortunately, Anne did not object as she began making even more money than she had before. So now Mary was in charge of a gang, which included six to eight men and women.

But Mary was not just a leader; she was also a good organiser. One evening she called all the members of her gang together and she told them that from now on they would play by a certain set of rules.

"Rules?" someone objected. "Like in the army or something?"

"Yes, rules," Mary insisted, "and here are some of them." She started counting them off on her slim fingers. "One. No-one can join our gang unless everybody here agrees."

"Good," a slightly alcoholic voice said. "Sounds fair enough. What's rule number two?"

"That no-one works on their own – everyone must be helped by at least one other member of the gang," Mary replied holding up two fingers.

"And three?"

"Any new member shall be on trial for a month and in that way learn our secrets."

"Ah," Anne said. "What if they leave after a month? They'll know everything about us."

"Don't worry about that, Anne. I doubt if anyone will leave when they know what they're making with us."

"Aye, they'd be very foolish to do that," Burly Bob said. "And besides, if someone did open their big gob after, that would be the last thing that they would do. Am I right, Tom?"

Tom nodded, listening intently as Mary told them that they would all be responsible for each other. "If one of you are caught," she said, "then the others will say to the watch or constable that it was impossible for say, you, Tom or George, to have done anything wrong as they were with you at the time doing some other innocent activity."

"Like looking in a shop window or going for a pleasant stroll with young Lizzie here," Tom added as he put his arm around Lizzie's waist.

"Exactly."

Sometimes Mary would have her gang mingle with the crowds who were pushing and shoving while listening to a priest or watching a hanging at Tyburn. Then they would dive into the many open pockets to earn the wages of sin. At other times, accompanied by members of her gang dressed as her maid and footman, a fashionably dressed Mary would suddenly 'faint' in the street. Then as several gallant gentlemen gathered around her to offer assistance, she would pick their pockets and swiftly pass on the stolen coins and watches to her waiting accomplices.

"Mary, you are so good at diving," one of the gang said, after yet another successful expedition on Drury Lane, "that we should change your name to Christine…"

Mary shook her head. "No, Jack, I don't like that. How about Jenny Diver? That way there'll be no connection to my past."

"Right, apart from your Irish accent," another member of the gang added.

And so Mary Young became Jenny Diver, and that was the name by which she entered the annals of England's criminal history.

One evening when the gang were sitting around the table in Jenny's lodgings counting out their profits of the day, Jenny came up with a new idea.

"You know the ploy we have where I suddenly faint in the street? Well, I suggest we try that again, but with a difference. I walk down the street arm-in-arm with one of you, who will be my beau or my husband, but this time we will make sure I faint just outside the front door of a rich man's house and..."

"Why?"

"Then we make a fuss," Jenny continued, "and my husband or whoever knocks on the door, and then when I'm taken in to be revived and…"

"And while we're inside and they are looking for smelling salts and the like, your husband is busy working the house over," George finished off with a smile.

"That's a good idea," Anne added. "But we can even improve on that. If you take young William with you, with his baby-face, he could be your son. Then we could have another pair of hands in the house. How about that?"

It was agreed to try out this new trick the following day outside the house of a rich tea merchant who lived in a fine house in the Strand. It worked like a charm. Jenny fainted, her 'husband' knocked on the door for aid, and an hour later the 'young family from Hampstead' left the merchant's house richer in coin and silver cutlery.

Diver's run of luck could not last forever. One day while picking a man's pocket who was looking in a shop window, Jenny's hand became stuck in the loose lining. Feeling something strange, the man whirled around and grabbed Jenny by her hair before she could disappear into the crowds. The man told his friend to fetch a constable, and Jenny soon found herself committed to Newgate Prison.

She languished there for some time, but the hardship of her stay was alleviated as different members of her gang, disguised as her mother, cousin or other members of her large 'family', brought her fresh food and clean clothes. They also provided her with some money to bribe the jailers to give her a better cell and allow her more time to wander within the confines of the prison. However, despite her improved situation, it was still just a short trip from Newgate to the Old

Bailey. There she gave her name as Mary Young and thereby kept her other alias secret for future occasions.

"Mistress Mary Young," the judge announced in a bored tone. "You are hereby charged with the crime of privately stealing, that is, stealing goods worth more than one shilling from another person. Since your attempt was fortunately unsuccessful and that the potential sum involved was not large and that you did not act in a violent way, you will not be hanged."

"At least this time," his clerk was heard to say.

As Jenny breathed a sigh of relief, she wondered what her punishment would be. She did not have to wait for long.

"As this is your first offence, that is, being your first offence recorded here in the Old Bailey, your punishment is that you will be transported over the sea to Virginia on the east coast of the American continent. There you will pay for your crime by working in the plantations there for a set time, to be determined later. In the meanwhile, until a transport ship is ready, you are to be returned to Newgate Prison." The judge banged his gavel. "Case over. Bring in the next one."

Jenny spent the following four months in Newgate waiting for the next prison ship to be organised. When it was time to sail, she bribed one or two of the guards, who let her take more than the usual prisoner's possessions on board.

"What do you want all that stuff for?" one of the guards on the ship asked.

Jenny tapped the side of her nose as she slipped him a shilling. "Don't ask questions and there will be more from where that came from."

The result was that Jenny had an easier passage crossing the Atlantic than most of the other prisoners. Once she arrived in Virginia, she continued to exploit her wealth, her good looks and easy manner.

She was allowed to work in the governor's own house. It was not for the likes of Jenny Diver to break her back working outside in the hot sun in the tobacco fields hour after hour. One evening several months after she had arrived, having spent a pleasant time flirting with the governor of the penal colony while his wife was away, Jenny asked if he would give her permission to return to England.

"It's not that I don't like it here, sir," she said as she allowed him to slide his hand down the inside of her blouse. "It's just that I miss my family so much," she lied and began sobbing quietly into her handkerchief. "And I want to see my ageing grandmother before she dies," she continued, allowing him to caress her breasts.

A month passed and Jenny found herself back on a ship bound for London. The governor had allowed her return, and by using her good and a few gold coins, she found a sea-captain willing to take the reformed prisoner, as she now described herself, on-board his merchant ship. Fortunately, favourable winds were on her side, the passage was smooth and uneventful, and she arrived in London a few weeks later. As soon as she stepped off the ship, she made her way to Anne's house, and that night they celebrated her return home with a noisy party.

"Isn't it a capital crime to come back to England before your time is up?" Anne asked as they finished off a bottle of gin together.

Jenny nodded, but told Anne that she had a signed document from the governor who had given her his special permission 'for services rendered'.

"And how are you going to pay your rent?" Anne asked. "Offering the same services, or diving?"

"Diving," Jenny replied immediately. "It's much more profitable and less hard on the body."

And that is what she did. For the next few months she went back to her old tricks. Soon she was doing so well that she re-established herself as the leader of the gang. Sometimes she would 'faint' in the streets, while on other occasions she would make sure that she was carted into the house of a rich merchant, banker or aristocrat after 'passing out' by their front door. Helped by a friendly member of her gang who 'happened' to be close by, she soon recovered and later returned to the street considerably richer.

"Tomorrow," she said to Anne and a few others one night, "I suggest we go to Canon Alley."

"Near St. Paul's?"

Jenny nodded. "Yes, we haven't been there for some time. We should have good pickings there. All these good Christian folks off to visit the cathedral. I'm sure that they believe in helping the poor and the downtrodden like us."

The next day was 4 April 1738. Despite the rough life she had led, somehow she had still managed to retain her good looks even though her fingers were becoming a little less nimble. She was now thirty-eight years old, middle-aged in terms of the 18th century, and now it took her more time to sew and repair any of her gang's clothes. Age and arthritis were inexorably taking their toll. And take it they did on that spring day.

As Jenny was trying to steal Mistress Rowley's purse, she and her two partners in crime were caught red-handed. Mistress Rowley started shouting, "Thief! Thief!" and within a minute a crowd had gathered around the poor woman, a crowd which did not let Jenny and her partners escape.

Once again, she found herself in Newgate prison, and again she found herself facing the authorities. Fortunately, she was up against a young magistrate who had not heard of her or of her past reputation.

"What's your name?" he asked.

"Mistress Jane Webb," Jenny answered, fluttering her long eyelashes at him and bobbing a curtsey.

"I see," he said as he riffled through the pages through a large black ledger. "Well, young lady," he continued. "I don't see your name recorded here, so this must be your first offence."

"Yes, Your Honour," Jenny said demurely. "I was just trying to make some money to pay the doctor for looking after my sick old mother. She…"

"Well, that may be why you did so, but picking people's pockets is not the way to finance such situations," the magistrate said, deliberately sounding pompous and trying not to be seduced by Jenny's charm. "Therefore, seeing that your name is not recorded here, instead of demanding the death penalty, something I may add that you richly deserve, I am sentencing you to be transported to Virginia. And until then, you will be incarcerated in Newgate prison."

Two nights later while Jenny was sitting in the corner of her cell thinking about her past life and her return voyage to Virginia, she was interrupted by several members of her gang who had come to visit her.

"Jenny, Jenny," a noisy one began.

"Hush, Bill," Jenny said, laying a finger to her lips. "They know me here as Jane, not Jenny."

"It doesn't matter, lass," Anne said, pushing her way forward. "The magistrate might not have known but the newspapers did."

"What do you mean?" Jenny asked. This did not sound like good news.

"The *Evening Post* has worked out that you, Jenny Diver is the same person as Jane Webb," Anne explained. "There's even an article about you on the first page."

Jenny put her hands around her neck. "So does that mean that they want to hang me?"

"I don't think so," Anne replied, "and I'll see if I can persuade them to keep you in prison here instead of sending you to Virginia."

Anne's efforts failed. The result was that two months later, on 7 June 1738, Jenny Diver found herself once more on board a prison ship, the *Forward*. Once again, she was sailing westwards over the choppy seas of the Atlantic Ocean back to Virginia. The voyage was worse than the first and she was very pleased when the ship sailed into the harbour and she could step once again on *terra firma*.

But what was not different was the way she worked in Virginia. As before, a now pregnant Jenny bribed her way out of working hard on the plantations and, also as before, she managed, after a few months, to persuade the governor to permit her to return to England. Now, together with her baby, she landed in Liverpool and from there took a carriage to London. But when she turned up in the capital, a nasty surprise awaited her. Her old gang was not there to meet her. In fact, it no longer existed.

"Where's Bill?" she asked One-Eye'd John, one of the gang's oldest members she happened to see in a tavern near the Old Bailey.

"'Anged," came the reply. "Three months ago. 'E was caught nicking a watch from this gent in 'Yde Park."

"And where's Anne?"

One Eye'd John shrugged. "Said she was going to Oxford one day and we never saw her again after that."

"And Fat George?"

The answer was a grubby finger drawn across an equally grubby neck. "Tyburn. In June. But 'is younger brother, y'know, Joe, well 'e was luckier. They shipped 'im off to the Caribbean. Seems like they don't like 'anging them when they're that young."

And within a few minutes Jenny learned that the old gang, her gang of friends, supporters and fellow thieves was gone, it's members either dead or dispersed. Only three of them lived in the area and they weren't interested in returning to their former lifestyle. Not even under Jenny's expert leadership.

That night, over a few drinks Jenny caught up with the local gossip. From what she learned she decided that if she were to continue diving, then she would do it alone. Or if not alone, then only with one or two selected 'experts'. One of these was Elizabeth Davies.

Elizabeth was younger and more attractive than Jenny, but Jenny did not mind at all. She saw Elizabeth's pretty face, grey-green eyes and fetching figure as a business asset. Sometimes the pair of them worked together, one distracting the victim while the other robbed him, while at other times Elizabeth would bring along a young man – she knew quite a lot of suitable characters – to help them in their criminal ways.

One evening, while the two women were sitting in Jenny's lodgings, Jenny told Elizabeth of her latest idea.

"Listen, Liz," she began, "this one should be very easy. A bit like that trick I used to do when I fainted in the street."

Elizabeth listened. This sounded like the old Jenny Diver she had heard so much about.

"We'll use one of your gentlemen friends. One of the more handsome ones. We'll get him to help the ladies when they have to cross that muddy patch in Sherborne Lane."

"Near the Royal Exchange?"

Jenny nodded, "And then, when he's smiling at them as he helps them cross over on those wooden planks there, we'll dive into their pockets. Should be dead easy. They'll be thinking about not slipping and…"

"We'll be busy diving," Elizabeth smiled.

And that is what they did. Two days later, on a grey wintry morning in January 1741, the two pickpockets, together with one of Elizabeth's young men, put their plan into action. They planted the fellow near the plank-covered, muddy patch, and using his most winning smile he guided the ladies over the temporary 'bridge'. As he did so, Jenny and Elizabeth were busy diving.

That night back at Jenny's lodgings, they counted their profits and then divided them up accordingly. They decided that it had been a good day and that if it wasn't raining, they would do the same again on the following Saturday, 10 January.

The day in question dawned bright and clear. Clear that is if you didn't count the few grey clouds that always seemed to appear in London's wintry skies. As before, Elizabeth's beau was well-dressed in a maroon jacket and matching cravat, a white shirt, beige breeches and highly polished black boots. And as before, he was strategically placed near one end of the muddy patch ready to help the ladies, young and old, cross to the other side.

All went well for the first hour. The young man smiled and helped, smiled and lent a willing hand to the ladies as they negotiated the planks crossing the muddy patch. In the meanwhile, Jenny, with her quick fingers and Elizabeth with her even quicker ones were beginning to amass enough money to render quite a few of their other underworld friends jealous.

Then Mistress Judith Gardiner appeared. She was a tough, thin-faced woman on her way to meet a friend on Upper Thames Street. She was not in a hurry and so she had the time to make her way carefully across the wooden planks that were providing a goodly income for Jenny and her partners.

As Judith was looking down and making her way across one of the wider planks, Jenny dived into her pocket and quickly grabbed her purse. But this time she wasn't quick enough. As she was about to withdraw her hand, she felt Mistress Gardner clamp her long bony fingers around her wrist.

Jenny tried to shake her hand free but to no avail. Then she hit Judith on the head with her other hand, but her victim still held on. At the same time Mistress Gardiner shouted, "Thief! Thief!"

Within seconds Jenny and Elizabeth found themselves surrounded by a threatening crowd. The boyfriend was nowhere to be seen.

One or two people shouted for a constable and soon the two female thieves found themselves locked up in the 'compter' – the local jail. They were questioned the next day by the magistrate who decided that they should be transferred to Newgate Prison.

By now, the next stage in the judicial proceedings was familiar to Jenny. From Newgate she would be taken to court and put on trial. Her major worry now was that the authorities would link Mistress Jane Webb and Mistress Jenny Diver with the criminal who was now facing charges before them. If that happened, then the outlook wouldn't look good for her.

"Oh, Liz, I'm so worried this time," Jenny confided in her friend. "I've heard that Mr Justice Wright is going to try us. He's a really mean bastard and we cannot expect any mercy from him."

But if Jenny's assessment of her situation was correct, her information was not complete. The 'mean bastard' Justice Wright was not going to be the only judge who would try her, Elizabeth and over a dozen other criminals that day. He would be joined on the bench at the next Sessions by Sir John Strange, the Recorder of the City of London, Sergeant Urlin, the Deputy-Recorder, Humphrey Parsons, the Lord Mayor, Baron Probyn, the Lord Chief Justice and Mr Justice Fortescue.

"Mistress Jenny Diver, you are charged with 'privately stealing' in Sherborne Lane," Justice Wright said as he opened the Sessions for London and the county of Middlesex. "Do you understand the charge and have you anything to say?"

Jenny stood up, showing as much of her full bosom as she dared, and flashed what she hoped was a winsome smile at the five stern faces sitting opposite her on the bench. Then in as convincing a voice as possible she admitted that she understood that she had broken the law but had only done so in order to buy some medicine for her sick mother. The judges did not look impressed.

"And in addition to the above charge of 'privately stealing', that is, picking pockets to the value of more than one shilling, you are also charged with having returned home to this country from Virginia, to where you were transported. How do you plead?"

"Innocent, Your Honour."

"Innocent? How can you say that when you are standing here in this court in London when by rights you should be somewhere in Virginia?"

"That's true, Your Honour, but I was given permission in writing by the governor to return to England."

"And do you have that document with you now?"

"No, Your Honour. It is in my lodgings."

"Oh, how inconvenient. Well, we'll see about sentencing you later today. In the meanwhile, I will deal with your accomplice. You may step down."

"But, Your Honour," Jenny began, fluttering her eyelashes again and pushing out her chest. "I just want to say…"

"Constable, take the accused down and bring her accomplice, Mistress Elizabeth Davies, before us."

Elizabeth was brought forward and asked similar questions to those Jenny had been asked as to her whereabouts on January 10. Like Jenny, she thrust her chest forward, but had no real defence as she had been caught red-handed. In addition, like Jenny, she was subject to the prosecution's chief witness' statements, that is, those made by Mistress Judith Gardner. This victim of the 'private stealing' described the robbery and proceeded to exaggerate the violence that she had suffered at the hands of the two accused.

"Oh, it was terrible, Your Honour," she said, crying a little into her handkerchief. "They beat me up so hard and left bruises all up and down my arms. I was so frightened," she sniffed, "that I thought that day would be my last day on earth."

"And can you show the court these bruises on your arms that you suffered?"

Mistress Gardner shook her head. "No, Your Honour. I'm afraid not. They have healed since then, but I can assure you that every word I have said is Gospel-true."

Justice Wright nodded sympathetically.

"And how many of these pickpockets set upon you?"

"Well, Your Honour, I can't be sure. It happened so fast. I know that there were these two women, and I think there was another man or two. A regular gang, so to speak. I had no chance against them. They stole thirteen shillings and one half-penny, Your Honour. That's a lot of money for a poor woman like me. I mean to say…"

"Yes, yes, Mistress Gardner," Justice White cut her off. "We'll see about any compensation, if there is to be any, later. You may step down. Now I wish to cross-examine some of the other witnesses."

Two hours later, Jenny, Elizabeth and the fifteen other accused were brought forward to hear the Recorder of the Court read out the verdicts in their cases. Of the seventeen men and women who stood in the dock, thirteen of them, seven men and six women were sentenced to death, and the remaining four to transportation. Jenny and Elizabeth were in the first group.

"But please, Your Honour," Jenny and Elizabeth called out in unison, "we wish to 'plead our bellies'."

"Are you both with child?"

They both nodded.

"Then in that case, I'll have a panel of matrons examine you. In the meanwhile, you are to be returned to Newgate from whence you came."

Later that week a couple of not very gentle matrons prodded and poked the two accused and declared that they were certainly not with child. This information was passed onto the court.

The following day a court official visited Jenny and Elizabeth in their cell to inform them what the court had decided.

"I have good news and bad news," the fat official began, taking out a document from his pouch. "The good news is that Mistress Elizabeth Davies is not to be hanged. She is instead to be transported to Virginia."

Jenny immediately put her hands up to her neck as the court official continued in a dry voice, "But you, Mistress Jenny Diver, are to be hanged by the neck until you die. This will take place at Tyburn at the next hanging session." And having said that, he left. Not a word of comfort or even of castigation.

Jenny spent the following two months in Newgate, again using her wealth to ease her stay there. It was now that she realised she had reached the end of the road. No more bribery for a stay of execution, no more voyages to Virginia. Her next journey would be from east London to west – to the gallows at Tyburn – to the infamous 'Tyburn Tree' or 'Triple Tree'.

However, in the meanwhile, it seems that Jenny found religion. Now, after twenty years or so of robbing people, cheating and charming her way out of grim situations, Jenny began to seriously wonder about the Christian faith, especially about Heaven and Hell; about the fate of her soul in the afterlife. Every so often she would sit with a priest in her cell, who would exhort her to confess and repent her wicked ways.

"If so, you will avoid going to eternal damnation in the fires of Hell," the earnest black-coated clergyman said. "You are going to die; about that I do nothing. But at least, if you show some remorse you will go and meet your Maker as a penitent soul."

Jenny took his message to heart. Together with all the other prisoners who were due to hang on Wednesday, 18 March 1741, she was taken to the chapel in the prison. There, sitting in one of the Condemned Pews and facing a coffin, she listened to a service which concentrated on the condemned prisoners' crimes, repentance and the hereafter. Three days later, on the eve of her execution, the bellman rang his bell and recited the following:

> *'All you that in the condemned hole do lie,*
> *Prepare you for tomorrow you shall die,*

*Watch all and pray, the hour is drawing near
That you before the Almighty must appear;
Examine well yourselves in time repent,
That you may not to eternal flames be sent.
And when St. Sepulchre's Bell in the morning tolls
The Lord above have mercy on your souls.'*

On that fateful day in March an unusual large number of felons were due to be hanged. Jenny was one of the most well-known among them, and the authorities made sure that a regiment of horse and foot soldiers were on hand to keep the public order. The felons' procession made their way west along Tyburn Way (now Oxford Street) to the 'Tree' (now the site of Marble Arch). Owing to the press of the crowds, the carts taking the condemned could sometimes take as long as three hours to make the three-mile journey. However, according to the *Gentleman's Magazine* of the day, Jenny did not travel in a mere cart, but was transported in a suitably attired mourning coach. She was veiled and heavily guarded and possibly somewhat inebriated, as tradition had it that the condemned prisoners were allowed to stop off at the *Bowl Inn* at St

Giles (near Centre Point today) for a last time drink of strong liquor or wine. Eventually arriving at Tyburn, Jenny and her fellow felons were greeted by a raucous crowd of tens of thousands of cheering Londoners. They were all there to enjoy the site of twenty-four unfortunates being strung up and left kicking and dangling in the wind. Again, to quote the *Gentleman's Magazine,* Jenny was:

> *'...strongly guarded, there being a design form'd to rescue her...She appeared gaily dressed even to the last, yet deeply affected with her approaching fate. Her concern was so sensibly expressed, when she took leave of her little [three-year-old] child, a few days before her execution, that it drew tears into the eyes of the Turnkey.'*

Perhaps the last thing that Mary saw before the hangman placed a black hood over her head was some disreputable man or woman worming their way through the crowds, picking the pockets of those who had come to see her 'turned off'.

Chapter 8

Jack Sheppard (1702-1724)

Jack Sheppard (1702-1724) was probably the most well-known villain in early 18th century London. In fact, he was so famous that Sir James Thornhill, the celebrated painter of huge murals in the Royal Hospital, Greenwich and on the inside of the dome of St. Paul's Cathedral came to Newgate Prison to paint his portrait before he was hanged. To have achieved such fame within the last two years of his life in the capital, a city

infested with hundreds if not thousands of thieves and pickpockets, was no mean feat.

The city's population loved him in the way they had adored the exploits of the fictional Robin Hood many centuries before. Like a modern film-star or singer, Jack Sheppard featured in many ballads and broadsheets. Here was a working-class man who had fooled the authorities through his many robberies and his association with poor prostitutes. Above all, he was admired for the four times he broke out of prison, including the notorious Newgate Prison, in order to continue his criminal career.

And not only did he become a legend during his lifetime, but his thieving and escapes were immortalised in literature, both in plays and novels. John Gay featured him as 'Macheath' in The Beggar's Opera *in 1728, while in 1840, one hundred and twenty years after Sheppard's untimely demise, William Harrison Ainsworth, the writer who had turned Dick Turpin into a hero, wrote a best-selling novel called* Jack Sheppard. *In 1969, the film* Where's Jack, *also known as* Run, Rebel, Run *in the UK, appeared, starring the cockney Tommy Steele, pop-singer turned family entertainer and film actor.*

*

Jack Sheppard (real name, John) was born into a poor family in the tough area of Spitalfields, London, in

1702. His father was a carpenter and his mother probably a housewife. The father died while Jack was young and so too did Jack's sister. His brother, John, after whom he was named, had died before Jack was born. It was probably due to the family's poverty that young Jack was very thin and grew to be only five feet four inches tall. This would prove to be a great advantage for him in his future jail-breaking career.

Since it was hard for his mother to support her family by working in a shop, she sent six-year-old Jack to a workhouse near St. Helen's, Bishopsgate. Here, in Mr Garrett's school, the boy became apprenticed to a cane-chair maker, but his master died soon after. The young Jack was then re-apprenticed to another cane-chair maker, but unlike his first employer, this second one mistreated his new apprentice.

Despite this, Jack remained there for four years, and then in 1712 went to work with his mother in a wool draper's shop in the Strand. It was during this period of Jack's life that a Mr Kneebone taught him to read and write, but this did nothing to help him in his future career. Five years later, in April 1717, fifteen-year-old Jack signed the necessary papers to begin a seven-year apprenticeship in carpentry in Wych Lane, Covent Garden.

It seems that the young man was doing well, when two years before the end of his apprenticeship, he drifted into the world of crime. He used to drink at a local tavern called the Black Lion, and there he met

Elizabeth Lyon, a prostitute also known as Edgeworth Bess, and her friend, Molly (alias Polly) Maggot. It is very probable that it was these criminal connections that caused Jack to leave the 'straight and narrow'.

"Hello, there," Jack said, studying the young woman's full figure and pretty face. "You're Edgeworth Bess, aren't you?"

"Yes," she replied, enjoying his attention. "And you are Jack Sheppard, no? You're a carpenter. Am I right?"

Jack nodded. "How d'you know? I don't come here very often."

She tapped the side of her pert nose. "I make it my job to know about people. After all, that's what I get paid for – knowing people. Especially handsome fellows like you."

From this the subject changed to money, with Jack saying that he needed more. It did not take Bess long to introduce him to several members of the underworld who promised him that they would help him solve his financial problems.

Two of these villains included Joseph Hayne, a button-moulder and Joseph 'Blueskin' Blake. The latter was a mixed-race, partly educated thief who loved to quote the classics and was to become Jack's future partner in crime.

Jack threw himself enthusiastically into this world of drinking, whoring and crime, and as a result, his woodworking skills suffered. Encouraged by Bess,

Jack began to steal and shoplift to pay for his new riotous lifestyle, his first recorded theft taking place at Charing Cross. Here he stole two silver spoons, and when he saw that he had got away with it he went on to rob some of the houses where he was working. He then passed on the stolen goods to Bess to fence for him.

As well as Bess, he also worked with another prostitute, her friend, Moll Maggot. She persuaded him to rob the house of a Mr Bains who worked in the rag trade.

One night, Jack broke into Bains' house in White Horse Yard and stole a length of fustian, a heavy cotton cloth. Seeing that it was easy to carry out this robbery, Jack returned to the unfortunate Bains' house again and, after removing some of the bars from the cellar window, stole more goods and money to the tune of twenty-two pounds (two thousand, one hundred and fifty today). These he passed on to Moll to fence for him.

Jack had not finished his apprenticeship with William Kneebone, who in the meanwhile had become very suspicious about the young man's behaviour. Once he noted that Jack had not been home for two days, and so he looked inside Jack's trunk and found the stolen fustian cloth. Jack saw what had happened and broke into Kneebone's house and stole the cloth back from him before his master could use it as evidence against him. But this was not the end of the story.

Kneebone reported what had happened to Bains, who then noticed that a length of fustian was missing. Bains decided to have Jack arrested and taken into custody. Jack's response was to deny it all and say that it was his mother who had bought the cloth in Spitalfields market. When questioned, Jack's mother backed up her son's story, although she was somewhat vague on the details about this purchase. Bains saw that it would be a long job to get his goods back, so in the end he dropped the whole matter.

As Jack became more and more successful as a thief, he came into contact with more of London's villains of the 1720s. The chief of these was Jonathan Wilde, the dangerous and vicious robber, gang-leader and self-styled 'Thief-taker General'.

Since Jack had ended his apprenticeship, he had no need to live near Covent Garden. Making out that he and Bess were married, they moved south of the river to Fulham where they lived for a while. From there they moved to Piccadilly.

While there, Bess was arrested and locked up in St. Giles's Roundhouse – a small prison. When Jack found out, he marched over to the prison and demanded to see her. The guard, a beadle called Brown, refused Jack's demand, so Jack beat him up, broke in and released her.

This exploit gained him his first public credit with London's underworld of prostitutes and thieves of all descriptions. This act of physical violence involving a prison would be the first of many in Jack's career. This time he broke in. In future, he would be breaking out.

Jack continued with his criminal career, often together with his 'wife' and his already convicted brother, Tom. Jack picked pockets, and possibly because he still had much to learn, he was arrested and thrown into the St. Anne's Roundhouse. While there, Bess, as the dutiful 'wife' came to visit him. This was a bad move on her part, as she was recognised, arrested and locked up together with Jack. From here they were sent together to New Prison in Clerkenwell and locked up in the same cell, one known as the Newgate Ward. From here Jack was to make the first of his several escapes from prison.

"Oh, Jack, I'm scared," Bess said, moving as close as she could to him considering the fetters around her legs. "What are we going to do? They can hang us for what we've done."

For an answer Jack held up a file and a pointed rod of iron. "Don't worry, lass. This is what we're going to do. First, I'll file these chains off and then I'll make a hole in the wall with this," he said, holding up the iron rod. "The iron bar on the window is loose, and so is the wooden one next to it. I'll pull them out and then we can climb out."

"Yes, but Jack, we're too high up. We're not on the ground floor."

"I know, and that is why we'll make a rope out of these sheets and blankets to lower ourselves. Don't worry, lass," he added, caressing her shoulder. "I'm sure it'll work."

Jack was right. He filed off their fetters, loosened the metal and wooden bars on the window and then using their sheets and blankets, they lowered themselves uninjured to the ground. But then they had another problem – New Prison was surrounded by a twenty-two-foot-high wall. Nevertheless, by using the locks and bolts on the high gate as footholds, the short Jack and the plump Bess managed to scale the wall and escape to freedom.

Soon after this Jack met Joseph Blake in the Black Lion.

"Hello, Blueskin. How are you?"

"All right, lad, and how's yourself?"

Jack shrugged. "I'm doing well, I suppose, but I'm in need of some money. And I'm having trouble with that Jonathan Wilde character."

"Why, what does he want from you?"

"Well, it's like this. After I escaped from Clerkenwell I robbed a few houses where I used to do some carpentry. Wilde got to hear of it."

"So?"

"He wanted me to fence the stuff through him and I refused. I knew I could get a better price if I got rid of the stuff on my own and…"

"And Wilde didn't like it."

Jack nodded. "So now I have to watch out for him and his two-faced ways. He'll hand me over to the authorities if he gets the chance. He's not the sort to say no to forty pounds a head."

Blueskin waved his hand dismissively. "Forget him, Jack. Here, I'll buy you a drink and then we'll talk about a plan I have in mind. A plan that will put a lot of chinks in our pockets."

The result was that in July 1724 Jack and Blueskin robbed the house of William Kneebone, Jack's former employer. Among the goods they stole were several bolts of heavy fustian cloth.

Wilde heard about this and demanded that they fence their loot through him. Jack and Blueskin refused and decided to use the good offices of William Field instead. In the meanwhile, they stored all the loot from this robbery and others in a rented stable near the Horse Ferry, Westminster.

Unfortunately for Jack, the phrase 'when thieves fall out' became more than a figure of speech. The fence, William Field, was really one of Wilde's men, and at the same time he informed on Jack and Blueskin to the 'Thief-taker', he broke into the stable and took the loot stored there for himself.

It was now that Wilde, Field's 'boss', decided that the time was ripe to have his own revenge. One day he met Edgeworth Bess in Temple Bar and plied her with strong drink. In her befuddled state she betrayed Jack, who was promptly arrested soon after by Quilt Arnold, one of Wilde's henchmen. He was taken to Newgate Prison, and this being his third arrest for the same crime, Jack was sure that he was going to hang this time. But, as he was waiting for his trial, he worked out how he was going to escape. He noticed that one of the iron bars in the grille in his cell could be cut or forced out and that would be his key to freedom.

Jack was taken to the assize court in the old Bailey in August 1724 and charged with three counts of theft. He was lucky that the authorities did not have enough evidence against him for two of the charges, but for the third, the stealing of one hundred and eight yards of woollen cloth and other items, Jack was in serious trouble. An aggrieved William Kneebone, supported by William Field, gave evidence that Jack had robbed his former employer's house, and for this he was sentenced to hang. Fortunately for him, this sentence was not to be carried out immediately, but on one of the next 'hanging days' at the 'Tyburn Tree'.

In the meanwhile, Bess quickly realised what she had done, and she rounded up her old friend, Molly Maggot, and together, wearing their most enticing dresses, they went to visit Jack in his cell.

"Listen, Moll," Bess said before setting off. "This is what I'm going to do. I feel real bad about what I've done to Jack, so now I'm going to help him escape."

"How?"

"I'll slip a few tools in here," she said, pointing to her deep cleavage, "and pass them on to him. I'm sure he'll know what to do with them. None of the guards will search me there," she added, pointing to her well-rounded chest.

Bess was right. Jack did indeed know how to use the small hammer, chisel and bar that she smuggled in. He also told them that he had worked out how to loosen one of the bars, but he needed the girls to distract the guard. For Bess and Molly this was no problem. It was all in a day's work. Having got rid of the tools, Bess and Molly sidled up to the fascinated guards and allowed them to happily ogle and fondle.

As the guards were enjoying themselves, Jack removed the bar, and being thin, slid through the gap in the grille and made his way out through a sooty chimney flue. He then put on a dress the girls had smuggled in, and thus disguised, made his escape.

Jack realised that it would not be safe for him to remain in London. After meeting an old friend, a butcher named Page, they left the city to lie low in Chipping Warden, Northamptonshire, some sixty miles north of the capital. "You'll like my family there," Page promised. "They're very friendly folk."

Page was wrong. His family did not like Jack; in fact, they were quite indifferent to him and within a week Jack and Page were back in London.

By now Jack Sheppard was a celebrity. Everybody knew about him and this proved to be a major problem. In 1724, London had a population of 600,000 (roughly that of Coventry, or Ft. Worth, USA today). His escapes were the talk of the town, and after robbing a watchmaker's shop in Fleet Street, he saw that he had to keep a low profile if he did not want to return to Newgate and the hangman's rope.

He moved to Finchley Common, on the northern outskirts of the city, but Wilde, still thirsting for revenge, discovered where he was. He sent some of his men after Sheppard, who arrested him a few days after he had returned to London.

Once again, he was taken to in Newgate, from where again tried to escape. Unfortunately for him, the guards twice found files that friends had smuggled in, and so he was transferred to the strong room known as 'the Castle'. This time, to be sure he wouldn't get away, the authorities had him handcuffed and attached by heavy iron chains to two iron staples set in the floor.

All sorts of people, rich, famous and otherwise, came to visit him. The guards were pleased about this as they charged admission for the honour of seeing such a well-known personality locked up in their prison. The visitors were frisked by the guards to ensure that none of them brought in a file or anything else that Jack might find useful. Nevertheless, like a prototype Houdini, Jack still made his escape. He found a bent nail on the floor of his cell and discovered that if he wriggled it around enough in the huge horse padlock, he could open it.

In the meanwhile, Wilde's men also arrested Blueskin Blake, who was brought to court the following week, on 15 October 1724. Wilde and Field gave evidence against him and although there were discrepancies in what they said, Blueskin was convicted. He was so angry at Wilde, his former friend and fellow thief, that he attacked him in court with a pocket-knife, slashing his throat. Fortunately for Wilde, although the wound was serious, it was not fatal.

The noise and commotion at the end of the trial caused a similar ruckus to break out in the nearby Newgate Prison. While this was in progress, Jack managed to unlock his handcuffs and remove his chains. According to the *Newgate Calendar* he then made a hole in the chimney of the 'Castle' and began his escape through the ceiling. At first his way was blocked. But then he managed to wrench an iron bar out of the side of the chimney and used this to break into the 'Red Room' above. His next problem was to get out of the 'Red Room', a cell that had previously been used to imprison captive soldiers.

According to the *Newgate Calendar,* Jack managed to:

> *'...work upon the nut of the lock and with little difficulty got it off and made the door fly before me.... The door of the entry between the 'Red Room' and the chapel proved a hard task, it being a laborious piece of work; for here I was forced to break away the wall and dislodge the bolt which was fastened on the other side.*

This occasioned much noise, and I was very fearful of being heard by the Master Side debtors. Being got to the chapel, I climbed over the iron spikes and with ease broke one of them off for my further purposes and opened the door on the inside.'

The riot below must have been so noisy and chaotic that none of his guards came to check on their famous prisoner in his cell awaiting the death sentence. In fact, after working hard to break into the prison chapel near the roof, Jack returned to his cell and grabbed a blanket which he then used to help him slide off the roof onto a neighbouring house, a dwelling belonging to one William Bird, in order to complete his escape.

It was now night, and being careful not to wake anyone up, Jack broke into Bird's house, sneaked downstairs and walked out onto the street through the front door. He made his way over to Tottenham and hid in a cowshed, where he was spotted.

"Who are you, and what are you doing skulking around my cowshed?" the surprised farmer asked.

"Don't worry, master. I was just resting here for the night."

"So why are you wearing them chain things on your legs? You're an escaped prisoner, aren't you?"

Jack nodded. There was no other reply he could give. "Yes. I escaped from Bridewell Prison and I'm trying to get home."

The farmer held his pitchfork out in front of him. "What was you in for? Murder? Robbery?"

Jack had to think very quickly. If he gave the wrong answer the chances were that he would be back in Newgate soon. "No," he said quietly. "The judge sent me there because I didn't have enough money to buy food for my bastard child, and because I couldn't give any security to the parish, they put me in the Bridewell."

The farmer sympathised with Jack, but he was not able to remove the fetters. So then Jack found a joiner and told him the same story, promising that he would give him twenty shillings (two hundred and fifteen pounds today today) if he would give him the necessary tools to remove the fetters, which were beginning to hurt him. The joiner borrowed the tools of his neighbour, a blacksmith, and soon Jack was completely free.

To celebrate he went to a cellar in a Charing Cross tavern, and so as not to be recognised he tore his woollen hat, coat and stockings and made out that he was a beggar. He then enjoyed the evening's conversation, much of which was about him and his escapes and his future prospects if he would be caught again. He repeated this act the next day in a small alehouse near Piccadilly. There he told a female customer that it would be impossible for Jack Sheppard to escape out of the country and that "the keepers would have him the next day". The woman cursed anyone who wished to betray him and, feeling uplifted by this, Jack continued his merry way in disguise until he came to the Haymarket. There among a crowd of ballad singers he heard people still talking about Jack Sheppard and his miraculous escape.

Jack remained free for two weeks, during which time he kept a low profile. Still dressed as a beggar, he made contact with his mother in Clare Street through a young woman. His mother came to visit him in a garret in a poor house in Newport Market.

"Jack, Jack," she asked as soon as she had stopped hugging him. "How are you, son? I was so worried about you when I heard you was in Newgate. Everyone was telling me that this time they'd hang you."

"Well, look at me, mother. Do I look hanged to you?"

His mother gave a weak smile and hugged him again. Then she pulled herself away and looked at him full in the face. "Listen to me, son. This has got to stop. You must leave London. You must get out of the country. Go to America. Go anywhere. Just don't stay here. Do you promise me?"

Jack nodded, but in his heart of hearts he knew that he would stay in London.

"Do you have any money for the fare?" she asked.

"A little, but don't you worry about that. I'll get some more soon."

And he did, but not for the boat fare to America. He broke into the Rawlins brothers' pawnshop in Drury Lane, where he stole some clothes, rings, watches, a silver sword and a wig. In his new clothes he spent the money and his time with two women. As the *Newgate Calendar* reported:

> *'...in company with my sweetheart aforesaid and another young woman her acquaintance, we went into the city and were very merry at a public house not far from the place of my old confinement. At four the same afternoon, we all passed under Newgate in a hackney coach... in the evening I sent for my mother to the Shears alehouse in Maypole Alley near Claremarket and with her drank three quarters of brandy; and after leaving her I drank in one place or other about the neighbourhood all evening till the evil hour of twelve...'*

It was as if he knew the game was up. Two days after breaking into Rawlins' shop, on 1 November 1724, he was arrested again. He was still disguised in his fine stolen clothes and wig, and was still groggy with drink.

This time the guards at Newgate had learned their lesson. They put him in the Middle Stone Room next to the 'Castle' where he was kept under very close and constant observation. In addition to the usual locks and chains, they added three hundred pounds of weights to his fetters.

As before, his guards decided to make hay while the sun shone and charged his visitors four shillings each to see him. This is when the famous painter, Sir James Thornhill, painted his portrait. Some of his more important visitors even petitioned King George I to have Jack transported like his brother instead of being hanged. But the authorities, who doubtlessly felt that they had been fooled by him too often, would have none of it.

He was taken to the Court of the King's Bench at Westminster Hall (the site of the trials of Anne Boleyn and Catherine Howard) and there was offered a chance to save his neck.

"Master John, otherwise known as Jack Sheppard," Mr Justice Powis declared. "This court will commute your sentence of hanging if you inform us of your associates. Which is it to be?"

"Your Honour," Jack said proudly. "That is something that I will never do."

"Well, in that case, it is my duty to confirm upon you the death sentence. You are to be hanged at Tyburn next Monday. Case dismissed. Take him down."

Jack was returned to Newgate, where apart from being visited by all and sundry, he attended prayer services in the chapel. He continued laughing and joking among the other prisoners and did not behave as if his day of reckoning was due.

According to the writer Daniel Defoe, Jack was still planning to escape and is alleged to have said, "One file is worth all the Bibles in the world," to Reverend Wagstaff, one of his many visitors.

One day shortly before he was hanged, a friend of Jack's, after 'garnishing' or bribing his guards to have a drink and not listen in on their conversation, had this to say to the condemned man.

"Listen, Jack, we've worked out a plan to save you. First of all," he said, quietly handing over a small parcel wrapped in paper, "take this penknife and keep it well hidden. You'll be able to use it to cut yourself free from the bonds they'll tie you up in in the cart, and also to cut the hangman's rope if you get that far."

"Why, what do you mean, 'if I get that far'?"

"Because, Jack, once you've cut your way free, you are to jump out of the cart when it approaches Turnstile Street."

"And what will I do then?"

"Fear not, my friend. We'll have some of our people waiting for you there and when they shout for you to jump, then you jump. From there you'll escape down that narrow alleyway known as Little Turnstile, and that will take you to…"

"Lincoln's Inn Fields."

"Right. Have you understood all that?"

Jack nodded and quickly stuffed the knife inside his shirt as he thought he heard one of his guards belch and start coming towards his cell. The friend looked along the gloomy corridor. "It's all, right, lad. No-one's there. Now listen to the rest of the plan."

"There's more?"

"Aye, listen carefully. Now if all of what I've just told you fails and you do get scragged at the Tree, some of us will be standing there in the front. The plan is that we'll grab your body and rush you off to a nearby surgeon who will bring you back to life and…"

"Like what they did to Half-hanged Smith twenty years ago?"

"Exactly. But now, Jack, I've got to go. So don't forget to keep that knife hidden and you'll be around for a lot longer." And with those final words of encouragement, he left as the guards, having finished their drink, returned to Jack's cell.

That night Jack Sheppard slept well knowing that his friends were looking out for him.

On Monday 16 November 1724, he was hauled out of the Middle Stone Room, bound, and under heavy guard was bundled into the cart which was to take him to Tyburn. He was smiling. He knew that he still had a trick left up his sleeve; however, he was destined never to play it.

As he was leaving the yard at Newgate, a prison official called Watson searched Jack and found the penknife. Then Jack endured the traditional ride from Newgate Prison to the Hanging Tree. This meant being visible to the world in an open cart as it slowly made its way along the crowded Tyburn Road (now Oxford Street). Two hundred thousand people – one third of the population of London – were there to see him and his guards stop at the Bowl Inn, one of the taverns *en route*, so that everyone could have a jolly time.

Here the condemned victim would crack the joke that he'll have a drink now and pay for it on the journey back. For his part, Jack drank a pint of 'sack' – a sweet sherry-type wine made famous by Shakespeare's Falstaff. He is also alleged to have said with a smirk, "Give the remainder to Jonathan Wilde." Drinking this strong wine meant that on more than one occasion, condemned prisoners were quite drunk and oblivious about what was happening to them as the hangman slipped the noose around their necks.

The macabre procession continued on its way, with Jack smiling and joking as his well-wishers cheered him on. This was the adulation that Jack revelled in but, despite all the jollity, Jack still had one more plan up his sleeve. After being hanged, probably by hangman Richard Arnet, Jack was counting on his friends to cut him down while he was still warm, whisk him away and revive him. This had to be done quickly as it had been done in the past with other villains, and

Jack hoped that it would work with him as well. It did not. Because he was so famous, huge crowds surrounded the gallows, preventing his friends from taking his body right away. Jack Sheppard, the thief who had escaped from jail four times, including the dreaded Newgate Prison, had reached the end of his road.

After hanging for the regulation fifteen minutes he was cut down. As soon as this happened, riots broke out all around the Tyburn Tree and it was now in the following chaos, although somewhat late, that his body was taken by his friends to the Barley Mow public house in Long Acre, Covent Garden. The rioting continued there, with windows being smashed and the unruly crowd having a good time drinking while others looted nearby houses and shops.

That night, a coach with an armed guard took Jack's body to St. Martin in the Fields churchyard where he was quietly buried. He was twenty-two years old.

But that was not the end of his tale. Jack Sheppard lived on. And how!

Soon after, an anonymous poet wrote the following poem linking Jack Sheppard's name with that of Sir James Thornhill:

> *Thornhill, 'tis thine to gild with fame*
> *The obscure, and raise the humble name;*
> *To make form elude the grave,*
> *And Sheppard from oblivion save.*

Though life in vain the wretch implores,
An evil on the farthest shores,
Thy pencil brings a kind reprieve,
And bids the dying robber live.

This piece to latest time shall stand,
And show the wonders of thy hand;
Thus former masters graced their name,
They gave egregious robbers fame.

Apelles Alexander drew,
Caesar is to Aurelius due;
Cromwell in Lely's work doth shine,
And Sheppard, Thornhill, lives in thine.

Only two weeks after Jack was hanged, John Thurmond wrote *Harlequin Sheppard*, a pantomime which immediately appeared on the stage at the Drury Lane theatre. Following this success, other writers cashed in on Jack Sheppard's name. In 1728, Jack was reborn as 'Macheath' in *The Beggar's Opera*, while Jonathan Wilde, his arch enemy, was resurrected as 'Peachum'. This play was popular for the next hundred years, and it was copied or plagiarised under such titles as *The Quaker's Opera* and *The Prison-Breaker*. In

1928, Gay's play formed the basis of Berthold Brecht and Kurt Weill's *The Threepenny Opera.*

In addition to Jack Sheppard's crimes being immortalised on the stage, he also featured in several best-selling novels such as *Jack Sheppard* by William Harrison Ainsley, a volume illustrated by George Cruickshank, and it is thought that Jack's life influenced some of Charles Dickens' descriptions in *Oliver Twist.*

If all of this was not enough, Jack Sheppard's escapades live on in the modern world in popular culture. His story featured in the 1971 song *Don't Hang Jack* by the British rock band Chicory Tip, while films featuring him were produced in 1900, 1923 and 1969. Jake Arnott, the famous Hollywood film director, wrote about him in his novel, *The Fatal Tree* (2017) and Jordy Rosenberg wrote another novel about him in 2018, *Confessions of a Fox.* Meanwhile in the 19th century, Jack Sheppard's name crossed the Atlantic. The American bank-robbing brothers, Frank and Jesse James, used his name when they wrote to the *Kansas City Star.* Apart from other robbers, such as Dick Turpin, none of the other villains mentioned in this book ever received such posthumous fame.

Chapter 9

Dick Turpin (1705-1739)

We tend to think of Dick Turpin as the typical romantic and brave highwayman – the man who defied the stuffy authorities as he galloped speedily away on his faithful and equally heroic horse, Black Bess. We see him as a latter-day Robin Hood, robbing the rich in their fancy carriages in order to help the poor. Not so. None of this is anything like the truth. So, what was the truth? How did the myth of Dick Turpin ever come about and how did it end up being nothing like what really happened some three hundred years ago?

*

"Young man, is this meat really venison? I've heard that you sell only good meat here."

"Yes, ma'am. It really is venison."

"And is it truly fresh, not like the meat I bought from that other butcher in town last week?"

Dick Turpin nodded. "Yes, ma'am. I can assure you that this meat is perfectly fresh."

"Well, how are you so sure?"

"I killed it myself. Just two days ago."

"Ah, so in that case I will purchase five pounds of it."

And saying that, the young butcher weighed out the meat, wrapped it up and thought of the money he was making.

For all of his young life, Dick had always worked around meat and serving the public. He had been born in September 1705 at the Blue Bell Inn, Hempstead, Essex. His father, John Turpin, had been a butcher and an innkeeper and had insisted that his fifth child learn to read and write. No doubt he and his wife, Mary Elizabeth, had high hopes of their son entering a trade that was somewhat more respectable than theirs. They also knew that the young Turpin did not enjoy preparing veal cutlets and other meat dishes, and he certainly did not like being servile to the arrogant and pernickety housewives who demanded good meat at cheap prices. Nevertheless, when the time came, Turpin Junior did take over the family business.

But the truth was that the young butcher would always want more excitement out of life, and more money for his expensive tastes. His marriage to Elizabeth Millington, mainly for her money than her plain looks, confirmed this need for his pockets to be better lined than those of his hard-working and respectable parents, and a conversation in the local inn was to provide the newlywed butcher with some of the answers to his problems.

"Dick, I hear that you are not happy being a butcher," his tubby drinking companion, Walter, said as they sat there in the corner supping ale and eating meat pies.

"Too true, my friend. I'm sure there must be more to life than cutting up chunks of meat, always having blood on my clothes and smelling of offal wherever I go. And," he added. "I'm not making so much money out of it, either. In fact, I'm in debt and my wife is forever screaming at me like a fishwife about how I can never afford to buy her jewellery and trinkets like her friends' husbands do."

"But why are you in debt? You certainly don't charge cheap prices."

"I know that, Walter, but I have to pay a hearty part of my profits to the hunters and farmers who supply me."

"Huh! That's no problem. Go and hunt your own meat. That way at least, you won't have to pay the hunters."

Dick slapped the table-top. "Now that's a good idea. Why hadn't I thought of that myself? Walter, you're a genius! Let me buy you another tankard. What is it you'll be wanting?"

Soon after, following another evening meeting in another tavern, but one more isolated, Dick had a meeting with several men and one woman. "Aren't you all called the Gregory Gang?" he asked the leader, the scar-faced, heavy-set Samuel Gregory.

"Yes," replied his brothers, Jasper and Jeremiah, together. "And we're also known as the Essex Gang."

"But whatever you call us," Joseph Rose added, "we work together, and we can supply you with as much venison as you can sell and..."

"Aye," joined in John Jones, "for much cheaper prices, too."

"And if we're talking about money," the young woman said, "I manage the gang's finances. I'm called Mary Brazier and I am the fence. They get the meat," she said looking around the table at the gang, "and I sell it. No problems." She pointed to her full figure but cast her eyes down demurely, adding, "Who is going to suspect a sweet-looking lass like myself?" And she was right. With her brown curly hair, sparkling eyes and a figure that many of her customers longed to wrap their hands around, who could resist her?

From now on, Dick Turpin's profits increased and his wife Betty's attitude to him vastly improved, especially as he was able to give her more jewellery. He became known as a purveyor of good fresh meat and that he could be relied upon to supply his uppity lady customers with the very best. Naturally they did not ask any awkward questions about where it came from. They didn't care. All *they* were interested in was being able to keep their husbands happy with a fine joint of tasty beef, mutton or venison.

But if Dick's financial and general situation had improved, that of the Essex Gang had not. Although they were able to supply him with large amounts of venison and other illicit meat that they had obtained from killing the King's deer and stolen cattle and sheep, this was not enough for them. Like Dick Turpin, who as well as supplying his own customers, cut their meat up and sold it on to unscrupulous London butchers, the gang members wanted to make even more money. At one of their gang meetings they decided that the time had come for them to do more than just shooting deer and rustling local herds of sheep and cattle.

"Y'know, Sam," Thomas Rowden began, "I was talking to a friend of mine and he told me about how he and a friend of his had broken into this place in Waltham Abbey and stolen some jewellery worth two hundred quid."

"So?"

"So what I'm saying is, we should switch from merely thieving cattle and stuff and start nicking jewellery instead."

"Aye," pale-faced John Wheeler joined in. "Bracelets is smaller than cows and they should be much easier to get rid of than cows, eh?"

And so the gang decided to change their *modus vivendi* and go in for house-breaking and robbing churches. It was not long before their activities became well-known in the area. They robbed housed and churches and sold their ill-gotten gains – money, jewels, chalices and church plate – to dealers in London who didn't ask too many questions.

It was certainly a cleaner way of making more money quickly, and Dick Turpin decided to join them. One evening just before Christmas 1734, Dick and five other members of the gang broke into the house of a Mister Ambrose Skinner and stole goods worth about three hundred pounds. Two days later they robbed a Mister William Mason, a Keeper of Epping Forest. The gang was lucky to escape the hue and cry when Mason's servant ran off and succeeded in rousing the neighbours, who returned hoping to catch the robbers red-handed. However, by the time several other neighbours arrived, the gang had fled with their loot, leaving the house in a complete state of disorder.

These robberies continued for the next few months and as they did, they became more violent. Stories were told that when the gang entered a house, they demanded to know in no uncertain terms where the owners kept their riches. If they were not given a clear answer immediately, then the gang would attack their unfortunate victim, sometimes even torturing him or her. A report in the local *Weekly Journal* (8 February 1735) read:

> *'On Saturday night last, about seven o'clock, five rogues entered the house of the Widow Shelley at Loughton in Essex, having pistols etc. and threatened to murder the old lady, if she would not tell them where her money lay, which she obstinately refusing for some time, they threatened to lay her across the fire if she did not instantly tell them, which she would not do.'*

Later in court, the widow's son stated that Turpin had threatened his mother, saying, "God damn your blood, you old bitch. If you won't tell me, I'll set your arse on the grate!" As a result of which, the son promptly told the intruders where the money was. That night the Gregory gang made off with one hundred pounds (nearly twelve thousand today) in cash, some silver plate, a silver tankard and 'all manner of household goods'.

This robbery was merely one in a whole series that ranged from the county of Essex to the northern and southern parts of London. Very soon afterwards, at a gang meeting held at the Black Horse Inn, Westminster, they planned the robbery of a Mr Joseph Lawrence of Earlsbury Farm, Edgware, a village on the outer edge of London.

Samuel Gregory opened the meeting. "I know this man well," he said, wiping the ale off his untidy moustache. "I used to be a blacksmith in the area and this Mister Lawrence used to pay his workers a good sum, and in cash, too. None of this paying them with food and eggs. Cash, and lots of it."

"Does he live there on his own?" Jeremiah asked.

"No, not as far as I know, but I don't think we'll have much trouble with his servants. That ol' bastard doesn't keep many and anyway they'll all be too busy looking after their own skins, no? And besides," he added, "the old man is nearly seventy if I'm not mistaken."

"Oh good," Dick said, finishing off his third tankard. "Then it should go off without any problems."

As a result, soon after the gang rode north, and on approaching the farm, they hitched their horses to some trees a few hundred yards away as they wanted to approach the farm quietly. However, just as they reached the edge of the farmyard, they were spotted by a servant boy rinsing out some buckets. Immediately two of the gang caught him, one of them clapping his dirty hand around their surprised and frightened victim's mouth.

"What's your name, boy?" John Wheeler hissed, thrusting his pistol in the boy's stomach.

"Em-Emmerton. James Emmerton."

"Who's in the house and how many are there?"

"Th-there's just Master L-Lawrence, J-John Pate, a s-servant and M-Mistress Dorothy and a c-couple of m-maidservants."

"Well, if you want to live, young Jimmy, you'll shut up and not shout out."

"Aye, but for safety's sake, we'll tie you up anyway," Jeremy Gregory added.

After taking him with them to open the front door the gang burst into the house brandishing their pistols and shouting, shocking the people inside. Three of the gang beat up two maidservants and threw them into a small room with the now bound and thoroughly frightened James Emmerton. In the meanwhile, Dick Turpin and Samuel Gregory lashed the old farmer to a chair.

"Where's your money, old man?"

"I-I don't have m-much…"

This was not the answer they wanted to hear, and the old man was swiftly beaten about the head.

"I'll ask you again. Where's the money?"

No answer. Just a few groans.

"I'll ask you for the last time," Dick said, pointing a pistol at the old man's bleeding face.

But still the old man refused to tell them.

Oh, it's going to be like that, is it?" Gregory snarled. "Dick, do to him what we did to that other stubborn bloke last week."

Turpin untied the old man, brutally turned him around and yanked down his breeches. Then using his pistols, he beat him on the buttocks, while at the same time Gregory beat the unfortunate man's head. It was only after that they had done this and dragged him around the room by his hair that the old man broke and divulged where he kept his money.

"I-It's over th-there behind the d-door," he gasped at last. And while the gang went to find the farmer's strongbox, Samuel Gregory dived into the room where the female servants had been thrown. From there he forced Dorothy, the most buxom of the two, upstairs and raped her. After satisfying himself, he rejoined the gang, who left the ransacked farm to return to their horses. Once they reached their horses tethered behind some trees, one of the gang forced the strong box open.

"How much is there?" Wheeler asked.

"Thirty pounds."

"*Thirty pounds?* Is that all? Are you sure?"

A quick recount proved that that was all. All that planning and violence for thirty pounds. They had expected ten times as much.

Since this robbery had taken place in the London area and was soon followed by a similarly violent one in Marylebone, the King was informed. He issued a pardon to any of the gang who would betray the others. This was to be followed by a reward of fifty pounds, paid on conviction. None of the robbers succumbed to the temptation. This was not surprising as they usually made more than the reward from each of their robberies.

However, at this stage the gang started to disintegrate. While on their way to another robbery in north London, the gang had stopped at the Nine Pins and Bowl Inn, a watering place owned by Richard Wood. As luck would have it, Mister Wood was soon afterwards walking down the road near Marylebone when he recognised the horses standing near the alehouse door. He called a constable and, together with some assistants, they burst into the alehouse and subdued the very surprised John Wheeler, John Fielder, William Saunders and a woman. They bound them up, took their pistols and marched them off to face the nearest magistrate.

As a result, and after being threatened with the rope's end, John Wheeler, the youngest and least-hardened member of the gang, broke and turned King's evidence. Following his 'ample confession' he, Saunders and Fielder were sent to prison to await trial.

But this was not the end of the gang's bad luck. Soon after, three other members, Joseph Rose, Humphrey Walker and Mary Brazier were also caught while drinking in a London tavern. Two of the party responsible for catching them included Farmer Lawrence's two sons and his servant, John Pate. They were out for revenge, and while in London were fortunate to recognise the men who had brutally beaten up their father and raped one of their servants.

Despite the gang members' denials of their alleged crimes, stolen goods were found where they were staying. This resulted in them being committed to Newgate Prison.

While there, young John Wheeler continued to 'squeal' on his former associates, and when asked to describe the missing Dick Turpin, this is what he said:

> *'A butcher by trade, is a tall fresh coloured man, very much marked with the small pox, about twenty-six years of age, about five feet nine inches high, lived some time ago in Whitechapel and did lately lodge somewhere about Millbank, Westminster, wears a blue grey coat and a natural wig.'*

In addition to Wheeler's confessions being used at the capital trial of four of the gang, the authorities now had more detailed descriptions of the other gang members who were still at large. Along with the above description of Dick Turpin, they learned that John Jones 'was five and a half feet high, fresh coloured, pock marks in his face and wears a brown wig'. Samuel Gregory was about the same height and also wore a brown wig and was similarly fresh coloured. In addition, he 'has a scar about an inch and a half long on his right cheek and is 23 years old'. Thomas Rowden was also 'fresh coloured' and pock-marked and was described as a 'little man, well set and full faced'. Herbert Haines was about the same height as Gregory and Jones and also wore a brown wig and was 'of a pale complexion'.

While they were still free, the authorities decided to deal with the gang members they were holding in custody. Walker, Sanders, Rose and Field were tried at the Middlesex General Session at the end of February 1735 and charged with robbing the house of Ambrose Skinner. Dick Turpin and Samuel Gregory were also charged *in absentia* for the same crime.

Humphrey Walker missed being hanged as he died in Newgate Prison. At fifty years old, he was the oldest member of the gang and had likely been seriously roughed up in prison while awaiting trial. His fellow criminals, Sanders, Rose and Field, were found guilty and hanged at Tyburn on 10 March 1735.

For a while, the luck of the remaining members of the Essex Gang continued to hold, before finally running out.

"You know what we should do," Samuel Gregory said to Jeremy one evening. "We should go south where we are not known. Y'know to Brighton and Shoreham."

And that is what they did. But after a few robberies on the south coast, crimes which didn't yield very much money, they decided to return to London where there were richer pickings. On their way back north, and not wishing to waste any valuable opportunity, they robbed the portly Sir John Osborne near Godalming of his gold watch and much money. They then tried to rob the landlord of the Red Lion in Guildford. However, this would-be victim was lucky and managed to escape his fate.

"Come, Jeremy," Samuel said to his brother soon after, "we're working too hard. We need some recreation. Let's go and see the cockfight near Petersfield. It's not too far away. About a dozen miles west of here and it'll make a nice change."

And a change it certainly was. For while they were sitting there watching the angry cocks battling each other, Samuel's coat came open and those sitting near him saw a pistol stuck in his belt. Immediately they started talking and speculating who he was.

"Ever seen him here before?"

"No, but I wonder why he's armed."

"Hey, wait a minute, doesn't he look like that bloke who robbed Sir John Osborne?"

"Yes, I think you're right."

And within minutes the crowd had forgotten the cockfighting and had begun chasing the two Gregory brothers. They were stopped at a local alehouse and surrounded by a mob holding swords, pistols and scythes. A large noisy scuffle broke out in which Jeremy was shot in the thigh and Samuel had the tip of his nose cut off by a sword. The two gang members were forced to surrender and soon after found themselves being hauled in front of a local Justice of the Peace. He committed them to Winchester gaol, where they were later confronted by Sir John Osborne himself.

At first, they denied any wrong-doing, but because of this, Samuel admitted who they were and even confessed to having carried out the robbery at the Lawrence farm in Edgware. Soon after, Jeremy died of his wounds, and a heavily guarded Samuel Gregory was taken to London to stand trial.

It cannot have been an easy ride for him as he was surrounded by more than half a dozen guards and his feet were chained together under the belly of his horse. He was taken to the New Prison, where Wheeler confirmed that Gregory had indeed taken part in the Edgware robbery. From there he was transferred to Newgate and then taken to the Old Bailey for trial. Here he was charged with robbing the houses of William Francis and Joseph Lawrence, stealing Thomas Humphrey's horse (a major crime in those days) and raping Dorothy Street during the Edgware robbery. Each of these crimes carried the death penalty. Gregory was hanged on 4 June 1735 and his body was sent to

Edgware to hang in chains alongside those of the rotting bodies of his past comrades.

Within a few months almost all of the remaining members of the Essex gang had been rounded up. Herbert Haines was hanged two months later, and Mary Brazier was transported to America. Only Dick Turpin, John Jones and 'little' Thomas Rowden continued to escape His Majesty's justice.

One evening, in a quiet tavern near where the county of Essex bordered London, the above trio had a council of war.

"I think the time has come," Turpin began as he finished his first tankard that evening, "for us to change what we do."

"Do you mean that we should go out and work…"

"Or join the Church?"

"No, no," Turpin replied quickly. "No, I think we should stop robbing houses for a while and turn our hands to highway robbery. It seems to be a quicker way of getting money and jewellery. Y'know, we stop a carriage, grab what we can and race off into the forest. If we cover our faces, no-one will recognise us. Not like what happened to the others, heh? What do you think?"

They agreed – it certainly seemed a safer way of getting their hands on a lot of money fast.

Nevertheless, after a couple of successful robberies in Epping Forest and east London in April 1735, the new gang's fortunes began to unravel.

Somehow, someone had recognised them, and on 10 July the following notice appeared in the press:

> *'Last Thursday night about eight o'clock Mr Vane of Richmond, and Mr James Bradford of the Borough of Southwark, going from thence to Richmond were attacked between Wandsworth and Barns Common by two highwaymen supposed to be Turpin the butcher and Rowden the pewterer, the remaining two of Gregory's gang who robbed them of their money &c, dismounted them, made them pull off their horses' bridles, then turning them adrift they rode off towards Roehampton where a gentleman was rob'd, as is supposed by the same highwaymen, of a watch, and about £3 4s in money.'*

Despite the unwanted publicity and with a new price of one hundred pounds on their heads, Turpin and Rowden continued their activities in south London. However, it seems that in the autumn of 1735, and perhaps after hearing that that the third member of this trio, John Jones, had been caught, Turpin and Rowden decided to have a break and lie low for the time being.

But apparently Rowden did not lie low enough. In July 1736 he was caught in Gloucestershire and put on trial for carrying out one of his old tricks – passing counterfeit coins. He was sentenced to be hanged for this and other past crimes. However, the judge decided to be merciful and commuted Rowden to transportation to America. Now Dick Turpin was the only member of the Essex gang who was still free.

No one is sure of where he was from mid-1736 until February 1737, when his name together, with that of his wife, Elizabeth, her servant Hannah Elcombe and a Robert Nott, appeared in the press. It is thought that he may have gone to the Netherlands for a while, but there is no evidence of this apart from a few alleged sightings of him there. But wherever he was during this period, he was definitely seen in England at the beginning of 1737.

During the spring of that year Dick Turpin teamed up with two other highwaymen, Stephen Potter and Matthew King, and with them he continued his nefarious activities in Leicestershire for a period before heading south to London. There, near the Green Man Inn in Leytonstone, one of the gang stole a horse called 'Whitestockings'. The owner of the horse, Joseph Major, reported his depressing news to the Green Man's assertive landlord, Richard Bayes, as the latter served him with a tankard of ale. Bayes decided that Major should not take the matter lying down.

"I'll tell you what I'll do," Bayes said to the unhappy Major. "I'll ask around about your horse and see what happens. I mean, with those white stockings, it's a very distinctive looking animal."

"That's very true, and it's very kind of you to help me, sir, but what good will it do? My horse could be anywhere by now."

"Fear not, Master Major. It often pays to ask questions. And besides, me being a landlord, I know lots of people who work in the trade – y'know, in inns and taverns and even in stables. You never know your luck."

A few days later Bayes met the still depressed Joseph Major in his inn. "Cheer up, Mister Major," he smiled, offering him a full tankard of ale. "I have some gladsome tidings for you."

"You've found my horse?"

"Yes, one of my friends in the victualling trade, well, he believes he has spotted your horse at the Red Lion in Whitechapel."

Joseph Major clapped Bayes on the back and asked what they were going to do about it.

"So this is what I've been thinking," Bayes replied, his eyes sparkling. "I'll round up a few stout fellows and we'll lie in wait at the stables at the Red Lion. Someone is bound to come along to collect her. You don't leave a good-looking horse like that standing around in a stable for long, do you?"

And that is what happened. On 1 May 1737, Matthew King's brother, John, entered the stables and was about to unhitch Whitestockings when he was surrounded and overpowered by Bayes' men. As they held him down, he said that the horse was not for him but for another man waiting outside in the yard. Bayes went to see if this was true and found that it was. Waiting there confidently was Matthew King, waiting to take claim of the stolen horse. Unfortunately for him, Bayes recognised the highwayman and later described the following altercation thus:

> *'King immediately drew a pistol which he clapped to [my] breast; but it luckily flash'd in the pan...Turpin, who was waiting not far off on horseback, hearing a skirmish, came up, when King cried, "Dick, shoot him, or we are taken by Gog," at which instant Turpin fir'd his pistol and it missed [me] and shot King in two places, who cried out, "Dick, you have killed me," which Turpin hearing, he rode away as hard as he could. King fell at the shot, though he liv'd a week after and gave Turpin the character of a coward.'*

But the shootings were not over. Turpin rode off to Epping Forest, where he had a hiding place in a hidden cave, and where he was seen by Thomas Morris and a local trader. Morris knew the forest well as he was a servant of a forest keeper, Mr Thompson.

Turpin, who thought the two men were poachers and wanted them to go away, shouted, "There are no hares in this thicket."

Morris then shouted back, "But I have a Turpin."

At this point, Turpin grabbed his carbine and promptly shot and killed him. Before Turpin could shoot the other man, he fled and alerted the authorities. At this point they doubled the reward for catching the murderous highwayman to two hundred pounds, and a detailed description of him was posted everywhere. According to the handbills and the press, Turpin was:

> *'...very much mark'd with the Smallpox, his Cheek-bones broad, his Face thinner towards the Bottom, his Visage short, pretty upright, and broad about the Shoulders.'*

Turpin clearly needed to get far from the scene of this latest crime, and one month later, now travelling as a horse-dealer named John Palmer, he appeared in East Yorkshire. There, wearing fashionable clothes and acting in a manner that was new to him, he became friendly with some local gentlemen and hunters. However, he was only able to keep up this front for so long. Even though he affected the style of a country gentleman and began hobnobbing with the best of the local gentry, there were some who were suspicious of this new man in their midst.

"What do you know about him, George?"

"Not much, Arthur. From the way he speaks, he's from the south and he certainly knows his horseflesh."

"Yes, I'll grant you that, but there's something about him that's strange. I'll tell you later if I can think what it is."

And Arthur did.

"George, have you heard, that John Palmer character we were talking about recently, you know, the one we thought isn't really as much of a gentleman as he makes out? Well, he shot his landlord's gamecock."

"What, he shot that fine bird? When?"

"A few days ago. It was like this. At the beginning of the week Palmer was returning from a hunting expedition with a few of the local gentry when the gamecock started strutting around in the street right in front of his horse. Now that Palmer fellow, who I think can be very short-tempered at times, drew out his pistol and promptly shot the bird."

"Just like that?"

"Aye, just like that. And when one of the neighbours, a Mister Hall or Mister Robinson, rebuked him – I mean, that bird was worth a fortune – Palmer replied that if he would wait around while he reloaded his pistol, he would shoot him as well. Now doesn't that prove what I was telling you about him? That Palmer is certainly no gentleman even if he does wear fancy clothes and ride a fine horse."

Apparently, several other local dignitaries thought the same. Turpin was arrested and taken into custody. Three Justices of the Peace heard the complaint and demanded that he pay a surety for his future good behaviour. Refusing to do so, perhaps due to a lack of funds, he was committed to the House of Correction at Beverley. For once, he did not try to escape.

"Ah, Mister Palmer, Mister John Palmer," Justice of the Peace Marmaduke Constable began his investigation. "Is that your real name?"

"Yes, sir."

"Are you sure?"

"Why, sir?" Turpin replied, beads of sweat appearing on his forehead.

"Because we had been informed that your real name is Richard Turpin," George Crowle JP replied. "Otherwise known as Dick Turpin."

"Oh, no, sir. John Palmer is my real name. My father was called…"

"Well, we'll get to the bottom of that later," Hugh Bethel, the third JP said. "Now tell us about yourself and let's see if it matches the information that we have already been told about you."

Turpin took a deep breath, wiped his forehead and began. "My name is John Palmer and I trade in horses. This means that I have to travel all over the place and that about two years ago I lived in Long Sutton…"

"In Lincolnshire?"

"Yes, sir, and there I traded as a butcher. But then unfortunately I fell into debts and had to leave the county."

"I see, "Bethel said. "So, in other words, you fled without paying your debts?"

Turpin hung his head. "Yes, I suppose so," he muttered, "but I was going to pay them back after I had made enough money here."

"I see, "Bethel repeated. "Then how is it you've been living, as we have been reliably informed, in such a goodly style in Yorkshire?"

"I changed my trade, sir. Instead of killing animals for meat, I began dealing in them."

At this point the three JPs went into a huddle and all Turpin could see and hear was a bobbing of heads and muttered whispers. At last the three heads separated and George Crowle faced a nervous Dick Turpin.

"Mister Turpin," he began quietly. "We do not believe your story. We think it is a whole pack of lies. Therefore, in order to get to the bottom of the truth, we are going to hold you over while we make more enquiries about you. Do you understand?"

Turpin nodded. He had no alternative and was immediately returned to the House of Correction.

In the meanwhile, a special messenger was sent to a local magistrate in Long Sutton, who replied that a Mister John Palmer had indeed lived in the area but that he had never been connected with trading in or butchering of animals there. The magistrate said that a John Palmer had been accused of rustling sheep and had been held in custody for doing so. However, he had made his escape, and had later been linked with stealing horses in other places in Yorkshire and Lincolnshire.

When the three justices received this information, they thought it would be wise to transfer Turpin to the more secure gaol at York Castle. While there, a Mister John Creasy claimed that the new prisoner had once stolen a mare worth three pounds and a foal worth twenty shillings from him.

Despite these accusations, as there was no positive proof that Turpin was a robber or horse-thief, he was listed as a labourer – a general catch-all description for all prisoners without a specific trade. He was kept in gaol for several months, this being the first time he had come down so hard on his luck.

During this period, the Duke of Newcastle, Thomas Pelham-Holles urged for Turpin to be tried in London rather than York. He wanted the London Assizes to have the honour of trying the by now notorious robber and highwayman. However, the Yorkshire judicial circuit ultimately won its right to the trial.

While waiting to go to court Turpin wrote a letter to his brother in Essex. Unfortunately for him, this letter was to prove fatal to his case, as in his defence he claimed he was really an innocent party named John Palmer. This is what he wrote:

'York, Feb 6, 1739
I am sorry to acquaint you, that I am now under confinement in York Castle, for horse-stealing. If I could procure an evidence from London to give me a character, that would go a great way towards my being acquitted. I had not been long in this county before being apprehended, so that it would pass off the readier. For Heaven's sake dear brother, do not neglect me; you will know what I mean when I say,
I am yours,
John Palmer'

As was the norm before 1840, it was up to the recipient of a letter to pay the postage. Turpin's brother refused to do so and therefore the letter was returned to the post office in Essex. There it was by chance spotted by James Smith, a local schoolteacher, who had taught Turpin to write. He recognised the writing, opened the letter and concluded that John Palmer and Dick Turpin were one and the same.

James Smith contacted the Essex magistrates who sent him to York to confirm that the man they were holding in prison there was definitely Dick Turpin. Now his trial could go ahead.

The now notorious rustler and murderer's trial at the York winter assizes opened on 22 March 1739. Due to the accused's infamy, the court was packed as Dick Turpin 'alias John Palmer,' was charged with stealing two horses, a capital crime since 1545. Technically, the charges against him were incorrect, stating that the crimes that he had committed had taken place at Hecklington, Lincolnshire and not Welton, Yorkshire. The authorities also made a mistake with the date of the crime. Turpin had allegedly stolen the horses in August 1738 and not in March 1739.

After the judge, Sir William Chapple, had read out the charges, Thomas Place, the King's Counsel and Recorder of York and Richard Crowle (brother of abovementioned George Crowle) opened for the prosecution.

As was the custom of the time, Turpin had no defence counsel and was therefore represented by the judge. Two of the prosecution witnesses included Thomas Creasy, the owner of the stolen horses, and James Smith, the Essex postmaster.

Thomas Creasy was the first witness to be called.

"Do you swear that the two relevant horses in this case were yours?"

"Yes, Your Honour."

"And how did you retrieve them?"

"I found them, Your Honour, through the good offices of my neighbour. I had told him that my horses were missing, believed stolen, and that my neighbour had heard about them through some information he had heard in Brough. He had gone there after visiting the fair at Pocklington..."

"Pocklington, about nine miles east of York?"

"Yes, Your Honour, and then I decided to follow up this information."

"And the animals in question were indeed your own?"

"Yes, Your Honour," Creasy continued assertively. "It was no problem at all for me to identify the mare as I had bred her myself and indeed, I had kept her for ten years. And as such as I was able to see that the mare was my own, so too was I sure that the foal was also mine."

"I see," Sir William said and then turned to Dick Turpin. "Do you have anything to ask the witness? Could he have made a mistake in identifying these horses?"

Turpin looked up and faced the judge. "Your Honour, I cannot say anything, for I have not any witnesses come this day, as I have expected, and therefore I beg of your Lordship to put off my trial 'til another day."

The judge refused this request and called Captain Dawson to give witness.

"Yes, Your Honour," he began, looking hard at the disappointed Dick Turpin, "I did indeed know the aforementioned mare and foal and that they had belonged to Mister Thomas Creasy."

Dawson was followed by Richard Crassby who, apart from giving evidence about the relevant horses, asked if he would be permitted to say a few words about the accused. The judge agreed and Crassby continued.

"He had no settled way of living that I know of at all, Your Honour. Though he was a dealer, yet he was a stranger and lived like a gentleman. This I thought was very strange."

After calling up George Goodyear to reinforce what had been stated earlier, Sir William called up the Essex postmaster, Mister James Smith, to give evidence.

"Now you, sir," the judge began, "have come up here all the way here to these assizes in York from Essex. Is that right?"

"Yes, Your Honour."

"And you did so by the express order of the justices of that county to prove that this John Palmer to be Richard Turpin, the noted highwayman?"

Smith nodded and said, "Yes, Your Honour," continuing, "I knew him at Hempstead in Essex where he was born. I knew him when he was a child and that I knew his father and all his relations, and that this Dick Turpin man that you have before you married one of my father's maids."

"I see," Sir William said, rubbing his hands. He was feeling good as the case was going the way he had planned. "Now, sir, please tell us about the letter that the accused wrote to his brother."

Smith did so and Turpin was asked if he wished to cross-question the postmaster.

"I never knew him," Turpin replied, a reply that was strange seeing that the postmaster claimed that it was he who had taught Turpin to write when he was a young boy in Essex.

After stepping down, the judge called on Edward Saward to give evidence. He was sworn in and proceeded to state that he had known Dick Turpin when he was a young boy and a butcher in Hempstead.

"Upon my soul," he said for the third or fourth time, "I knew him well and I knew his family well. Yes, Your Honour, upon my soul, I..."

"Excuse me, sir," Thomas Place, KC interrupted, "you do not have to keep saying, 'upon my soul' all the time. You have already been sworn in. Once is enough."

"Yes, sir," and he continued. "As I was saying, I knew his family and indeed his father well. Yes, it was many the time that my good lady-wife purchased some meat from the accused's father, Mister John Turpin, or that I shared a tankard of ale with him at the Blue Bell Inn in Hempstead. Yes, sir, upon my soul, I remember his son, Dick, well and I..."

At this point he was asked to step down, it being clear that he had identified the accused as Dick Turpin from the south, and that he was not a Yorkshireman called John Palmer.

When asked, as he had done so with the postmaster and his past schoolmaster, James Smith, Turpin also denied knowing Edward Saward.

Smith was then recalled to give further evidence. "Your Honour, when I first identified the accused in the prison in York Castle as Dick Turpin, he said to me two or three times, 'Let us bung our eyes in drink'. I did indeed drink with him and as I stated before, the man in the dock is definitely Dick or Richard Turpin."

Sir William then turned to Turpin. "Do you have anything to add before I pass sentence?"

Turpin straightened himself up and looked directly at the judge. "Your Honour," he began, "it is true that I called myself John Palmer because I had been long out of trade and had run myself in debt." He then went on to describe a protracted hard luck story, which he hoped would convince the court in its mercy to transport him to America instead of hanging him. Flashing his most winning smile at the jury and the crowded courthouse, he noticed that one or two ladies were crying into their handkerchiefs, but that was all. The judge had heard too many sad stories by the accused brought before him in the past to be affected by this latest tale of woe.

After hearing more details regarding how Turpin claimed to have bought the foal in Whitechapel, Judge Chapple then called on the jury to give their verdict. They returned a verdict of 'guilty' on both counts – of stealing both the mare and the foal.

Before hearing the judge pass his sentence, Turpin, now feeling somewhat desperate, tried one more ploy. "Your Honour," he began, bowing respectfully to Sir William and the jury, "I thought I should have been removed to Essex, for I did not expect to be tried in this county, therefore I could not prepare witnesses to my character."

"I see," Judge Chapple commented. "And can you give me any reasons why you should not be executed? After all, stealing horses is a capital crime. And you have been charged with stealing not only one but two of them."

Turpin, trying to look remorseful, repeated his line of defence, "It is very hard upon me, my Lord, because I was not prepar'd for my defence."

As before, the judge did not look impressed. "Why was you not? You knew the time of the assizes as well as any person here."

Turpin did not admit this, but instead told Judge Chapple, "Several persons who came to see me assured me that I should be removed to Essex to be tried there, for which reason I thought it needless to prepare witnesses for my defence."

Looking at him straight in the eye, Sir William Chapple replied, "Whoever told you so were highly to blame; and as your country has found you guilty of a crime worthy of death, it is my office to pronounce sentence against you." He paused for a moment, looked around the crowded courtroom and declared, "Richard Turpin, for the stealing of two horses: a mare and a foal, you are to be hanged on 7 April 1739. Take him down."

Turpin was returned to York Castle to await his execution. One of the first things he did after being convicted was to write to his father asking him to intercede with a certain gentleman and lady of quality. He wanted them to exert their influence and have his death sentence commuted to that of transportation. His father did his best but failed – no-one would take the side of such a notorious robber and highwayman. The only reply he received was one from his father urging him to 'beg of God to pardon your many transgressions which the thief upon the cross received pardon for at the last hour'.

Now understanding that there was nothing he could do to escape his fate, Dick Turpin was determined to enjoy himself to the end. He entertained a large number of visitors who wined and dined his remaining few days away. The scene within the confines of his cell was such that the prison chaplain wrote:

> *'He seemed to pay but little regard to the serious remonstrances and admonitions of the reverend gentlemen who attended him, and whatever remorse he had on his*

conscious for his villanies, he kept them to himself.'

During his last days on earth, Dick Turpin decided he would leave the world in style. He ordered and paid for a new fustian frockcoat and a pair of pump-type shoes. In addition, he paid five poor men ten shillings apiece to follow the cart taking him to the gallows as mourners. He also distributed gloves and hatbands, while leaving a ring and some other items to a married woman in Lincolnshire with whom he had been acquainted. It seems that he left nothing for his wife and family in Essex.

On 7 April 1739 he was taken from his cell in York Castle by cart to Knavesmire, the traditional hanging site just outside the city. While on his way, the *Newgate Calendar* reported that Turpin 'bowed to the spectators with an air of the most astonishing indifference and intrepidity'. On arriving at the gallows, a triangular structure similar to the better known one at Tyburn, London, he climbed the ladder without appearing to be afraid.

He then chatted with the hangman, Thomas Hadfield, a pardoned highwayman, for a short while before throwing himself off the top of the gallows. Unlike many other unfortunate criminals who took over twenty minutes to die, Turpin was dead within five minutes. To make sure he was truly dead, his body was left swaying gently in the wind for a while before it was cut down. It was then taken to a tavern in Castlegate, York and the next morning was buried in St. George's Church graveyard, Fishergate. But this was not the end of the story.

A few days after the burial, it was reported that body-snatchers had stolen the body, probably to sell it to some institute for research purposes. This was a common if not highly approved practice. However, these particular body-snatchers were not to get away with their crime. They were discovered and Turpin's body was reburied, this time under a layer of quicklime. Thus ended the brief life of Dick Turpin, hung at the age of 33 who, despite his relatively short and vicious career, has gone down in history as the archetype of the dashing and gallant highwayman. How did this happen?

Almost immediately after Turpin's demise, Richard Bayes, the landlord of the Green Man who had helped retrieve Whitestockings the horse, published *The Genuine History of the Life of Richard Turpin.* This chapbook or pamphlet was written to cash in on the hot news of Turpin's exploits and death. It was a mixture of fact and fiction and became the source for future similar literature. It contains a picture of a man hiding in a cave, as Turpin was supposed to have done in Epping Forest, but it does not contain any portrait of him. In those days, only the rich could afford to have their portraits painted.

As for Turpin's fantastic ride from London to York on his faithful horse, Black Bess, this legend first appeared almost one hundred years later, in William

Harrison Ainsworth's 1834 novel, *Rookwood*. This story was probably based on a much earlier escapade recorded by Daniel Defoe in 1727; a William Nevison had committed a robbery in Kent in 1676 and then allegedly rode to York to prove he had been nowhere near the scene of the robbery at the time. However, it must be stated that all of these stories about tremendous rides and heroic horses were impossible. From London or Kent to York is two hundred miles, and there is no way that a horse, however strong or faithful, could make that journey in a single day.

Ainsworth's dramatic tale was an inspiration for cheap magazines – known as 'penny dreadfuls'– such as *Black Bess or The Knight of the Road* in 1867-1868. Not only did these lurid publications continue to immortalise the fabulous horse-ride, they also turned Turpin from a pock-marked vicious criminal into a smooth and dashing Robin Hood-type figure.

Aside from literature, the romanticised image of Turpin was strengthened further when in 1846 Madame Tussaud had a wax figure made of our hero to be exhibited at her popular museum in Baker Street, London. Later, Turpin became the focus of various stage and screen productions. These included Fred Ginnett's 1906 silent movie, *Dick Turpin's Last Ride to York*, as well as London Weekend Television's twenty-six-episode series, *Dick Turpin* (1979-82). This last production, in accordance with the tradition started by Richard Bayes in 1739, was very loosely based on the truth. And so nearly three hundred years after his death, Dick Turpin continued his gallant but fictional career well into the twentieth century.

Chapter 10

Laurence Shirley, 4*th* Earl Ferrers (1720-1760)

Early in the morning of 5 May 1760, a huge crowd began to gather at the site of the infamous Hanging Tree at Tyburn, west London. They had come to watch a man get strung up for killing a fellow man in cold blood. But this man was no ordinary murderer. He was an aristocrat, an earl, a member of one of the highest ranks in Britain's long-established aristocracy. He had murdered his faithful servant in cold blood and now he

was due to pay the price. The crowd was delighted. Why, if you could hang an earl as well as a commoner for murder, didn't this show that there truly was equality in the country?

And everyone in the crowds, from the upper classes to the lower was eager to see justice being served. Of course, the rich could afford to avoid mixing with the noisy crowds and not come too early. For ten pounds, they had reserved seats for a good view from one of Mother Proctor's Pews. But for everyone, high class or not, it would be an entertaining sight: to see the Earl kick and swing for a minute or two as his life was choked out of him.

And this time, to add something new, the hanged man would be sent on his way by the 'new drop method'. He would not be left there swinging and strangling to death for a while. No, he would be stood on a platform which would suddenly give way, and that would be the end of the story. He would not have time for the usual 'pissing when you can't whistle'. This would be an entirely new show.

In the meanwhile, the crowds spent their time waiting, fighting and brawling, pushing and shoving, as well as eating and drinking what they could buy from Tiddy Doll and other well-known hawkers. And of course, there were those who would not be watching the grim spectacle unfolding on the scaffold. They would be exploiting the time by sneaking among the packed crowds and, using their past experience and long fingers, would have a profitable day picking pockets and going home with their newly gained money and watches. Ironically, if the lawmakers had hoped that hanging criminals in public would show that crime did not pay, then here was proof that this old adage simply was not true.

But why had the man who was to be hanged, the 4th Earl Ferrers, killed his faithful servant in the first place? What had the poor old man done to be forced to leave this life earlier than he had thought? Here is his story: the story of why it was not always good to be loyal and to dedicate yourself to your rich master as devotedly as you can.

*

"Sir," the servant bowed. "Your uncle has asked me to tell you he wishes to speak with you in his study."

The young man looked up from where he had been concentrating at the card table. "When, dammit?"

"He said now, sir. He says there is something important he wishes to discuss with you. Shall I tell him you're coming?"

"Yes, yes, I suppose so. Tell him I'll just finish this round and I'll be on my way."

"Yes, sir," the servant bowed and left his lordship to finish yet another game of cards. How many times can he play the same game of Faro? the servant wondered as he made his way to his master's study.

Ten minutes later, the heir to Earl Ferrers found himself standing in front of his uncle.

"Yes, sir, what do you want?" asked the twenty-two-year-old Laurence Shirley, as he turned back to close the huge double doors. "Is this conversation so important that you had to interrupt my game?"

"Yes, Laurence, it is. I think the time has come," the Earl began, "for us to talk about your future."

"Why? What about it? You are the third Earl Ferrers and one day I will be the fourth. What is there to talk about?"

"Plenty. For example, how do you occupy yourself these days apart from playing endless games of cards or practising your target shooting with those pistols of yours?"

"I practise my French and…"

"Yes, yes, the French you learned when you spent your time in debauchery in Paris and bringing shame on the family name."

The heir to the Ferrers estates ignored this. "Uncle, you forget, I was also a student at Oxford and…"

"I know, and you left in the middle. You never completed your studies. All you learned there was how to use a sword and a pistol and how to deflower young maidens. And that's to say nothing about how you now carry on with anything you see wearing a skirt."

"Uncle, I protest," the young man replied, holding his head up defiantly. "I learned something about the Classics."

"Such as?"

"Well, you cannot expect me to remember everything I learned there, can you? It was some time ago, after all."

"No, I don't suppose I can, especially when you spend much of your time now with that Margaret Clifford wench instead of with Mary, your truly wedded wife. No, I can't expect much of you, can I?" The old man paused and looked up at his nephew. "But tell me, my boy, have you given any thought of how you're going to run your estates once I've gone?"

The young man hung his head. "Well, not really, uncle. All I know is that…"

"Yes, that's what I thought," the Earl said and with a deep sigh, and with a dismissive wave of his hand indicated that this conversation was over. "Go away and start thinking, boy. I'm not going to be here forever and then what will you do?"

The uncle was right. He died soon afterwards, and Laurence Shirley stepped into his aristocratic shoes to become the 4th Earl Ferrers. Now he was responsible for the family estates in Leicestershire, Northamptonshire and Derbyshire. He lived with his wife, Mary Meredith, in the family home, Staunton Harold Hall, in northwest Leicestershire. The marriage was not a happy one. He terrified her with his outbursts of violent behaviour and more than once, she, as well as their servants, were the victims of his fists or the flat of his sword. Apart from this, she could not stand his drinking, gambling and womanising. And if this weren't enough, she hated having his four illegitimate daughters, the offspring of his union with his beloved Margaret Clifford, wandering around their estates.

One day, after six years of marital hell with her hot-tempered and drunken husband, Mary told him that she could no longer stand being with him. She was going to request an official separation.

"You can't," he retorted, throwing a wine glass at her. "The law says you have to live with me. Don't you remember, for better or for worse, for richer, for poorer, in sickness and in health? You can't get rid of me," he gloated, "but *I* can get rid of *you*."

He was wrong. In 1758, Mary managed to obtain a separation from him by an Act of Parliament. And not only that. Parliament decreed that Mary Shirley, née Meredith, was entitled to receive an income from the rents from some of the Earl's estates. This greatly annoyed him, however he had no choice but to comply. As a result, old Mr John Johnson, the family retainer, against his will was made a trustee - a receiver of these rents. The old man was forced into becoming the buffer between the explosive Earl and the ex-wife he so despised.

One day things came to a head between the Earl and the trustee.

"Ah, Johnson," Ferrers said to the old man whom he had ordered to come to his study. "No, don't sit down. You won't be here long."

"But sir, my old legs are killing me. It's the arthritis, you know."

"No, I don't know, so just answer me this. Who gave you permission to pass on fifty pounds (ten thousand pounds today) to that old hag I was once married to, eh?"

"Well, sir, it was like this," Johnson began, not daring to look at the Earl in the eye. "She told me that she couldn't afford to have any new clothes made and as the winter was coming on, I thought that you surely wouldn't begrudge her a few pounds to have a new coat and some dresses, sir."

"A few pounds! Do you call fifty pounds a few pounds? Go on and get out of here! I don't want to see your miserable face again. And don't, I repeat, *don't* you dare do anything like that again. Any money that wretch will be given, will be given through me. Is that understood?"

Johnson bowed. "Yes, sir," he muttered and left the study as quickly as his aching legs would allow.

"And Johnson," the Earl called to his retreating back. "If the rumours that I hear about you carrying on with that miserable bitch are true, then woe betide you."

The rumours were not founded on the truth. Sometime later, Mary married Lord Frederick Campbell, a Scottish nobleman and politician.

On Sunday 13 January 1760, the Earl went over to Mr Johnson's house, The Lount, and told the trustee that he was to come and see him at Staunton Harold Hall on the following Friday. Ferrers had a few business matters to sort out and the sooner they were done, the better. Johnson duly turned up a few days later on the 18th. at the appointed time, three o'clock in the afternoon. However, before the meeting began, the Earl made sure to send Margaret Clifford and her daughters out of the study and told them to go for a long walk around the estate.

"Margaret, I don't want the sounds of the children to disturb me," he told her. "Go and pay your father a visit and then come back in two or three hours' time. And yes, before I forget, tell the rest of the servants that they can have this afternoon off. I'll just have Elizabeth…"

"Elizabeth Burgeland? The maidservant?"

"Yes, her and two others here in case I need anybody."

As soon as the old retainer entered, the Earl attacked him verbally. "You're a liar and a cheat, old man! Everybody thinks you're honest, but I know differently."

"But, sir, I don't know what you're talking about. I have truthfully recorded…"

"*Truthfully recorded nothing!* Now get down on your knees!" he shouted. "No, man. Not on one knee. Both of them! Now!"

Outside, the three servants heard the shouting and felt pity for Mr Johnson, but there was nothing that they could do to help him. They knew their master well enough and feared his fiery temper.

The shouting continued. "Now declare that you have acted against me," the Earl continued. "Your time has come! *You must die!*"

And saying that, the 4th Earl Ferrers drew a pistol out of his pocket and shot the kneeling servant. Fortunately, he did not kill him. The wounded man managed to stand up, hold onto the back of a chair and began pleading for his life.

"No, no, sir. Please do not…"

But just then, the maidservants gathered up enough courage and burst into the study. As they did so, their furious master marched out leaving them to deal with the dying trustee.

"Quick," Elizabeth ordered one of the others. "Go and fetch Mr Kirkland, the surgeon. He shouldn't be far away. He lives at Ashby. Go! Go now and we'll see what we can do for the old man in the meantime."

They put Mr Johnson in a bed, wiped the blood off him and waited for the surgeon. Just then, the Earl re-entered the room, and pushing the maidservants out of the way, went up to the old man and asked how he felt.

"I'm dying," John replied, as his daughter entered the room. At this, Ferrers applied a pad of soft wet cloth to the wound and tried to staunch the flow of blood. However, impatient that he could not see any immediate improvement in the old man's situation he stood up and left. He then went over to his private quarters and started drinking. It was only when he heard Mr Kirkland arrive that he put his bottle aside and told the surgeon that he had shot the trustee.

"I tell you," he told Kirkland, "it is true that I shot him, but I only wanted to frighten him." Ferrers looked down at his pale victim lying gasping on the bloodstained bed. "I tell you, sir. He's not really hurt. More frightened than anything else. The man is a villain and deserved to die, but I spared his life. Now do what you can for him."

"Well, sir, I don't think I can believe you," the bending Mr Kirkland said, standing up. "See what I have found." And he showed the bullet to the Earl.

"Well, whatever you've found, you're not going to scare me, so just you continue and clean him up. And now," he declared to nobody's surprise, "I'm going out for a drink."

Ferrers stormed out of the room and went to find himself another bottle. When he had drunk most of it, he burst into the room where the surgeon and the maidservants were doing their best to make the old man comfortable. Reeking of alcohol, he marched up to the bedside, pushed the others aside and started shaking the dying servant.

"You're a villain, you old goat!" he shouted. "Do you hear me? I should shoot you through the head and rid myself of you forever!"

Seeing this, Kirkland and the maidservants ran forward and pulled the Earl away. He immediately stormed out of the room again.

That evening, after Margaret Clifford had returned and managed to calm down the fuming aristocrat, she suggested that they should take the wounded man to his own house where his daughter and their friends would look after him.

"That is not going to happen," the 4th Earl stated. "He shall not be removed; I will keep him here, to plague the villain." Then in a surprising move, he turned to Johnson's daughter and told her that if her father died he, Laurence Shirley, 4th Earl Ferrers, would take care of her and her family, "on condition, of course, that you don't prosecute me."

That night, Ferrers went to bed sometime between eleven and twelve o'clock. However, before retiring for the night, he must have realised the seriousness of the situation. He had shot a man in cold blood and there were at least three witnesses. He therefore decided to have a word with Mr Kirkland.

"Sir," he began, "I would be most grateful if you could make sure that news of this unhappy event is not broadcast to the world. And," he added, "I certainly do not wish to be seized for having shot that old man. Besides, I have a fearful headache and I must away to my bed now. Therefore, we will continue this conversation further in the morning. Good night."

Dr Kirkland, however, had no intention of leaving the dying Johnson under the mercurial Earl's roof for any longer than necessary. As soon as Ferrers had gone to bed, the surgeon rounded up a couple of servants and with their help, made a type of sedan chair out of an armchair and two long poles. Then, carefully sitting the old man in it, they carried him over to Johnson's own house. There he died the next morning at about nine o'clock.

By this time, word had got out around the estate and neighbourhood of what Ferrers had done. The local population, armed with sticks and a blunderbuss or two, soon gathered around Staunton Harold Hall aiming to arrest the Earl and hand him over to the authorities. As the crowd of locals approached the Hall, they saw the Earl walk over to the stables.

"Stop there," a man called Springthorpe shouted, his pistol raised.

But Ferrers did not stop. Instead he put his hand into his coat and Springthorpe thought that he, too, was about to produce a pistol. That did not happen. Ferrers simply ran back to the Hall and slammed the door behind him. The crowd of estate workers and their supporters did not follow him. The Earl was trapped inside his house and, for the time being, that was enough.

The crowd remained outside in the grounds wondering what to do. Then after two hours, Ferrers stuck his head out of one of the upper windows and shouted, "How is Johnson?"

"He's dead and it was you who killed him," came the reply from below.

"That's a lie," shot back the enraged Earl. "Now be off with you and get back to your work! No, no, come into the Hall and I'll get my servants to furnish you with food and drink."

Suspecting this was a trap, no-one moved. They remained there waiting patiently. Two hours passed and suddenly a collier called Curtis ran up to where the crowd was wondering what to do next.

"I've seen him," he said. "He's on the bowling green and he's armed."

"With his pistol?"

"No, with more than that. He's carrying a blunderbuss and a brace of pistols and I saw a dagger in his belt."

There was a quick discussion what to do and, in the end, Curtis ran off and approached the Earl. Ferrers was surprised to see him standing there, suddenly planted in front of him, not moving. "Give up your arms," Curtis shouted and to his astonishment, the Earl meekly handed his guns over to the collier. By now several others had arrived and seeing that he had no alternative, Ferrers allowed himself to be led away to a public house in Ashby-de-la-Zouche where he was retained in custody until he could be held in a more secure jail.

Two weeks later, Laurence Shirley, 4th Earl Ferrers, was removed from Leicester gaol to London where he was ordered to be held in the Round Tower of the Tower of London. There he was well-guarded and, because he was an aristocrat and had the wherewithal to pay for an easier stay, he wined and dined well. His confinement was also made easier as one of the prison guards had told him that Margaret Clifford, his mistress (or common-law wife), had also come to London with her daughters to visit him. However, the authorities would not allow her to do so and therefore she had to content herself with writing letters to him instead.

Two months later, on 16 April 1760, Ferrers was escorted out of the Tower under heavy guard to Westminster Hall where he was to stand trial. Although there was no question that the hot-blooded Earl had shot his servant, Ferrers' defence was that of insanity. To everyone's surprise, he conducted himself well and supported his claim by quoting his and his family's medical past. None of this helped. His peers found him legally sane and therefore he was guilty of murder. Sir Charles Pratt, the Attorney-General, then declared that the 4th Earl Ferrers would be hanged by the neck until he was dead and that this, as was the custom, would be followed up with the dissection of his body. This grim sentence was to be carried out on Monday 21 April 1760.

Then this was changed. Due to the condemned man's status, and in order to allow him to have suitable arrangements made for his family and property, the sentence was to be postponed until the following month on Monday 5 May.

All of this came as a shock to the forty-year-old Earl. To be hanged by the neck in public. And at the hanging Tree at Tyburn! This was the death sentence performed on common criminals, not earls. He applied to King George II to be beheaded instead. He received a negative reply. Beheading was for aristocrats who had committed treason, not murder.

Ferrers made his will and left four thousand pounds (eight hundred thousand pounds today) to each of his four illegitimate daughters, and two hundred pounds to Sarah Johnson.

The day of the execution arrived and Ferrers, dressed in his light beige-coloured wedding suit was, under a heavy guard, escorted in his own carriage from the Tower of London right across London to the 'Fatal Tree' at Tyburn. This journey through the packed streets of the capital's centre took nearly three hours. Everyone was there. Who did not want to see the villainous Earl pay for his sins? When Ferrers arrived at the special scaffold, he saw that it was covered in black baize. In addition, the authorities had supplied two black cushions for the condemned man and his chaplain to kneel on before he was hanged. There was not an empty place anywhere surrounding the scaffold, and the

King's Guard were there in full to maintain public order among the huge and potentially riotous crowds.

The 4th Earl Ferrers mounted the scaffold and his chaplain, Mr Humphries, told him that he should offer up a prayer before meeting his Maker. Before reciting the Lord's Prayer, Ferrers commented that he thought "so large a mob had collected because the people had never seen a lord hanged before." He then mounted the drop and Turlis, the hangman, tied his arms behind his back with a black silk sash. Saying his last words, "Am I right?" Ferrers' white nightcap was pulled down over his head and, following a given signal, the drop opened and Laurence Shirley, 4th Earl Ferrers, was no more.

After being left to hang for the allowed time, the body was cut down, placed in a coffin and transported to Surgeon's Hall for dissection. Later his remains were taken back to Staunton Harold Hall, Leicestershire, the site where this cold-blooded murder had taken place.

Following the 4th Earl's hanging, Staunton Harold Hall was taken over by his brother who demolished most of it in the 1780s. This is the building that one can see today. From the mid-19th century, the fortunes of the family declined and most of the estate was sold to pay off debts. One hundred years later in 1954, this stately but somewhat rundown hall was converted into a Leonard Cheshire home for disabled ex-servicemen. In 1980, it was converted into a hospice which closed twenty years later. The family reclaimed it in 2003. Today Staunton Harold Hall is run as a stately home and is open to the public – Laurence Shirley, 4th Earl Ferrers being known as its most well-known past resident.

Chapter 11

William 'Deacon' Brodie (1741-1788)

One aspect of the human psyche that has fascinated people for many years is how people behave in a completely unexpected fashion. How is it that the polite, mild mannered next-door neighbour who 'wouldn't say boo to a goose' can act in an extremely violent way, even killing his wife and children? Is this a classic case of 'Nature versus Nurture'?

If you study this topic, you will see that many people who use their brains a great deal, such as John Nash, the 1994 Nobel Prize winner for mathematics, may have a tendency to suffer more from mental troubles than others. Other famous people who are said to have suffered from severe mental problems include Van Gogh (artist), Beethoven (composer), Zelda Fitzgerald (novelist and painter), Abraham Lincoln and Charles Dickens. Perhaps the most famous example in literature is the protagonist of the story The Strange Case of Dr Jekyll and Mr Hyde *by the Scottish writer, Robert Louis Stevenson. This book however will receive more attention later.*

In the meanwhile, another Scot, William Deacon Brodie (1741-1778) preceded the famed fictional split personality by one hundred years. This man was both a respectable pillar of the Edinburgh community and a celebrated housebreaker and gambler.

*

"Dad," the small boy asked, as he walked along the Lawnmarket section of Edinburgh's Royal Mile, "why does that pub sign up there have a different picture on each side?"

"Ah! That one with the picture of Deacon Brodie on it," the father smiled. "Yes, Robbie, that *is* unusual since most pub-signs have the same picture on both sides. But here, the man in that picture, Deacon Brodie, was a most unusual man. In fact, my son, he was more like two men. One man during the day, but a completely different sort of man during the night. So that may be why the sign has a different picture on each side."

The small boy scratched his head. "But Dad, that doesn't make sense. The same man being two different men. How can that be?"

"I'll tell you what, son. We'll go into that café over there and I'll tell you all about this unusual man."

And this is the story the father told.

William Brodie was born in Edinburgh in 1741 into a family of professional respectability. His two grandfathers were well-known lawyers, and his father, Francis, was a famous carpenter and cabinetmaker. His professional reputation was so high that he became the leader or 'deacon' of a guild of skilled tradesmen which catered to the whims of the city's upper crust. In addition, Francis Brodie also had a seat on the city council. All in all, young William Brodie had everything to look forward to – a future living and working among Scotland's high society.

When Francis Brodie died in 1780, William inherited a flourishing cabinet-making business as well as ten thousand pounds, a workshop and house on Edinburgh's prestigious Royal Mile. In addition, he was a member of the Edinburgh Cape Club, a former tavern-based club, which was now more like a posh social club. There he would rub shoulders with the leading artists of the day, and it is thought that he also met the poet,

Robbie Burns, there. Like his father, by 1786 William Brodie had become the Deacon of the Incorporation of Wrights – that is, the head of Edinburgh's guild, a professional association which protected the rights of its members.

William Deacon Brodie had reached the peak of his career; professional, honoured and respected by all. But this is only half of the story. Like many of the cream of Georgian society, he also had another, less respectable side. He was a gambler, he loved a 'drop of the hard stuff' and he kept two mistresses who bore him five illegitimate children. In many ways these last deviations from the norm were not too seriously frowned upon, and in the end, it was his love of gambling that brought him down, causing his name to be forever associated with crime and the leading of a double life.

It all began in 1768 when he was twenty-seven years old. The scene: a seedy tavern in Fleshmarket Close, a back alley in Edinburgh. The air is thick with tobacco smoke and the grubby place stinks of unwashed bodies and alcohol. Brodie is sitting at a table with three or four others, dice in his hands and stacks of coins on the table between himself and his fellow gamblers.

"Well, Brodie, you mean bastard, are you going to pay me the twenty pounds you owe me, or not?" the unshaven man asked, as he reached for his tankard.

"John, it's like this," Brodie replied, pushing a small stack of coins over to the man, hoping that he would accept them, "I don't have even two pounds right now, and I have to give something to, er, two ladies that I know. Listen, I'll give you an I.O.U. now and pay you next week."

"Aye, that's what you said last week when it was only ten pounds. Now it's twenty, so forget your I.O.Us. I want my money and I want it now!" This was followed by the sound of a heavy fist crashing down on the table.

Brodie looked at the other three men. "Can any of you help me out here? Just for a week or so?"

His question was answered with cynical grins. One of the men spat on the floor. "It's your problem, man, and it's up to you to solve it."

"How?"

"How? You're a cabinetmaker, aren't you?" said a thin man with a scar running down the right side of his face. "Why not get some of your customers to help? You know," he winked, "paying you more than you ask for."

And that is what happened, although perhaps not in the way the criminal-minded scar-face had thought.

The first time was when he was still working with his father. They were busy installing some cabinets and tables in a government office when William Brodie noticed that the clerk, who had gone out to see his superior, had left the keys to the safe on the table. Brodie slid over to the table and, without his father noticing him, slipped the keys into his pocket.

Saying that he wanted to go outside for a moment, he took out the key for the safe and the front door to the office and pressed them into a wad of putty that he had brought in a tin box for this purpose. Now he had an impression of the necessary keys. Later he would make a duplicate copy of them for himself. He quickly returned the keys to their original place and continued helping his father.

Brodie was somewhat smarter or perhaps less impetuous than most burglars. He bided his time. He did not want anyone to think that the men who had been working in the office had anything to do with the forthcoming robbery. A few weeks later Brodie returned to the office, unlocked the safe and helped himself to the eight hundred pounds that was waiting there for him. This went a long way in paying off his debts, but it wasn't enough – Brodie had been well and truly bitten by the gambling bug. From now on, other than paying for his mistresses and his illegitimate offspring, all of the money that Brodie would steal over the next twenty years would go either to pay off his gambling debts or to act as a stake for future bets.

For year after year, Brodie's incredible luck stayed with him, at least as a burglar, if not as a gambler. On one occasion he was recognised by a friend while he was 'on the job'. However, the friend knew that if he informed the authorities about what he had seen, he knew that William Deacon would never reach his full three score years and ten. The hangman's rope would make sure of that. The friend did not want another man's death on his conscience.

On another occasion he was seen by the old lady whose house he was robbing. Brodie had assumed that she would be in church at the time, but she was lying sick in bed. When questioned later about the robbery, she denied that she had seen him.

"Are you sure, madam, that the thief wasn't Master William Brodie?"

"Oh, no Your Honour. That couldn't be. How could such a respectable man bring himself so low as to rob my humble home?"

But if Brodie had a weakness for gambling, he had another weakness too. This was to rob more and more, and to try to make ever larger yields each time. But he could not do this on his own. He had to have some help. He therefore teamed up with three accomplices: Andrew Ainslie, a shoemaker and a similar minded compulsive gambler, John Brown, a convicted trickster who was trying to keep one step ahead of the law to avoid being transported, and a George Smith. This last-mentioned criminal was also a grocer, travelling salesman and a part-time locksmith. He was able to make good copies of the keys from the putty impressions that Brodie made.

They pulled their first job in October 1786.

"Listen up, you fellows," Brodie said one night as he sat in a dark and grimy tavern not too far away from Edinburgh's Royal Mile. "There is a goldsmith's shop in town, about half a mile from here, and I've heard it said that the owner is not too careful where he leaves his keys during the day. I suggest that I pay him a visit to see if this rumour is true."

The rumour was well-founded, and soon Brodie was handing two putty impressions to George Smith, one for the goldsmith's shop's front door and the other for his safe. Shortly afterwards one of Edinburgh's goldsmiths found that his precious stock had disappeared into the murky night.

Brodie and his gang gathered together to divide the spoils. "Are we going to do this only once?" Andrew Ainslie asked. "I need some more money to pay off some of my gambling debts. There's this Macpherson character who'll beat me up if I don't pay him the fifty pounds I owe him by the end of the month."

"Fear not, laddie," Brodie replied. "I have made a list of our future jobs. It includes some jewellery shops, silk merchants and tobacconists."

"And what about grocers?" George Smith asked. "They often keep a lot of money, and I mean, who would think of robbing a grocer's shop?"

Brodie continued living as a respectable businessman during the day while robbing all sorts of places by night. Brodie and Co. broke into many shops and businesses in Edinburgh, stealing both money and the sort of goods that were easy to sell off to disreputable buyers. Items such as gold rings, necklaces and costly teas soon passed along the chain from the unfortunate shopkeepers to Brodie and then onto his dubious contacts in the underworld. In October 1787, as a way of celebrating their first year working together without being caught, they broke into the University of Edinburgh's prestigious library and stole the institution's ceremonial silver mace.

But still it was not enough. Brodie and the others wanted more.

"Drink up, lads," Brodie said a month later to his three accomplices. "I've worked out a brilliant idea which will make us *really* rich. None of this cheap shillings and pennies stuff we've been doing so far." They were sitting in one of their favourite taverns, a place known for its cheap ale, buxom lasses and no-questions-asked atmosphere. On hearing their leader talk like this they sat up, and John Brown even stopped caressing the barmaid's well-rounded rump to ask, "How?"

"Well, it's like this," Brodie began. "Which government office in town has a safe or two, maybe even three or four, bursting with money?"

This question was followed by silence as the three robbers tried to find an answer in their alcohol befuddled brains.

"The Excise office, of course," an impatient Brodie said, answering his own question.

"But how do you know the safes there are full of money?" George Smith asked.

"Because I've been there, my friend," Brodie smiled. "I had to take some furniture there a few months ago and I saw the safes in the office. One of them was open and I saw how full it was with all the tax money the citizens of this town pay the government. Well, while I was repairing one of the cabinets, I made sure to remember the plan of the rooms – where the doors, windows and safes were. In fact," and here he pulled a much-folded piece of paper out of his pocket, "this is the plan of the rooms I made as soon as I returned home that evening. I didn't want to forget it."

Now, the four men were leaning over the candle-lit table studying the plan. You could almost hear the wheels spinning in their heads as they worked out how to enter the room with the safes, grab the money and escape.

"How much do you think is kept in those safes?" Ainslie asked, his eyes glinting in the candlelight.

Brodie shrugged. "I don't know, but it must be hundreds of pounds. Think of all of the taxes, customs duties people have to pay."

"You are right, man," Brown said. "It could be thousands, and all of it just sitting there waiting for us." And saying that, he rubbed his hands together and ordered another round of ale.

That night they decided that Messrs. William Brodie and George Smith would pay a visit to the Excise Office. They would ask some routine questions about taxation – questions that any solid citizen might need to ask regarding their business interests. While there, Brodie would distract the official by asking a few more detailed questions about some obscure points of taxation law. Meanwhile, Smith would quietly take the front door and safe keys off the nail by the door where Brodie had discovered they were kept. He would immediately make putty impressions of them and then quietly replace them within a minute or two.

"Sounds too easy," Ainslie scoffed when he heard the plan. "It's not going to work."

But he was wrong. It did work. At least in part.

On the evening of 30 November 1787, using their newly forged keys to open up the cashier's office, they set to work. However, this time the keys did not work on the safes and they had to leave quickly before the night watchman made his rounds. They were forced to leave the door open as their keys could not close it. This meant that the guard and the tax men were now expecting a robbery of some sort.

But Brodie was a patient man. For four months he continued acting as a worthy tradesman before putting his plan into action again. On 5 March 1788 they returned to the office, but this time they were armed. In addition, remembering the problems they had earlier in forcing open the door, they brought a coulter – a small blade from a plough – with them. Imagine their disappointment when they saw that their loot amounted to only sixteen pounds.

"*Sixteen quid*! Is that all?" Brown exclaimed. "You told us we'd find a King's ransom in here! Not just sixteen bluidy quid!" (two-and-a-half thousand pounds today). Perhaps fortunately for them, as it would have rubbed salt into their wounds, they did not know that within a few feet from their greedy hands, six hundred pounds was stashed away hidden under the cashier's desk.

"Hush, man! Someone might hear you!" Smith hissed. And someone did. A deputy solicitor who had forgotten some papers returned to the office. Brown and Smith were about to shoot him, but at the last moment they decided to let him flee the scene unharmed. It was time for them to flee, and the high hopes and dreams of the four men crashed to the ground. Sixteen pounds to be divided up between the four of them!

John Brown wanted more than four measly pounds, and soon after he learned that there was a two-hundred-and-fifty pound (forty thousand pounds today) reward for anyone who could identify the robbers; an identification that would lead to their capture. He knew the money would be his if he 'squealed' to the authorities, so wearing a large cap to hide the top of his face and pulling up his collar to hide much of the rest, John Brown paid a visit to the office of the sheriff of Edinburgh.

Looking around warily, he began. "I hear that there's a reward of two hundred and fifty pounds for anyone who can identify the men who robbed the Excise Office last week."

"Aye, that is correct," the sheriff replied. "Why, do you know anything about this?"

Brown nodded. "And, sir. If I tell you, will my other minor crimes be taken into account?"

"What d'you mean?" the wary official asked.

"I mean, if I'm found guilty of some other small crimes, will they be taken into account? I mean, can I claim the 'King's evidence' and be let off for them?"

The sheriff told Brown he would look into this matter and that Brown should return to the office the following morning.

The next day, after Brown had been informed that all of his past crimes would be wiped off the slate, relieving him of the possibility of being transported to Australia, he was informed that he would receive the two hundred and fifty pounds if he betrayed his accomplices. He spilled the beans and Ainslie and Smith were arrested, but for the moment, Brodie's luck still held.

He fled the city and took a ship from Leith to London. On board, calling himself Mr Dixon, Brodie gave some letters for Ainslie and Brown to Thomas Geddes, another Edinburgh man and fellow passenger. However, by the time Geddes returned to Edinburgh, Brodie's two accomplices were well and truly 'inside'.

Geddes handed the letters over to the authorities, who then raided Brodie's house. There they found a cache of burglar's tools together with the silver mace he had stolen from the University of Edinburgh's library. Not knowing that he had given the sheriff proof of his involvement in his past crimes, Brodie continued with his escape plan.

From London he sailed to Holland, from where he intended to escape to America. But here his luck ran out. A few days after landing in Amsterdam he was tracked down, arrested and brought back to Edinburgh.

"I'm innocent," he protested all the way back as the ship sailed north over the choppy North Sea. "I've been in Holland all this while and besides, why would I, as a successful cabinet maker and tradesman, have anything to do with robbing the Excise Office?"

"That we'll find out when we return," was the curt reply. "If you are as innocent as you say, then we'll let you go. If not…" and the official drew his long finger across his bony throat.

Brodie now realised that he was in it up to *his* neck – the neck that would feel the hangman's noose unless he could do something about it. Still protesting his innocence, he reminded the authorities that he was an upright citizen and tradesman and that he had helped the sheriff by acting as a past juror. He had even served as a town councillor, but none of this helped. Ainslie, like Brown, in the hope of saving his own neck, also gave 'King's evidence,' and similarly betrayed Brodie and Smith.

William Deacon Brodie's trial was a sensational event. No-one could believe that this supposedly honourable citizen, this pillar of the community, was truly responsible for all the crimes of which he was now being accused. In fact, the Edinburgh authorities were so sure that public pandemonium would break out, they called out the army to prevent any possible rioting and to preserve public order.

On 27 August 1788, William 'Deacon' and George Smith, with chains around their ankles, were escorted into the High Court of Justiciary in Parliament Square from their cell in Edinburgh Castle. Although their trial took twenty-one hours, the verdict was a foregone conclusion. Apart from the prosecution's use of Brown and Ainslie's testimony against them, the housebreaking tools and the stolen university mace were silent proof of their criminal lives.

Brodie tried to prove his innocence by writing to several influential past friends to support him, but none of them replied. He tried to earn the court's sympathy by complaining about his treatment in prison; how he was not allowed to shave or be given any sharp cutlery, but none of this helped. In order to distance himself from his miserable and blubbering partner, George Smith, Brodie appeared in court confidently dressed in a new coat and silk breeches as he acted respectfully towards the judge throughout the proceedings. It was all a waste of time.

However, before he was finally sentenced, his defence lawyer raised an interesting point of law.

"Your Honour, so far the prosecution has based much of its case on testimony submitted by two criminals: John Brown and Anthony Ainslie. I submit that this testimony is inadmissible because the former, if not the latter, is a convicted felon."

Unfortunately for Brodie and Smith, this line of defence did not work. The prosecution was so determined to find the two men guilty that they arranged for Brown and Ainslie to be pardoned under English, not Scottish, law and so the trial continued on its inexorable way, leading to its grim verdict and sentence. Brodie's trial was therefore not only about crime and punishment, but it also involved the question of who was in charge of Scotland's judicial processes.

Inevitably, the two men were found guilty. Their punishment was to be the hangman's noose. One month later, on 1 October 1788 at half-past two, they were hanged at the Edinburgh Tolbooth in front of a record crowd of forty thousand spectators. But this was not the end of the story. Rumours immediately circled that Brodie had not really died. It was claimed that he himself, using his carpentry skills, had designed the gallows in such a way that they would not kill him.

Other rumours flew saying he had treated the trapdoor mechanism for the same purpose. If these stories were not enough, others claimed that he had swallowed a metal pipe so that he would not be strangled, or that he had made a deal with the hangman and the doctor on duty to have him pronounced dead almost immediately, after which his friends had spirited him away, allowing him to escape to France. However, the truth is that he was hanged, and then buried in an unmarked grave.

But the story of William 'Deacon' Brodie lives on. In addition to the café, street and pubs in Edinburgh, New York and Ottawa, Brodie's name came to be linked to a best-selling novel. Thomas Stevenson, a well-known engineer and lighthouse designer had bought some furniture from William Brodie. His son, Robert, was brought up on the stories of this infamous fellow Edinburg resident, and he together with W.E. Henley, wrote a play called, *Deacon Brodie or The Double Life.* Despite the play's fascinating material, it failed. Almost one hundred years after Brodie's criminal demise, Robert Louis Stevenson, still fascinated by Brodie's double-life, turned his earlier play into a novel – *The Strange Case of Dr Jekyll and Mr Hyde.* In addition, the heroine of the novel, *The Prime of Miss Jean Brodie,* claims to have been one of Brodie's descendants. In this way, William Deacon joins Robin Hood, Dick Turpin and Moll Cutpurse as a villain who unwittingly made a major contribution to English literature.

Chapter 12

Isaac 'Ikey' Solomon (1787-1850)

Few 'fences' – dealers in stolen goods – during the first half of the nineteenth century achieved the fame or dubious glory that Isaac 'Ikey' Solomon did. For not only was he a successful fence running a lucrative business, but he was also a renowned thief. Half-way through his criminal career he enhanced his already

celebrated reputation by making an amazing escape from the forces of law and order in the centre of London.

This may have been enough for him at the time, and perhaps his name would have died with him, but later it was to be immortalised, as it is widely thought that Ikey Solomon, the highly successful trader in stolen property, was the model for Fagin, the loathsome underworld character in Charles Dickens' novel, Oliver Twist.

Unlike most of the villains mentioned in this book, Isaac Ikey Solomon had 'itchy feet', in that he was a truly international criminal. His career took him from London to Denmark, New York and Hobart, Tasmania. Several of these journeys he paid for himself, others were financed by the British government, though not out of a desire to pander to his wishes.

*

"Dad, watcher goin' to do with all those lovely stones you've got on the table?"

"Ikey, keep your thievin' 'ands off 'em! They're for the business they are."

The ten-year-old boy took his hands off the table where he'd been playing with some of the sparkling jewels. "But what are you goin' to do with them?" he asked. "I only want to know. Are you goin' to give them to Mummy so she'll look all pretty?"

"No, I'm not going to give 'em to your mother. I'm going to flog 'em and make some money out of 'em."

"Like in a shop?"

"Yes, son. Somethink like that." And Henry Solomon swept up the jewels, rings and bracelets into a soft velvet bag and stuffed it into the deep pocket of his somewhat grubby coat.

"Can I come with you when you flog 'em, dad? I'm sure it'll be more exciting than sitting at home and playing with the cat."

Henry Solomon hesitated for a minute, then grudgingly said, "All right, son. But don't forget to keep your mouth shut when I'm talking to people in the market. D'you understand?"

Ikey nodded, grabbed his cap and hurried out along Houndsditch after his father in the direction of Whitechapel High Street. He could not know that this was to be his first lesson in 'fencing' – dealing in stolen goods.

He watched carefully as he saw his father stop and talk to other disreputable characters on corners or in dark alleys. He noted how his thin, pock-faced father would always look around cautiously before taking the velvet bag out of his pocket when he was 'trading', as he described his business activities to his son.

"Dad, why are you always lookin' around so much, especially when you stop to talk to one of your friends?" the sharp-eyed boy asked.

"'Cos I'm looking out for the Watch and the constables. Now keep yer own eyes peeled an' tell me if you see any around. Understand?"

"Yes, Dad."

It did not take long for Henry Solomon to notice that along with his son being smart, he was quick. When Henry was selling jewels, rings, bracelets and necklaces from his shop in Bell Lane, it was often young Ikey who was the first to spot a constable lurking about between the other run-down shops. It was also the young lad who was quick to spot any 'mistake' that a customer made when trying to cheat his father.

"Yes, young Isaac," his father said kindly to him one day after his son had caught a sailor trying to cheat him out of five shillings. "You're catchin' on fast. One day you'll be able to run your own business like mine. You're certainly faster than your brothers. *That* I can tell you."

And Henry Solomon was right. As Ikey grew up, he learned how to buy, sell and fence stolen goods just as well as his father. If not better. He was quick, both of hand in picking the odd pocket or two, and also in working out the profits and losses of his father's shady exchanges. In fact, he was doing so well, that in 1807 when he was twenty years old, he married Anne ('call me Hannah') Julian and began his own family. When his father-in-law, Moses Julian, asked Ikey if he would like to come into the coach business with him as a coachmaster, Ikey turned him down, saying that he was doing quite well, thank you.

And it was true. For the next three years, Ikey's quick fingers and sharp brain were easily able to provide for his wife and children. They lived near his father's shop, a business which his father called a pawnshop, and it was here that the young man made many profitable deals.

Then disaster struck.

On 17 April 1810 Ikey, together with his business associate, Joel Joseph, were caught red-handed. They were mingling with a large crowd at a public meeting outside Westminster Hall when someone spotted the pair of them stealing forty pounds in banknotes and a 'dumby' – a pocketbook – from a Mr Thomas Dodd. Ikey and Joel immediately took to their heels, but the police caught them inside the Hall, from which there was no escape. Joel tried to swallow the banknotes as Ikey tried to get rid of the pocketbook. None of this helped and the two men were promptly arrested. Soon after they found themselves up in front of the 'beak' at the Old Bailey.

Whereas Joel Joseph said in his defence:

> *'I was coming along the bridge to Westminster and I picked this* [pocket]*book up, and looking at it I put the notes in my neck* [of my jacket] *for safety, and the next*

> *morning I intended to look in the newspapers to see if they were advertised, I meaned to restore them to the owner if they were advertised.'*

Ikey denied his having anything to do with the theft:

> *'Curiosity led me to go to the Westminster Meeting. I had not been in the crowd two minutes, the crowd was so great I ran out for fear of being hurt. I proceeded to Westminster Hall, and I had not been there one minute before somebody catched hold of me. Vickrey [constable] searched me and found five pound notes which was my own property, seven dollars and half-a-crown and a corkscrew and papers that I took along. I had no intention of committing a felony whatsoever. I am quite innocent of this business. I never had the pocketbook in my possession.'*

The judge, who had probably heard hundreds of cases like this before was not impressed. He saw his job as to clear the likes of Joel Joseph and Isaac Solomon off the streets of London, either to the hangman's noose or to distant Australia.

"For this detestable crime," he told the two criminals, "you are ordered to be transported to Australia, where, it is hoped, you will spend the rest of your miserable lives. However, before you are sent there, you will spend the interim in one of the hulks anchored off the coast at Chatham."

Joseph and Solomon were bound and taken to Chatham. Here, they were marched up the gangplank and taken aboard the *Zetland*. This vessel had been one of His Majesty's proud fighting ships-of-the-line. Now it was a miserable rotting hulk refurbished to incarcerate six hundred equally miserable convicts.

Our heroes soon discovered that the conditions on board were appalling. They were even worse than those of Newgate Prison where they had spent some time before their trial. Men were shackled together hand and foot, disease was rife, and the food was often rotten and inedible. Any infraction of discipline meant being severely flogged with a 'cat-o-nine-tails' or spending time in solitary confinement in a tiny dark and damp cell. Despite these inhumane conditions, the prisoners were expected to work. This meant at least, that even if the work was tough and backbreaking, they were able to breathe fresh air after having been taken off the hulk and rowed ashore always under the eyes of armed and brutal guards.

At some point after boarding the *Zetland*, Joel Joseph and Ikey Solomon became separated. Joseph was transported to Tasmania on the *Lady Nelson*, but the younger Ikey was kept on board the stinking hulk. He was to remain there for four years, and no reason for this has yet been found. At the end of this period, he was released and returned to the East End where he went back to the only life he knew – pawn-broking and dealing in stolen goods.

Perhaps it was good luck that despite his dubious lifestyle he managed to stay out of prison and, in general, keep away from the long arm of the law. According to the *Newgate Calendar*, Solomon was extremely successful in 'trading' during the thirteen-year period between his confinement on the *Zetland* and his next major brush with the law:

> *'His house was looked upon as the universal resort of almost all of the thieves in the metropolis; but so cautiously and so cunningly did he manage his transactions, as to render every effort of the police to procure evidence of his guilt unavailing. His purchases were, for the most part, confined to small articles, such as jewellery, plate etc. and in his house, under his bed he had a receptacle for them, closed by*

> *a trap-door, so nicely fitted that it escaped every examination that was made.'*

But then his success brought him other problems. He found that his house was not big enough to store all of his stolen goods. Also, in addition to sharing his affection with his wife, he had acquired a mistress, who of course he wanted to keep hidden from his wife. In order to solve both these problems he bought another house, this one in Lower Queen Street, Islington.

It was during this period that a spate of robberies of watches and jewellery broke out in Cheapside, London. Solomon understood that he would be a prime suspect, and so he left London for Birmingham for a while. However, during his absence his wife found out about his Islington bolthole. This of course did not improve the atmosphere in the Solomon household.

Then, on 25 April 1827, Solomon's problems were compounded when he was arrested for possession of stolen goods, including six watches, three-and-a-half-yards of woollen cloth, twelve pieces of Valentia cloth, several lengths of lace, seventeen shawls, some caps and various other articles. He was taken to Newgate Prison to await trial. By this time Solomon was a well-known figure in the criminal world and highly exaggerated pamphlets soon appeared describing his illegal activities.

While he was in Newgate, Solomon planned to carry out a daring escape. However, for the plan to work he would need the help of some of his underworld friends and his wife.

"So, lads, this is what we're going to do," Solomon began at a meeting in his prison cell. "I will demand a writ of *habeas corpus*..."

"Which means that they'll have to take you out of here to the Old Bailey."

"Right, there or somewhere else, and then on the way, we overcome the guards and I escape to a secret place in the city – a place we will organise in advance."

"Huh," his wife commented. "D'you really think it will really be as easy as that?"

Solomon smiled. "With your cooperation, my dear, and some drugs and strong drink, it should work out. And anyway," he shrugged. "What have I got to lose? It's either my neck or transportation."

And with that grim choice before him, this is what happened. After appealing for a writ of *habeas corpus*, Solomon was taken under guard to the Court of the King's Bench. Here his appeal was denied, but that was expected. In fact, it was part of the plan. The prisoner and his guards then set out for the return journey to Newgate in a hackney cab.

According to the *Newgate Calendar*, Solomon managed to persuade the guards, possibly through bribery, or possibly the promise of free drink, to make a detour to a local public house. There they were met by

Hannah Solomon and a couple of her husband's criminal associates. Then, with the guards being suitably wined, dined and drugged, and Solomon's father-in-law acting as the cab's driver, they made a detour in the direction of Petticoat Lane. Here Solomon jumped out, ran into a friend's house through the front door then disappeared out of the back. From here he went into hiding so successfully in the dark rabbit warren of east London streets that the authorities never found him.

Of course, looking for him in that dank and grimy maze would have been a waste of time anyway. For, after being sheltered by family and underworld friends in the East End and Highgate, Solomon's next stop was Denmark. Somehow, he found a way of dodging the authorities and managed to escape unnoticed on a ship bound for Copenhagen, where he spent three months before taking ship to New York.

There he found out that his money was running out. Seeing this, he felt he had to go back to his old ways, and so he started dealing in forged banknotes. But as this was not profitable enough, he wrote a letter to his wife asking her to send him a quantity of watches. These were to be cheap watches that were 'righteous' – that is, honestly obtained. She should make sure that she did not send him any which he had obtained 'on the cross'.

Unfortunately, the dutiful wife made a mistake and started handling Solomon's stolen watches. The authorities were keeping their eyes on her, and soon after, still on the far side of the Atlantic Ocean, Ikey Solomon had the following conversation with a fellow criminal.

"'Allo, Ikey. How are you? You're lookin' good," the new arrival to New York said, clapping him on the back.

Solomon shrugged. "Can't complain, I suppose, but I'm waiting for Hannah to send me some stuff. You know to…"

"'Annah, 'haven't you heard? They've got 'er."

"Who? What? What are you talking about?"

"The Runners or 'oever. It was in the papers. Didn't you see? They caught 'er dealin' in stolen property, y'know, watches an' stuff 'on the cross'. They arrested 'er and put 'er on trial. She got fourteen years."

"Fourteen years!"

"Aye, and while we're standin' here talkin', she's probably on 'er way to Van Diemen's Land now."

"Van Diemen's Land. To Australia?"

"Aye. I 'eard that she got fourteen years, not the usual seven, because the bigwigs were so angry that *you* 'ad got away, so they took it out on your missus instead."

"But how did they find out?" a shocked Ikey Solomon asked.

"Oh, that was easy. They got 'old of one of 'er relations who as they say is not completely 'onest, and they persuaded 'im to spill the beans."

"And in return for that, they'd reduce or cancel his sentence?"

"Exactly."

The news travelled fast between the English and the American authorities and soon Solomon felt that he too was being watched. There was only one thing to do. He couldn't return to England, so taking whatever money and goods he had, 'righteous' or not, his next stop was Hobart in Van Diemen's Land, (later to be called Tasmania). He travelled under the name of Slowman (it is not known if this was a deliberate misspelling or not) aboard the *Coronet* to Rio de Janeiro. Here the ship took on fresh supplies of food, water and the other essentials for the rest of the long voyage to Australia.

"Tell me, Mr Slowman," one of the crew asked him, "why are you going to Hobart? You're not a criminal, are you?"

Solomon smiled and laughed. "No, no, my good man. I'm going there solely to gain the society of an affectionate wife."

The crewman walked off wondering if this English passenger was telling the truth or not, but he did not pursue the matter any further.

On 6 October 1828, thousands of nautical miles later, Solomon arrived in Hobart. There, apart from his wife, he found many of his criminal friends who had been transported to this far outpost of the British Empire.

"Hello, my love," he said to Hannah when he first met her. "How long have you been here?"

"'Bout four months. I arrived here at the end of June. I came on the *Mermaid*. That was a terrible voyage. The captain was a really cruel bastard. He used to…"

"And what about the kids? Where are they?"

"They're all here. The judge said that, as the four little ones were under ten years old, they could come with me."

"And what about John and Moses?"

"Oh, they came on their own. They bought tickets to Sydney and then they made their way here to Hobart."

"And how's my dad? Did the law come down on him as well?"

"Yes and no," Hannah replied. "They charged him with theft and dealing in stolen goods, but as he was old – I mean he's nearly seventy, isn't he? – they let him off."

Solomon smiled and then asked, "And what are you doing for money, my dear? Anything illegal?"

"No," she smiled back. "In fact, I'm even working for the law. They gave me a job working for a Mister Richard Newman. He's a police officer here. I'm sort of his housekeeper, but I don't like it much."

"Why not?"

"He and his fat wife are watchin' me all the time, y'know, that I'm not thievin' anything like their candlesticks or silver spoons and stuff. There's that, and they also give me all the dirty jobs to do. I mean, I was a respectable housewife in London once, wasn't I? It's not for me to clean out the bedpans and stuff like that, is it?"

Ikey leaned over to his wife. "And are you thieving anything?"

"No, at least not yet, but I don't know how long I'm going to stay there. They're beginning to make me feel very jumpy all the time, the way they look at me."

Hannah was right. Soon after being reunited with her husband she had a blazing row with the police officer and his wife. They accused her of trying to steal from their house. Hannah, who could not restrain herself, shouted back at her accusers and soon found herself in the Female House of Correction.

Meanwhile, Solomon had met up with some of his past associates from London. When they asked him what he planned to do now that he was in Hobart, he replied that he was going to go 'straight'.

"I'm hoping to open a general store or tobacconist's on Elizabeth Street," he would reply. "I've brought some money over from America that should get me started. And some of you fellows are going to help me as well."

And that is what happened. Ikey Solomon, perhaps for the first time in his life, started trading as an honest shopkeeper, and once he had established himself, he petitioned Lieutenant-Governor George Arthur that his wife be assigned to work for him. His petition was successful, especially as several local citizens agreed to pay bonds of one and two hundred pounds on the promise that Hannah would not attempt to run away from Hobart. Apart from which, having her six children with her ensured that she was unlikely to flee.

And so, for a year all went well. Solomon was establishing himself as a solid citizen and his wife and children were living with him. However, unknown to him, the law in England had a long memory.

One year after Solomon's arrival in Hobart, the *Lady of the Lake* sailed into the town's harbour. And with her she brought a warrant for the arrest of Isaac Ikey Solomon. He was immediately taken into custody, but all was not lost. Solomon's lawyer entered a writ of *habeas corpus* and, owing to a technical error in the warrant, he was released immediately on condition he paid two thousand pounds in bail and four sureties of five hundred each. Unfortunately for him, his friends and acquaintances could not raise such huge sums.

Then Lieutenant-Governor Arthur issued a new warrant and Solomon was re-arrested soon after. He was taken on board *The Prince Regent* to begin the long voyage back to London. There, stretching over a period from July 1830 to May 1831, he was tried at the Old Bailey on eight charges of receiving stolen goods. He was found guilty on two charges and sentenced to be transported back to Hobart for fourteen years. He may not have considered this as such a bad deal, especially as his wife, family and friends were already there. It is thought that Charles Dickens, then working as a reporter, was present in the court, and that he used Solomon's trial as material for Chapter 52 in his novel *Oliver Twist*. If so, this was how the criminal, Ikey Solomon, came to be a model for Fagin, his co-religionist and fellow dealer in stolen goods.

Six months later, Solomon returned to Hobart on the *William Glenn Anderson* and was sent to Richmond Gaol. He must have been somewhat better than most of the other convicts there as he was promoted a 'javelin man' – a convict constable. After three years he was sent on to the Port Arthur Convict Settlement and one year later in 1835 was granted a 'ticket-of-leave'. This was a conditional form of freedom under which he was allowed to live freely so long as he did so at least twenty miles away from Hobart.

His new house was at New Norfolk, a small town north-west of Hobart settled mainly by farmers and 'ticket-of-leave' men and their descendants. One of the first things he did there was to try to reunite himself with his family. Unfortunately for him, this did not happen.

"Just look at us," Hannah shouted angrily one evening. "Just look where we are. Stuck out in the middle of nowhere! I miss my friends and the kids don't like it here, either."

"But, Hannah, my dear. I just want to…"

"Ikey, don't you 'Hannah, my dear' me. I keep telling you that I don't want to stay in this godforsaken hole!" Hannah yelled. "I'm used to living in cities like London, or at least Hobart. Not being surrounded by cows and sheep all day. If you want to know, I'm going back to Hobart as soon as I can."

"But you can't. What about the kids?"

"They agree with me. They also want to go back. They hate it here. There's nothing for them to do and they miss all their friends."

Solomon was not impressed. "And who's that Bill or George fellow who keeps hanging around here all day like a bitch on heat? What's he doing here?"

Hannah turned her back on her angry husband. "Oh, you mean the gardener? He's not doing nothing. Just planting some potatoes and stuff like that."

"Aye, I'm sure he's wanting to plant more than potatoes. Him and that other tall one I often see around here. Him in the red waistcoat with the long nose."

Their arguments grew more violent and vociferous and according to which documents you read, either Ikey threw her and the children out, or they threw him out. Whatever was the truth, Ikey and Hannah stopped living together as man and wife and she and the children returned to Hobart. Both Hannah and Solomon were granted conditional pardons in May 1840, and four years later he was issued with his 'Certificate of Freedom'. This meant that he was now a completely free man and could leave his isolated life in Van Diemen's Land and return to London.

However, perhaps because he was now fifty-seven years old, he chose to remain in New Norfolk. He re-opened his tobacconists' shop and even became a respectable seat-holder in the Hobart synagogue. He lived in the town for another six years before dying there on 3 September 1850, far away from his family and birthplace.

Ikey Solomon was buried in Harrington Street Jewish cemetery, Hobart, aged sixty-three. Apart from (perhaps) serving as a model for Fagin, the archetypal 'fence', all that we have of him today are the Old Bailey court records and a sketch-portrait made at the time by the Lambeth police. In this he is depicted as a severe, gaunt-faced man with a long, pointed nose and short hair. He is wearing a cravat and a high-collared buttoned jacket. Altogether, it is not a very pleasant portrait.

Perhaps, the most positive thing that may be said of him is that he does not seem to have been violent. He certainly appears to have been a friendly soul, as on more than one occasion his associates and fellow-criminals were willing to help him out financially, as well as supporting him when he escaped from the arms of the law in London before fleeing to Denmark and New York.

In addition, despite his affair with his mistress in Islington, he made the long journey from New York to Hobart on the other side of the world to be reunited with his wife and family. In those days, nearly two hundred years ago, when global travel, communications and international records were not like they are today, he could have easily abandoned her and started a completely new family life in the New World. No-one would have been any the wiser.

Chapter 13

William Burke (1792-1829) & William Hare (c.1792-1829):
'The Body Snatchers'

Most of the villains in this book gained their infamous reputation through their sticky fingers. The two who feature in this chapter, William Burke and William Hare, gained their immortal reputation through their bloody fingers. Like several of the other villains mentioned within these pages, Burke and Hare later inspired writers, dramatists and

filmmakers. Robert Louis Stevenson, who based his bestselling Jekyll and Hyde novel on Deacon Brodie, also featured Burke and Hare's exploits in his short story The Body Snatcher.

Nearly one hundred years later, novelist Margaret Byrd referred to these two criminals both in Rest Without Peace (1974) *and* The Search for Maggie Hare (1976), *a novel about William Hare's wife.*

Two films featuring the Burke and Hare story include Burke and Hare (2010) *and the earlier* The Doctor and the Devils (1985). *For some reason, this last film which was based on a hitherto unproduced screenplay by Dylan Thomas, changed the name of the body-snatchers to Fallon and Broom. Similarly, Dr Robert Knox, the medical lecturer who bought the bodies was rechristened Dr Thomas Rock. Other films based on the lives of Burke and Hare include* The Flesh and the Fiends (1960) *and* The Greed of William Hart (1948) *starring the aptly named actor, Tod Slaughter.*

Burke and Hare are among the two best-known criminal characters who may be defined as British, as opposed to English villains, since they were both born in the north of Ireland and yet carried out their murderous rampage in Edinburgh, Scotland.

*

The story began in a tavern in Penicuik, a small town some ten miles south of Edinburgh. William Burke and his female companion, Helen McDougal, were sitting down in the corner having a quiet drink and a meat pie when their conversation was interrupted by William Hare.

"Excuse me," Hare said, raising his hat to Helen. "May we, that is, me and my good lady-wife, Margaret, join you? All the other chairs have been taken and I know for one, I must rest my feet. They're killing me after a day working in the fields."

"Hey, aren't you the man I asked for a light for my pipe earlier today?" Burke asked. "Y'know, when I was walking down the road this morning?"

"That's right," Hare replied, sucking on his own pipe. "And I thought then that I could detect an Irish twang to your speech."

"Well, that's no wonder," Helen said. "My husband is from Ireland; from County Tyrone to be exact."

"Ah, another Ulsterman like me," Hare said, shaking Burke's hand. "Except that I'm from further north. From Derry. Fancy two Irishmen, and your pretty wife," he added bowing to the smiling Helen, "meeting up here in the middle of nowhere in Scotland. Come, let me buy you another drink."

He did so, and the four of them sat down to have a friendly chat.

"So, tell me about yourself," Burke began. "Apart from you being Irish and buying me and my wife a drink and that we work together, I know nothing about you. How old are you? All I know is that we are both working here on the harvest and that I used to work on the Union Canal. Digging away 'til I almost broke my bloody back."

The thin-faced Hare shrugged and fiddled with his cravat. "Well, there's not much to tell. Like you I'm from Ulster and I also worked on that damned canal. But I suppose I never saw you there 'cos there were thousands of us Irishmen and we must have been working in different parts. And as for my age, I don't know the exact year when I was born. But, looking at you, boyo, I suppose we're about the same age."

"Ah, that would make you about twenty-five years old," Helen McDougal concluded.

Hare nodded. It was clear that his age was of no importance to him. "So, as I was saying, I worked on a farm back home for a while before coming here to Scotland to work on the Union Canal..."

"Ah, and for how long did you work on it?" Burke asked.

"Oh, about seven years, I suppose, and then I moved to Edinburgh where I became a coal man's assistant."

"And?"

"And nothing," Hare said. "That's it. That's all I've done in my life so far. Nothing too exciting. After I've finished making some extra money here, I suppose we'll move back to Ireland or go to London. Now *that's* where the money is. In London." He took a large swallow of his drink and finished off his meat pie. "Now it's your turn to tell me about yourself."

Burke looked at Helen and then turned back to face Hare. "Well, like you, I too haven't had such an exciting life. I had an easy upbringing – perhaps it was too easy – as when I was old enough, I joined the army with my brother, Constantine, to have some excitement."

"And – was it exciting?" Hare asked.

Burke shook his head. "No, not really. I served in the Donegal militia for a while and then I left when I got married…"

"To this lovely lady here."

"No, no. To some bitch from County Mayo. But as you can see, it didn't work out. I had a fight with her father about my owning a piece of land, and when I saw he wasn't going to give in, I left that skinny bitch, yes, and her kid, and came here to Scotland to work…"

"On the canal?"

Burke nodded. "And then I met Helen McDougal, my Nelly," he added, giving her plump thigh an affectionate squeeze, "and so we settled down in Maddiston near Grangemouth and…"

"So she's not really your wife," Hare said, looking at Helen.

"No, not really," Burke smiled. "But who cares? Anyway, tell me, where d'you live in Edinburgh? Near the castle?"

"Aye, about ten or fifteen minutes north of it. In Tanners Close. Why?" Hare asked.

Burke smiled. "Because we're looking for somewhere new to move into. Our landlord has just put the rent up and we can't afford to stay there anymore."

"So why don't you move in with us?" Hare said. "We've got three rooms to let. One of them is used by a lodger, an old army pensioner called 'Old Donald' – I don't know his other name - but you could use the other two. How does that sound?"

Helen looked up at Burke. "That sounds like a good idea. Don't you agree, Will?"

William Burke smiled. "I agree. And when could we move in? Soon?"

Hare nodded. "As soon as you like, and that means we'll all be happy. You'll have a roof over your heads and what you pay me for the rooms will help me out of a fix."

Burke smiled. "That's the best news I've heard today. Come. Let's drink to it." And the story of Burke and Hare was born.

Sometime later, on 29 November 1827, Old Donald died of dropsy (today called oedema). This really annoyed Hare as his lodger had died before paying him the four pounds (about four hundred today) he owed him. To Hare, this was a fortune and he decided to talk about it with Burke. It did not take long for the latter to come up with a suggestion.

"We'll sell the body to one of the local anatomists," Burke said. "They're always looking for bodies for research purposes."

"D'you mean like at the university or somewhere like that?" Hare asked.

Burke nodded. "I'm sure of it, and anyway, we can't lose, can we?"

That same day they set off to find a carpenter who would make a coffin. Once the carpenter had left, Burke and Hare removed Old Donald's body from the coffin and filled it with bark from a local tanner' yard to give it some weight before sealing it shut. The coffin was then duly buried, the expenses being paid by the local authorities. Meanwhile, the old pensioner's body lay hidden under a bed in Hare's lodging house.

The next day they took the corpse to Edinburgh University. Here, after asking around, they were directed to contact the well-known Dr Robert Knox, a fellow of the university's Royal College of Surgeons. They were told that he was always ready to receive cadavers, especially as he advertised that he gave 'a full demonstration on *fresh* anatomical subjects' in his lectures.

Knox agreed to pay the two 'body snatchers' seven-and-a-half pounds, most of which went to Hare to pay for Donald's unpaid rent. And, perhaps what was just as important as Hare covering his financial loss, they were told that the doctor of anatomy would be pleased if they could furnish him again with a corpse 'when they had another to dispose of'. The doctor did not ask any awkward questions and they certainly did not divulge the source of their anatomical supply.

This business offer must have initiated much discussion between the two friends. Here was a source of income that could be obtained without having to work too hard. All that they needed to do was to provide the good doctor with bodies for his lectures. Bring a body and collect the cash. It was as simple as that!

At the beginning of 1828, Joseph, one of the tenants in Hare's lodging house, fell ill with an infectious disease. Burke and Hare saw the sick man as a source for future profit but there was another problem.

"You know, Hare," Burke said one evening after they had endured yet another half hour of Joseph's delirious groans, "we've got to do something about him upstairs. I think that old boy's fever is catching."

"And?"

"And if we don't, everyone, including us, is going to be infected."

"Aye, and then what will I do for rent if the others die?" Hare asked.

So that night, telling the old man that a drop of Scotch would be good for him, they gave the sickly Joseph a very large dram of whisky before smothering their inebriated victim with a pillow. To make sure he would not resist, while Hare held the pillow down over Joseph's face, the heavier Burke lay across their victim's body. In this way, the poor old man shuffled off this mortal coil without leaving any signs of violence on his body. As before, they took the cadaver to Knox, who was so delighted that he paid the murderous duo ten pounds.

Nothing succeeds like success, and over a period dating from November 1827 to November 1828, Burke and Hare murdered eighteen people: four men, thirteen women and one boy. And all to make money from selling their dead bodies.

As this pair of murderers did not keep any records of their activities, and it was only during their trial that any specific dates were first publicly recorded, it is not clear who their next victim was, either Abigail Simpson or another male lodger. We do know that the man, a travelling seller of tinder and matches from Cheshire, was staying in Hare's house when he fell ill with jaundice. Hare who, as before, was worried that that man might die before paying his rent, dealt with him in the same way as he had previously done with Joseph – he and Burke suffocated the sick man and then sold his body to Dr Knox.

At about the same time, Abigail Simpson, a pensioner who made a few extra shillings by selling salt, was invited in by Burke and Hare for either a social chit-chat or a business deal. She never left the house alive. On 12 February 1828, the only specific date Burke mentioned in court, the poor woman was made to drink too much alcohol. She agreed to spend the night after being convinced that she was in no state to return home to her house in the nearby village of Gilmerton. She was dispatched in the usual way and her body, packed in a tea chest, was sold to their cooperative lecturer in anatomy.

This unfortunate woman was soon followed by another. During Hare's absence, his wife, Margaret, invited their next anonymous victim into the lodging house. Like Abigail Simpson, she was plied with enough whisky to make her drunk. When Hare returned home, all he had to do was suffocate the inebriated woman and then, together with Burke, sell the cadaver to Dr Knox. She netted them ten pounds profit.

"You know, Hare, my friend," Burke smiled one evening over a glass of Scotch, "we're doing well out of this business. We've made something between forty and fifty pounds."

"Aye, so far, so good," Hare replied, rubbing his hands.

"D'you mean you want to continue?"

"Why not? No-one's asking any questions. My wife is working with us and the doctor hasn't asked us any awkward questions, has he?"

Burke had to agree, and soon the pair of them invited two women, Janet Brown and Mary Patterson, to come back to the lodging house and share a 'wee dram of guid Scotch whiskey'. Apparently, Mary Patterson could not hold her liquor well and soon fell asleep. Burke and Janet Brown continued their amicable discussion but were interrupted when Helen McDougal burst into the room.

"Who is this woman?" she shouted, pointing at the tipsy Janet. "I know. You're having an affair with this lass! I know you, William Burke."

"No, he's not," the half-drunk Janet replied, slurring her words. "I was just…"

"No, no, Helen," Burke shouted back. "You've got it all wrong. All we were doing was…"

"Aye, I can see what you were doing! Carrying on behind my back! Well, I'm going out now and when I come back, I expect to see her gone." And with that she stormed out of the house to find Hare and his wife.

By the time Helen returned together with Hare and Margaret, Janet had sobered up enough to make her own way home and had therefore unwittingly saved her own life. Then the two men told their wives to leave the room, whereupon they smothered Mary Patterson to death in her drunken sleep. They did not waste any time but wrapped the young woman's still warm body in a sheet before packing her into a tea chest and taking it to the university. However, before doing so, Helen, as a good Scottish housewife, muttering 'Waste not, want not,' removed Mary's petticoats and skirt and kept them for herself. This time, Fergusson, one of Dr Knox's assistants, *did* ask a couple of potentially awkward questions.

"Don't I know this woman?" he asked, as he pulled the white sheet off to expose the dead woman's face. "I'm sure I've seen her before."

"I doubt it," Burke replied quickly. "She's just someone who drank herself to death and we bought it, or rather her, from another woman in town."

Fergusson looked again at Mary Patterson's face, shrugged and asked Burke to close up the tea chest. A few days later it was the turn of the now sober Janet Brown to ask questions.

"Where's my friend, Mary?" she asked as she stood in the doorway of Hare's lodging house. "Y'know, the woman who was here with me a few days ago?"

"Ah, Mary," Hare replied, hesitating. "Er, yes," he said at last. "The last thing I heard of her was that she went to Glasgow with a salesman. I don't know what he was selling, but your friend seemed to be very pleased to go with him."

Janet walked off, not knowing whether to believe him or not.

Their next female victim, Mrs Haldane, was the opposite in build to Mary Patterson, or to use Burke's words from his confession, 'a stout old woman'. She went the same way as Mary Paterson. She became one of Hare's lodgers, was plied with strong drink, smothered to death while she was sleeping it off and her body sold to Dr Knox. She was not the only one of the Haldane family to shuffle off this mortal coil courtesy of William Burke.

A few months later, her daughter, Peggy, came to lodge at Hare's house. One evening when Hare was out (perhaps looking for a new victim), Burke invited the young lady to join him for a drink. She happily did so and soon was following the same route her mother had taken. This time Burke killed her by himself, stuffed her body into another tea chest and sold her to the ever willing Dr Robert Knox for eight pounds.

This young lady was followed by yet another lodger, this time, an older woman. We do not know her name, but as before, Burke killed her in his usual way and without involving his partner. He sold the cadaver to Knox, this time receiving ten pounds.

A cinder-gatherer, a person who scavenged through rubbish bins, was next. Her name was Effie, and Burke knew her as she had sold him some pieces of leather when he had been honestly employed as a shoemaker. Burke poured her a goodly dram of whisky, this time in the stable attached to the lodging house. Then Burke and Hare killed the unfortunate woman and sold her to Dr Knox for another ten pounds.

It was the long arm of the law who supplied the murderous duo with their next victim. One day Burke was walking through Edinburgh when he saw a constable holding up a woman who had clearly drunk too much of Scotland's national beverage.

"Can I help you with this young woman, officer?" Burke asked. "I just happen to know a good lodging house where she may sleep it off."

"No, it's all right," the constable replied, "I'm going to take her to her own lodging house."

"I see," continued Burke, the ever-concerned social minded citizen. "If you want, give me the address and I'll take her there myself and save you the bother."

Minutes later, after parting from the constable, Burke was helping the half-drunk woman on her way to a lodging house. *Hare's* lodging house. There she was sent off to meet her Maker in the usual way, making another ten pounds for the two serial killers.

June 1828 was also a profitable month. First, they killed an old woman, then quickly followed this murder up by killing her grandson, their only child victim. The grandmother and her grandson were both in the lodging house at the same time. The old woman was got rid of in the bedroom by the pair's usual method and then the 'dumb boy', to quote Burke, was taken to the same room and dispatched as well. Some reports say that this time the latest victim was not given any strong drink, but that Hare killed the boy by breaking his back across his knee. This time the two bodies were taken to the university in a herring barrel, the tea chest proving to be too small.

Towards the end of June 1828, Burke and Helen went to Falkirk to see her father. Despite Burke and Hare's recent 'successes', Burke knew that Hare needed more money quickly and that therefore he had pawned some of his clothes. You can imagine Burke's surprise that when he returned from Falkirk to find his murderous partner wearing new clothes and talking about the money he now had in his pockets.

"Ho, my fine friend. You're looking good, even like a lord," Burke exclaimed. "Where did you get the money from? Have you been busy on the side?"

"Och, man, of course not. I just found some money in the street behind the house and…" but seeing Burke's murderous expression, Hare confessed that he had indeed done away with an old lady and sold her cadaver for eight pounds. This did not stop the two men from coming to blows, with the result that Burke and Helen decided to leave Hare's lodging house and move into the house of Burke's cousin nearby.

However, this move meant the end of their very profitable 'business,' which neither Burke nor Hare wanted. That autumn, Hare decided to visit Burke while a Mrs Hostler (or Ostler), a laundress, was also present. Both men thought that here was a good opportunity to revive their mutual interests, so with their usual efficiency, they got her drunk, killed her and immediately sold her body to Dr Knox for eight pounds.

Before long, Ann Dougal, one of Helen's relations, became the source of their next windfall. She came to visit from Falkirk, was murdered in the usual fashion and her corpse was sold for yet another ten pounds.

Soon after this, when Helen was out of the house, Margaret Hare came up with a startling proposal. "Why don't you two kill Helen?"

"What?" Burke replied somewhat shocked. "Are you serious? Why?"

"Yes, I'm perfectly serious," Hare's wife answered with a straight face. "I don't think we can trust her anymore. I mean, think what would happen if she opened her big mouth and blabbed to someone about what was going on here. I'm telling you. It doesn't bear thinking about."

Burke did think about it, and he refused to carry out this murderous suggestion. However, this was not the end of his and his partner's bloodthirsty regime. The next person they killed was James Wilson, a killing which was to prove a serious mistake. The city of Edinburgh, with a population of 160,000, was small enough for everyone to know, or know of, 'Daft Jamie', a distinctive eighteen-year-old beggar. In addition to his strange gait caused by his deformed feet, he was also well-known for his torn clothes, bent back, low IQ and his unconventional behaviour.

One month after disposing of Ann Dougal, young Jamie was enticed into Hare's lodging house, plied with Scotch and was then set upon by Burke and Hare. This time the serial killers did not have everything go their way. As their victim did not like whisky very much, he was not too drunk when the pair set upon him. He fought back, but in the end the two men succeeded in overcoming him and he was duly killed. Before stuffing his body into the tea chest, Hare took Jamie's snuff spoon as loot, while Burke kept the young man's snuff box. Then following their usual procedure, they handed him over to Dr Knox.

However, the good doctor's next anatomical lesson did not go as smoothly as hoped, as several of his students recognised the well-known Jamie. Knox insisted that they were wrong. But then word got around that the young man was nowhere to be seen, and so Knox continued his dissection after first removing the head and feet.

One year after their incredible killing spree started, Burke and Hare murdered their last victim. Her name was Margaret Docherty and like the two men, she too had come over to Scotland from Ireland.

"Hello, there," Burke greeted her before 'chatting her up'. "Come and meet my wife, Helen. And yes, my mother was also a Docherty," he lied, "but come in and have a wee drop and we'll talk about where we used to live in the old country."

Margaret Docherty had no reason to doubt the friendly Mr William Burke and followed him into his cousin John Broggan's house. There, she sat and talked with Helen when Burke stood up to say that he had to go out for a minute to buy some more drink. In fact, he went to fetch Hare. However, there was a problem to be solved. Another pair of lodgers, James and Ann Gray, were staying in the house at the time, and the killers paid them to go and spend the night at Hare's lodging house instead.

Burke, Hare and their womenfolk had a merry drinking party with the unsuspecting Margaret Docherty. And even though the two men, probably under the influence of too much Scotch started fighting at one point, they succeeded in murdering their next victim and stuffing her body in a pile of straw under some furniture.

All would have gone well except that the following day, Ann Gray returned to the house and became somewhat suspicious of Burke's behaviour.

"Please let me in to collect some of the clothes I left behind."

"No, you can't come in now," Burke replied, blocking her way.

"But I need them. I need some clean stockings."

"Well, you cannot have them now. I'm busy. Come back tomorrow."

"But Mr Burke. I need…"

"Are ye deaf, woman? I said, come back tomorrow. Now, be off with you."

Unfortunately for the murderous pair, they were not able to remove the body as quickly as they had done so often in the past. That night, Ann Gray and her husband returned while Burke and Hare and their wives were out, and they found the hidden corpse of Mary Docherty. They immediately left to inform the police, but they were stopped *en route* by Helen McDougal. She tried to bribe them, but the Grays were not having any of it. They reported what they had found to the police, but not before Burke and Hare had already handed over their latest contribution to Dr Knox for his lectures on anatomy.

While the police were carrying out their investigation, they found Margaret Docherty's bloodstained clothes on the premises. Under questioning, Burke and Helen gave different answers about what had happened. Naturally, this aroused further suspicions and so the police went see Dr Knox and check out his laboratory. Here they found Margaret Docherty's corpse, and that, together with the Grays' claim that this was the woman they had seen the night before was enough for the two serial killers, as well as Burke's cousin, John Broggan, to be arrested.

Soon after, Broggan was released, but Burke and Hare and their wives were kept in detention as they were 'helping the police with their enquiries'. The police followed up their arrest by having a doctor and two forensic specialists examine Mary Docherty's body. This resulted in all four of the guilty party being charged with murder.

Robert Christison, one of the forensic specialists, then questioned Dr Knox. He explained that Burke and Hare found the bodies in poor lodging houses in the city and had bought them before any family claimed them for burial. Christison was not satisfied with this answer but decided that Knox had not broken the law and did not have him arrested.

However, due to the nature of Burke and Hare's *modus operandi,* there were no bodies apart from that of the unfortunate Margaret Docherty, something which caused the police several problems with the case. But then news of other murders and strange disappearances began to surface in the town. The terrible nature of these oral and newspaper reports was reinforced when Janet Brown went to the police and identified the clothes that her friend, Mary Patterson, had been wearing when they had been 'entertained' by Burke and Hare. In addition, a local baker claimed that he had seen Burke's son wearing clothes that had once belonged to Daft Jamie. Three weeks after Margaret Docherty had been brutally murdered, Burke and Hare and their wives were charged with the murder of Jamie Wilson.

The police wanted to finish the investigation quickly and they used the well-known technique of 'divide and conquer', offering Hare immunity from prosecution if he would turn King's evidence. He agreed to do so, and thereby saved not only his own neck, but that of his wife, as by law he could not testify against her. As a result of his confession, William Burke and Helen Dougal were charged with the murders of Mary Docherty, Mary Paterson and James Wilson.

Two months after their last murder, on Christmas Eve 1828, Burke and his wife faced their accusers in Edinburgh's High Court of Judiciary. The case aroused great excitement and hundreds of constables were brought in to keep the peace.

It was a complicated case and Burke and Dougal's lawyers claimed that the accused and his common-law wife could not be tried together. After several hours of legal wrangling, Burke and McDougal pleaded not guilty to murdering Mary Docherty. Over fifty witnesses were questioned, with Dr Knox and his assistants being questioned outside the courthouse.

"Mr Hare," the prosecutor asked, "was Mr William Burke the sole murderer of Mary Docherty?"

"No, Your Honour," Hare replied, not daring to look at his former partner in crime. "Helen McDougal, his so-called wife, was also involved concerning the death of that woman."

"Please elaborate."

"She was responsible for bringing Mary Docherty back to the house," Hare continued. "And she also helped Mr Burke take her body to Dr Knox."

Finally, the two doctors, Christison and Black, told the jury in that crowded courtroom that they suspected foul play but that there were no marks of violence on the body. After several days' deliberation, the jury declared that William Burke was guilty. This was followed by the Lord Justice-Clerk David Boyle passing the death sentence on William Burke and adding:

> *'Your body should be publicly dissected and anatomised. And I trust, that if it is ever customary to preserve skeletons, yours will be preserved, in order that posterity keep in remembrance your atrocious crimes.'*

One month later, on 28 January 1829, William Burke was hanged at Lawnmarket before a crowd of about 25,000 people, of which some paid high prices to have a good view of Burke breathing his last. Ironically, and as the judge had ordered, the man who had provided the university with eighteen bodies for dissection finally provided a nineteenth.

Professor Monro publicly cut up Burke's corpse in the Edinburgh University's Old College anatomy theatre. The dissection took two hours and at the end of it, Monro dipped his pen into the murderer's blood and wrote '*This is written with the blood of Wm Burke, who was hanged at Edinburgh. This blood was taken from his head*'. This dissection caused minor riots, and in order to restore the peace, no more than fifty students and members of the public were allowed to attend at any one time.

However, this was not the end of the case. Daft Jamie's mother and sister appealed the court's decision to grant Hare immunity and demanded that he also be tried for murdering their son and brother. Edinburgh's High Court of Justiciary debated this issue but in the end, after a vote of four to two, upheld the original agreement so that Hare was again declared a free man.

And what happened to the rest of the *dramatis personae* of this incredible story of murder and greed?

Hare was kept in custody for a few days before being allowed to leave in disguise. He was justifiably scared of being recognised in the town, and so he fled in a mail coach west to Dumfries. However, his plan to remain anonymous quickly unravelled – he was recognised *en route* by one of Jamie Wilson's lawyers, who then told the rest of the passengers who their fellow traveller was. Then, when Hare arrived at Dumfries, he was greeted by a large crowd at the hostelry where he had planned to stay. The local police arranged for him to get out of the building unseen, lodging him in the town jail for his own protection. But the good people of Dumfries found out and began to riot and attack the jail.

Early on the following morning, Hare, described at the time as a 'rude ruffian, ferocious profligate' and 'evidently the greatest villain of the two' was escorted out of the town by an armed guard and told to make his way to England, some forty miles to the south. This he did. He was reported to have last been seen heading east from Carlisle on the way to Newcastle-upon-Tyne. Other than his name appearing in books and film ever since, he was never heard of again. However, there are stories that he was later discovered and thrown into a lime quarry by an angry mob, as a result of which he eked out the rest of his life as a blind beggar in London.

According to the agreement where Hare testified against his fellow criminal, Hare's wife, Margaret, was not put on trial for her part as an accomplice. She was released on 19 January 1829 and fled to Glasgow. While waiting in the port for a ship to take her back to her native Ireland, she was recognised by several fellow passengers and beaten up. As with her husband, the police (probably unwillingly) rescued her and put her in the local police station for her own protection. She was escorted to a ship sailing to Belfast, but no more is known about her once she reached her destination.

Her fellow female accomplice, Helen McDougal, was also released and then recognised by an angry mob. She too was rescued by the police who took her to a local police station for her own good. The furious mob then besieged the building. The police smuggled her out through a back window, and she was taken to a better protected police station in the centre of Edinburgh. While there she asked if she could see her common-law husband, who was awaiting his execution. This request was turned down and she managed to leave Edinburgh the following day. Again, we do not know how she spent the rest of her life, but it has been claimed that she went to Australia.

As for the balding and bespectacled Dr Robert Knox, even though he was never put on trial, he became a hated and despised figure on the streets of Edinburgh. Newspapers printed mocking cartoons depicting him as a hairy, horned devil, happily harvesting bodies. One month after the trial an effigy resembling Knox was publicly burned outside his house.

Although a committee of inquiry exonerated him from involvement with the actual murders, he resigned his post and was subsequently 'sent to Coventry' by his fellow academics. He remained in

Edinburgh for another thirteen years before moving south to become a lecturer in London.

From here his career went into further decline. While working in London's Royal College of Surgeons, he broke some of the college regulations and was not allowed to continue as a lecturer. In 1848, twenty years after he had encouraged Burke and Hare to supply him with cadavers, the Royal Society of Edinburgh removed his name from their distinguished Roll of Fellows. He then became a regular doctor, working in the pathology department at Brompton Cancer Hospital in south London from 1856 until his death six years later.

Following a similar style 'murder-for-body-sale' in London's Bethnal Green two years later – the body being sold for anatomical research to King's College, London – Parliament passed the 1832 Anatomy Act. This stated that universities and other research institutes could only use bodies from workhouses which were unclaimed after 48 hours. In addition, this Act clearly stated that a person having lawful possession of a body could permit it to undergo 'anatomical examination' – dissection – provided that no relative disagreed.

Since then, this Act which effectively put a stop to Burke and Hare-style activities, as well as to robbing graves in order to sell cadavers for cash, has undergone several changes. Today, the latest relevant Act of 2004 - the Health Tissue Act (2006 in Scotland) – aims to 'regulate the removal, storage, use and disposal of human bodies, organs and tissue'. This Act allows anonymous organ donation but prohibits the selling of organs. In 2007, a man was convicted for trying to sell one of his own kidneys for twenty-four thousand pounds in order to pay off his gambling debts.

As mentioned in the introduction to this chapter, Burke and Hare's exploits, in a similar way to several of the other villains who appear in this book, have inspired writers and filmmakers.

In addition, the duo's exploits have been immortalised in the following cynical piece of doggerel:

> *Through the close and up the stair*
> *But and ben wi' Burke and Hare.*
> *Burke is the Butcher, Hare's the thief*
> *And Knox the boy who buys the beef.*

As for William Burke, his skeleton may still be seen in the Surgeon's Hall in the Anatomical Museum of the Edinburgh Medical School. It is also reported that several anatomy students had taken pieces of his skin and used them as card holders and book binders – a legend echoing what happened to the skin of Richard of Pudlicott (Chapter 1), the man who had stolen the King's treasury in 1303. A book made with Burke's skin can be seen at the Edinburgh police museum.

In February 2009, *The Guardian* newspaper published an article saying that a pair of plaster masks of Burke and Hare had been found at Inverary jail in

Argyll, Scotland. This is really a mystery, as neither of the murderers was ever incarcerated there and nobody was ever hanged in that prison. The death masks were found during a clean-up in one of the prison's storerooms, the building today being a museum.

Andrew Connell, the manager of the museums' collection at the Royal College of Surgeons, says that they have a copy of Burke's death mask, but adds, "I've not seen them anywhere else. I don't think they were like Charles and Diana souvenirs, churned out in their thousands. There was probably only a handful made." So it is that a mystery involving this murderous couple lives on nearly two hundred years after Burke and Hare duped so many innocent people to line their greedy pockets, their victims becoming anatomical specimens in Edinburgh university.

Chapter 14

Charles Peace (1832-1879)
The "Banner Cross Killer"

Charles Frederick Peace (1832-1879) was an accomplished cat-burglar and murderer, while at the same time a successful master of disguise. However, none of this did him any good in the end, as he spent

over eighteen years, more than one third of his life, behind bars. In addition, he spent many months in custody while he was 'helping the police with their enquiries'. His career, which included robbery, murder and seriously harassing at least two women, took him all over England, from the north and Midlands – Sheffield, Nottingham and Manchester – to south London and the south coast – Portsmouth, Southsea and Southampton. He passed on to greener pastures aged 47 at the end of the hangman's rope in Leeds. In the end, his talents had brought him nothing but immortal notoriety.

*

A human cry of pain and desperation rose above the noises of the heavy mechanical thump-thumping and hissing at the huge Sheffield steel plant.

"Help! Help! My leg! It's burning! Help me! Won't anybody help me?"

Four men rushed over to where the fourteen-year-old boy lay writhing on the dirty floor next to the steel-rolling machine. His face was contorted as he twisted in agony, pointing to his injured leg. There was no need to ask why he was in such pain – a red hot piece of iron was sticking out of his leg where it had penetrated just below the knee.

Someone immediately threw a bucket of cold water over his leg and shouted for others to do the same.

More cold water followed as the men threw bucket after bucket over the protruding iron bar to cool it down.

"Go for the doctor," a man called, and soon a doctor was bending down on the floor trying to calm the sweating boy.

"Send for his folks," he said. "This lad must go to the infirmary."

And that is where the young Charles Frederick Peace spent the next eighteen months, in Sheffield Infirmary. He recovered from his terrible ordeal but remained disabled for the rest of his life. When he was discharged, in 1846, it was clear that he would not be returning to the steel mill. He would have to find a new way of earning a living and helping his mother and three older siblings make enough money to put food on the table and keep a roof over their heads.

Even without having to pay Charles' medical bills, the Peace family's financial situation had worsened recently as the father, John, had died while Charles was lying in the infirmary.

"Do you want to follow in your father's footsteps, Charles?" his mother asked. "I know he showed you a bit about making and repairing shoes," she added, hopefully.

Charles shook his head. "No, Mother, I don't. I cannot think of anything more boring than that. I need to do something to get my blood flowing again after lying in the infirmary all that time."

It was true. Making and repairing shoes was the last thing Peace wanted to do. Nothing could be so boring. Where was all the noise and excitement in making a pair of lady's red leather boots? Nothing could compare to the heat, smell and clangour of the steel mills. True, that life had nearly cost him his leg, but on the other hand, he had earned good money for his age and he loved the rough camaraderie of working with the tough older men. *Huh! Making shoes, indeed!*

Charles Frederick Peace needed some excitement, a flame, a thrill in his life. Where would he find it? His damaged leg would not allow him to be a soldier, and he spent the next few years doing odd jobs. He was always looking for that certain something that would make his heart leap, always thinking about any potentially exciting situation. Then one day, without any planning, he found it.

While walking through the market, he noticed that an old man had, for some unknown reason, laid his large gold watch on a wooden box. He was looking at some fruit and comparing prices. Without any hesitation, Peace swiped the watch off the box while the old man was busy chatting to the pretty fruit seller. Seconds later, Peace was away. Walking briskly past the crowded stalls so as not to attract any attention, he ducked into a murky alley. Here he stopped in dark doorway, his heart beating hard as he became aware of the rediscovered excitement his life had been lacking. *Yes!* This was how he was going to make his living.

Crime. It would provide the food and shelter and it would supply the longed-for thrills.

From then on, and despite his bad leg, the nineteen-year-old Peace started burgling houses on a regular basis. All went well until October 1851 when a lady in Sheffield reported that her house had been broken into. In that small neighbourhood where everyone knew everyone else, the long arm of the law suspected Peace. His house was searched and some of the lady's property was found there. Peace was arrested and put on trial.

"Seeing that this is the first time he has broken the law," the judge asked, "has anyone anything good to say about the young man standing before us before I pass judgement?"

"Yes, Your Honour. I know this man well. At least I did," a former employer said. "He was a good man and a good worker. It was very unfortunate that he was badly injured at the steel mill. I'm sure that caused him a lot of pain. And I'm equally sure, Your Honour, that this burglary for which he is now on trial, will be the first and last time that he will ever commit such a crime."

"I see. Well, if that is the case," the judge continued, looking at Peace in the dock as he recorded the sentence in a large black ledger, "I will let you off with just one month's imprisonment. I am hoping that my being so lenient this time will be a lesson for you and that we will never see you in here again. And at the same time, may I take the opportunity to suggest to you, young man, that you take up a new, a non-criminal career. I am sure that you will find it to be a more profitable and a more honourable way to earn your daily bread."

Peace took the judge's words to heart. He learned how to play a one-stringed violin and began making money playing music at parties and other social gatherings. He called himself 'The Modern Paganini'. He also began to paint and draw, and this became another minor source of income.

As Shakespeare said, 'If music be the food of love,' but it did not provide enough food for the young musician and entertainer, who soon returned to robbing wealthy houses in the Sheffield area. Three years later he found himself once again facing a judge in court. This time there was no kind past employer to say any good words to mitigate his sentence.

The judge at the Doncaster Sessions sentenced him to four years penal servitude, while the two young ladies, his sister, Mary, and his girlfriend, who had been found in possession of stolen property, were each given six months 'inside.' Mary died soon after.

Unfortunately, Peace did not learn from this experience. On completing his four-year sentence, he went back to both his violin and burglary. But this time he carried out his housebreaking activities in Manchester. Although he changed his area of operations, his luck did not improve, and he was caught by the police while returning to pick up the stolen goods he had hidden in a hole in a field. It was August 1859.

This time, Peace had made two serious mistakes. The first was to return almost immediately to the scene of the crime in order to pick up his loot. The second was to try and kill the arresting officer. He failed, was arrested and sentenced to six years of penal servitude.

He was released in 1864, aged thirty-two, after having served one third of his life at Her Majesty's pleasure. This meant that Peace had spent more than ten years carrying out such tasks such as walking the treadmill, winding a crank handle, picking oakum and working on building sites. Most of this time was spent in heavily imposed silence, sleeping on hard plank beds and eating the same deliberately boring fare day after day.

Apparently, none of this affected Peace. After being released from his third prison sentence, he returned to Sheffield. Finding no luck there, he crossed the Pennines once again and went back to Manchester. There in Lower Broughton, north Manchester, Peace was caught breaking into a house once again. Having drunk too much beforehand, he was too befuddled in trying to escape from the law. He was arrested and this being his fourth conviction, he was sentenced to eight years penal servitude in December 1866. He was a true example of criminal recidivism.

This time Peace was not willing to complete his sentence within the grim walls of Wakefield Prison.

Despite the fact that he had a gammy leg and had lost a finger during his criminal carer, he decided to escape by emulating the deeds of Jack Sheppard, the 'Eighteenth Century Houdini' (Chapter 8). One day, while carrying out some repair work in the prison, he managed to smuggle a small ladder into his cell. Then using a home-made tin saw, he cut a hole in the ceiling. But then his plans began to unravel. Just as he was about to escape, a warder entered his cell. Peace hit him, climbed through the ceiling and ran along the top of the wall of the prison.

But again, he ran out of luck. Some loose bricks on the wall caused him to fall. To complete his escape, he sneaked into the governor's house, where he changed his clothes. Then, after waiting for a nerve-wracking ninety minutes to make his getaway, he was recaptured in the governor's bedroom and was forced to complete his fourth long prison sentence. Some of this time was even spent on the Rock of Gibraltar.

Peace was released in 1872 and returned to his family in Sheffield. He had earlier married Hannah Ward, a widow, and now he tried to live a 'straight and narrow' life. He went into the picture framing business and his family, without Peace, began attending services in the local church. Three years later, the now peaceful and law-abiding Peace family moved to Darnall, a suburb east of central Sheffield. There Peace became acquainted with a Mr and Mrs Dyson.

"Ah, so you went to America for a while," Peace said to Dyson as they sat knocking back a pint in the local pub.

"Aye, that's right," Dyson replied. "The move was all part of my job as a civil engineer."

"And did you take your wife with you?"

"Of course I did, Charles. You don't think that I'm going to leave a pretty lass like that here on her own, do you?"

"No, Arthur, I suppose not. And yes, I must agree with you. Your Katherine, er, Mrs Dyson, is indeed a very pretty lady. If she were mine," Peace added, "I certainly wouldn't leave her behind. You never know what could happen if you did."

From this point on, despite being a married man with a family, Peace became infatuated with Mrs Dyson. He began stalking her, and the situation deteriorated so much that Dyson wrote a note, 'Charles Peace is requested not to interfere with my family' and threw it into Peace's garden. It had no effect. Peace continued to stalk his former friend's wife.

That same day, as a form of childish revenge for her not returning his amorous intentions, he tried to trip up Mrs Dyson in the street. This, of course, did not increase any feelings of affection she may have had for him. That night, Peace added even more fuel to the fire when he threatened to shoot Mr and Mrs Dyson. In desperation, Mr Dyson took out a summons against Peace.

After this, Peace moved to Hull and, together with his wife, opened a café. Then one day he returned to Manchester, allegedly for business purposes, and while there he committed his first murder.

At about midnight on 1 August 1876 two policemen saw Peace breaking into a house at Whalley Range. Peace, knowing that another prison sentence would be much longer if he were caught, ran away as the police chased after him. In order to stop them, he took out his revolver and threatened to shoot. Constable Nicholas Cock ignored this warning and continued to chase Peace.

"Stop! or I will shoot you," Peace shouted, brandishing his gun.

Cock, truncheon in hand, kept up the pursuit.

Peace aimed at Cock but deliberately missed. Cock kept chasing him. Peace fired again, and this time he hit Cock, who fell to the ground, dead. Peace did not wait around. Despite his bad leg, he ran off as quickly as he could and made his escape.

As a result, two brothers, William and John Habron, who lived nearby and were 'known to the police', were arrested and charged with killing PC Cock. They were taken to Manchester Assizes and William Habron was found guilty of the murder of the policeman and sentenced to death. However, luck, in a way, was on his side. Two days before his scheduled execution, the judge, Mr Justice Linley, who had not been impressed by the prosecution's case, commuted

Habron's sentence to penal servitude for life. His brother, John, was found innocent. When Peace, who had attended the trial as a spectator, heard this verdict, he rejoiced and left Manchester and returned to Sheffield.

Meanwhile, the Dysons had moved back from Hull to Banner's Cross, another suburb in Sheffield. Here they hoped to escape from the bothersome and threatening Charles Frederick Peace.

Soon afterwards, Peace and a friend saw Arthur Dyson in the street. "If he offers to come near me," Peace said to his friend, "I will make him stand back."

Dyson was not deterred when he saw Peace holding his revolver.

"You stay away from my wife," he said. "She told me you'd said to her that you had come to Banner's Cross to annoy her."

"Aye, that's right," Peace replied. "And I'll annoy you and her wherever you go."

But threatening the Dysons was not enough. Peace wanted more.

One evening while keeping a look-out on Dyson's house, Peace saw Dyson come out of the back door, cross the yard and enter an outhouse at the back. Peace thought that now he had an opportunity to be alone with Katherine Dyson, so he knocked on the Dyson's door.

Katherine came out and was immediately confronted with Peace pointing his revolver at her.

"Say something," he said, "and I'll fire."

Screaming, Katherine Dyson fled back inside. Hearing the noise, her husband ran back to the house and saw Peace standing just outside holding his revolver.

Suddenly Peace turned around and ran down a side passage. Dyson raced after him. Hearing that he was being pursued, Peace turned around and fired at Dyson. He missed, and Dyson kept running. Peace fired again and this time Dyson fell, mortally wounded. Hearing the shots, Katherine Dyson ran into the passageway to her husband's side.

"Murder! You villain! You have shot my husband," she shouted.

As he had done previously in Manchester after shooting PC Cock, Peace did not wait to see if he had killed Arthur Dyson, and ran off without being pursued. Dyson died two hours later.

In the meanwhile, Peace had bought a train ticket to Beverley, East Yorkshire. However, to throw the police off his scent, he got off the train at Normanton, some twenty miles away and then made another thirty-mile train journey to York.

The next day he returned to Hull via Beverley where he went to his wife, Hannah's café.

"Where have you been, Charles? I was so worried," she said.

Peace shrugged and pointed to the kitchen. "I've been away, woman, on business. Now get me some food. I'm hungry."

Hannah knew better than to ask him any more questions. Just as he was getting down to his meal, Peace heard a knock on the door. He slipped out to a back room, thinking that it might be the long arm of the law. He was right.

"Excuse me, ma'am," one of the detectives asked. "Is your husband here?"

"No, officer."

"Have you seen him recently?"

Hannah shook her head again. "No, officer. He's been away on business for these past two weeks."

"Then you won't mind if we search your house, will you?"

"Try looking around at the back," a customer called out.

Hearing that, Peace went up to a back room and hid out on the roof behind a chimney stack until the detectives had left. He then shaved off his grey beard, dyed his hair and began wearing a pair of spectacles. He remained in Hull so disguised for three weeks.

The police did not give up. They put a prize of one hundred pounds (nearly eleven thousand today) on his head and publicised the following detailed description:

> *'Charles Peace wanted for murder on the night of 29th inst. He is thin and slightly built, from 55 to 60 years of age. Five feet four inches or five feet high; grey (nearly white) hair, beard, no whiskers. He lacks use of three fingers of left hand, walks with the legs wide apart, speaks somewhat peculiarly as though his tongue were too large for his mouth, and is a great boaster. He is a picture-frame maker. He occasionally cleans and repairs clocks and watches and sometimes deals in oleographs, engravings and pictures. He has been in penal servitude for burglary in Manchester. He has lived in Manchester, Salford, and Liverpool and Hull.'*

Even though Peace was actually forty-four at the time, the police later amended the above so that his age was given as forty-six. Another fact about Peace not given in the above description was that he had made himself a false arm. It was hollow and made out of gutta-percha, a natural rubbery material. Peace was able to put his own natural arm inside and by using a hook at the end of this device he could use a fork and other implements.

and so overcome certain problems difficulties that resulted from the loss of one of his fingers earlier in life.

After his narrow escape and short stay in Hull, Peace moved south to Doncaster and then on to London. From there he travelled to Bristol and then Bath. But this was not the end of his journey. After a short spell in Bath he continued to Oxford before taking the train to Birmingham. He stayed there for a few days and then went to Derby, where he stayed for one week before heading east to Nottingham. Here, in January 1877, Peace stayed at the house of Mrs Adamson, a woman who dealt in stolen goods, and where he met Susan Grey who later became his mistress.

Over the next few months Peace had some narrow escapes, but by threatening his pursuers with his revolver he managed to escape every time. Naturally he could not stay in one place for long, especially as notices offering fifty pounds for his capture were displayed in many of the shop windows across the country.

One day, while staying with Susan Grey on a return trip to Nottingham, he must have forgotten to lock the front door. A local policeman, seeing the door open came to investigate. The result was that Peace was almost caught while in bed with her.

"Excuse me, sir, and please excuse me for asking," the constable asked somewhat apologetically as Susan Grey pulled the blanket up to cover her chest, "but aren't you Mr Charles Peace?"

"Certainly not," an aggrieved Peace replied. "My name is John Ward and this young lady is called Mrs Bailey. And now would you do us the courtesy of leaving us to go to sleep in peace?"

"I'm sorry, sir but I cannot do that. Please could you get dressed and come downstairs? My chief will be here in a few minutes and he would like to speak to you."

"Well, alright," Peace replied grudgingly. "But I'm not going to get dressed while you are standing there. Please go downstairs and I'll join you in a few minutes and help you sort out this case of mistaken identity."

The policeman left the room and as soon as he had done so, Peace dressed himself and slipped out of the house. Later, from another part of town, he sent a message for Susan to join him. Soon after this he left Nottingham and returned to Hull. There he found that his wife's shop was still being visited by the police, and he decided that he would make his way south to London. In the capital where he was not known, he hoped, he would be able to operate with impunity.

He stayed in London for two years. He set himself up at first in Lambeth as a Mr Thompson, a dealer in musical instruments. However, like Deacon Brodie (Chapter 10), Peace lived a double life. By day he would buy and sell violins, flutes and oboes – by night he would break into houses in south London.

From Lambeth, Peace moved to Greenwich and there, in one of two adjoining houses, he lived with Susan Grey, alias Mrs Thompson. His wife and son, Willie, lived in the other – somehow, he had managed to persuade the genuine Mrs Peace and his son to move south and be near him. We do not know why she agreed to this strange arrangement, but perhaps it was due to the money he gave her.

However, 'Mrs Thompson' did not like living in Greenwich. She claimed that Peckham was much nicer. And so, in May 1877, the Peace households moved to their new address, 5 East Terrace, Evelina Road, Peckham.

Continuing to live as Mr Thompson, the respectable new neighbour, Peace let it be known that he was a gentleman of independent means. He and his family attended church services and a more honourable citizen could not have been found anywhere in south central London.

This was all one big con. Almost every night from the beginning of 1877 for the next year-and-a-half, Peace would break into houses all over south London. In addition, with his pony and trap, he went as far as Southsea, Portsmouth and even Southampton. However, on 10 October 1878 his career came to an end much nearer to home.

On that night, at 2 am., Constable Robinson saw a light suddenly start shining at the back of a house in St. John's Park, Blackheath. Together with two other policemen, they approached the house and rang the bell. Hearing it, Peace tried to escape via the garden. While doing so, he fired four bullets at Robinson, who had managed to grab hold of him. Luckily for Robinson, Peace only managed to shoot him in the arm with his fifth bullet. Despite this, the policeman did not let Peace escape, and soon Peace found himself in the local police station.

There he refused to cooperate with the police, and even though he was held there for a week, he would not tell them his name. But then he gave himself away. He wrote a letter to a business friend and signed it as John Ward. His friend revealed Peace's true identity to the police.

Meanwhile, the police were beginning to amass plenty of evidence against their uncooperatively silent suspect. They followed Peace's trail from Peckham to Nottingham, contacted Peace's wife and daughter, and found boxes of stolen property. In addition, a local policeman who knew Peace from Sheffield, was sent south to Newgate Prison and identified him immediately. "That's Peace," he declared, seeing him exercising in the prison yard. "I'd know him anywhere."

Despite this, when Peace was tried later at the Old Bailey, where he was charged with burglary and the attempted murder of PC Robinson, he was tried under the name of John Ward. This time the sentence was not for just a number of years – although the accused tried to make out that he was insane, Mr Justice Sir Henry

Hawkins was not fooled and sentenced Charles Frederick Peace to penal servitude for life. He was to begin his sentence at Pentonville Prison, north London.

Next, Peace was tried for the murder of Arthur Dyson, three years earlier. He was transferred from Pentonville prison to Sheffield by train for the first hearing. However, as Mrs Dyson's testimony was due to be heard at the next hearing, Peace was returned to London.

A week later, the enormous crowd waiting outside Sheffield Town Hall, where the hearing was to take place, was disappointed to hear that the case was to be postponed for eight days. While on the journey back to prison, distracting his guards' attention, Peace managed to leap out of the window at Kiveton Park in south Yorkshire as the train chugged its way north.

Unfortunately for Peace, his attempt to escape failed. He landed badly by the train track, was knocked unconscious and seriously injured his head. The guards immediately pulled the communication cord and the train shrieked to a halt.

After a search, the unconscious Peace was found and escorted to Sheffield police station. Here he was placed under heavy guard. Later, a doctor examined him and a new date, 30 January 1879, was set for his second hearing.

During this hearing, William Clegg, Peace's defence lawyer, a former football player for Sheffield Wednesday and England, attempted to prove that Mrs

Katherine Dyson had been more intimate with Peace than she had admitted. Clegg also tried to prove that Peace had shot her angry husband out of self-defence. Additionally, Clegg produced several pencil-written notes in court by which he tried to show how close Peace's relationship with Mrs Dyson had been.

She denied that she had written them, and there was a question if indeed they were genuine. As a result of this hearing, Peace was committed for trial in Leeds. The assizes were due to start at the beginning of February 1879.

The trial, which lasted one day, opened with both Peace's lawyer, Frank Lockwood, and the prosecution lawyer, Mr Campbell Foster Q.C. complaining about the sensational stories appearing in the press. They claimed that these reports prejudiced a fair trial, which prompted Peace to call out 'Hear, hear' from the dock.

Like his predecessor William Clegg, Frank Lockward tried to prove that Katherine Dyson had been on intimate terms with Peace.

"That's not true, Your Honour. It's true that we were friends for a time but that's all it was. Friends."

"But you were seen together, weren't you?" Lockward continued.

"Er, yes," Mrs Dyson blushed. "But only on a few occasions. My husband didn't like me seeing him, er, Mr Peace, that is."

"And did your husband, Mr Arthur Dyson, attack my client, Mr Peace on any occasion?"

"Oh, no, sir. It was him over there that did the attacking." And Mrs Dyson pointed at Peace.

Other witnesses were brought in, including a Mr Brassington. He said that he had seen Peace on the night Mr Dyson had been shot and that the defendant had told him that he would shoot 'those strange folks before morning'.

"Are you sure you were talking to my client?" Mr Lockward asked. "After all, you said that you didn't know him and that this meeting was at night, in the dark."

"I know that, sir, but there was a full moon that night and besides, he, Mr Peace, told me what he said he'd do while we was standing under gas lamp. On that I will swear to."

Later forensic evidence proved that the rifling of the bullet removed from Arthur Dyson's head matched the rifling of the revolver confiscated by the police from Peace.

At the end of the day, at seven o'clock that evening, Mr Justice Lopes summed up what he had heard for the benefit of the jury. "Members of the jury," he began, "during your deliberations, I want you to take the revolver that has been mentioned and see if you are able to accidentally discharge it – as the defendant claimed is what happened. In addition," the judge continued, "consider whether Mr Lockward was justified in trying to discredit Mrs Katherine Dyson's evidence regarding her friendship with Mr Charles Peace. However, please note, this case relies on more than that. As for the threats made by Mr Peace two-and-a- half-years-ago in July 1876 against Mr Dyson, please take into account that they have been corroborated by three other witnesses, witnesses you have heard here in this courtroom today. In fact, in my opinion, there was no scuffle that night between Mr Arthur Dyson and Mr Charles Frederick Peace. And hearing all of this, I charge you to do your duty to the community at large and also by the oath you have sworn."

The various representatives of the law and the public were not to wait long to hear the verdict. The jury retired and returned to the jury box ten minutes later. Their leader pronounced the verdict.

"Guilty, Your Honour."

Hearing this, Justice Lopes asked Peace, "Do you have anything to say before I pronounce sentence?"

Peace, still on his feet, looked up. "No, Your Honour," he replied quietly. "It's no use my saying anything."

"In that case, I will just say that I am passing a sentence of death and that this will be carried out at Armley Jail, Leeds, on February 25th, 1879."

Before Peace was hanged, he did manage to right one of the judicial wrongs he had caused. In a meeting with Reverend Littlewood, the vicar of Darnall, Peace confessed that in addition to killing Arthur

Dyson, he had, in August 1876, also shot Constable Cock. As a result, William Habron was exonerated, freed and paid eight hundred pounds (nearly a hundred thousand pounds today) compensation for the years he had spent in prison. Peace did however continue to claim that Katherine Dyson had been his mistress, although she strongly denied this.

Although Peace said he wanted to see Susan Grey before his execution, he gave in to his family's wishes and refrained from doing so. It was somewhat surprising that he did wish to see her as she had betrayed him with her evidence in court. Nevertheless, he sent her several forgiving and loving notes.

On the day before his execution, 25 February 1879, his closest family came to visit him. He asked them to restrain their feelings of sadness as he did not want them to disturb his own final happiness. He advised them to sell or exhibit several of his artistic works, and then they all knelt down to pray.

As his wife was leaving, Peace gave her a funeral card that he had designed himself. It said:

>*In memory*
>*Of Charles Peace*
>*Who was executed in*
>*Armley Prison*
>*Tuesday February 25th,*
>*1879. Aged 47*
>*For that I done but never*

Intended.

The following day was bitterly cold, as William Marwood, the hangman who had designed the 'long drop,' arrived at Armley Jail. Peace ate a full breakfast but complained about the bacon.

Before being hanged, he asked for a drink of water, but this was refused. As he was being escorted to the gallows, he suddenly called out to the prison chaplain:

> *'Sir, if I believed what you and the Church of God say that you believe, even if England were covered with broken glass from coast to coast, I would walk over it, if need be on hands and knees and think it worthwhile living, just to save one soul from an eternal Hell like that!'*

He was then hanged without any fuss and died immediately. He was buried in the prison grounds.

Chapter 15

Amelia Dyer: 'The Ogress of Reading' (1837-1896)

Of all of the villains and thieves, crooks and murderers described in this book, Amelia Dyer is by far the worst. While Jack Sheppard was a brilliant escape-artist and thief, and Mary 'Jenny' Diver and Elizabeth 'Moll'

Adkins stole and conned a lot of money out of gullible souls, none of them, and that includes the disreputable Burke and Hare, killed the number of people that Amelia Dyer did.

This plain-faced, often scowling woman with a penetrating gaze, lived in Victorian England (1837-1896) and started her career as a trained nurse before she went into baby-farming. During this period this was a recognised practice, where a woman would adopt and look after unwanted babies in exchange for money as a way of supporting herself.

In addition, Amelia Dyer loved literature and poetry, was a mother of her own three children and was a widow for the last twenty-seven years of her life. None of this would make you think that here was a woman who became one of the worst serial killers in English history.

After her murderous secret was revealed and her past history thoroughly investigated, it was discovered that over a thirty-year period she had probably killed up to four hundred people and that they were all babies! Not surprisingly, when she was finally caught, she was nicknamed the 'Ogress of Reading'. She never expressed any pride or regret about what she had done, and all she said before the noose was put around her neck was, "I have nothing to say."

*

"Mummy, what are you doing? I haven't done anything wrong," young Amelia asked as her mother picked up a frying-pan and looked as if she were about to hit her with it. "And please stop shouting," she pleaded. "You scare me so much when you behave like this."

"Sorry, love," the distraught woman said, shaking and putting the frying-pan into the sink. "I didn't mean to scare you. It's just that suddenly something came over me. I don't know what it was, but it won't happen again – promise. I don't know why, and I love you so much. Now let me give you a big hug and then you can go out and play with your sister, Sarah Ann. She's out in the back yard with her dollies."

Amelia walked out of the kitchen wondering why her mother kept acting so strangely. Usually she was quite loving, but recently her bouts of wild rage had become more frequent. Only a few days ago she had hit her youngest brother with a rolling pin, and they had had to take him to the doctor afterwards.

Amelia had heard that her mother's behaviour was something to do with typhus, but she did not know what typhus was exactly, or why it made her mother suddenly act up in such a wild manner. All she knew was that from time to time her mother would suffer from tremendous headaches and fevers and tell Amelia and her siblings to close the curtains as she couldn't stand the daylight streaming into the house. Sometimes, without any warning, she would be sick all over the floor, and then Amelia or one of the other children would have to clean it up. Amelia hated this smelly job and wondered why it happened. She saw that her mother's skin was covered in dark brown and red blotches which, with her scraggy looks, made her look like the wicked witch she had read about in her favourite story book.

Her father was not much help either. He, Samuel Hobley, was a shoemaker who was hardly ever home as he worked all day and sometimes all night to make sure that his wife and their five children had a roof over their heads and food in their bellies. The roof over their heads was in Pyle Marsh, a small village east of Bristol.

Amelia continued looking after her sick mother until 1848, when she died. The twelve-year-old girl then went to live with an aunt in Bristol before she was apprenticed to a corset maker.

In 1859, her father died, and her brother inherited his shoemaking business. In 1864 Amelia moved to Bristol, where she had lodgings in Trinity Street. It was at this time she married George Thomas William Dyer, a 59-year-old man over twice her age. Both of them lied to the authorities about their ages in order to make the age gap look more respectable. He said he was in his late forties and she said she was thirty-one.

It was at this point in her life that Amelia trained to be a nurse. However, she did not stay a nurse for long. Her life changed in 1869 after she met Ellen Dane, a midwife.

"Amelia, you look exhausted. What's happening to you?"

Amelia shrugged. "You know how it is, Ellen. George died recently and now I have to work all the hours of the day and night to make sure I have food and shelter. You know, nurses don't get well paid, and we are often looked down on. Y'know, it's the drunk ones who give us such a bad name." She sighed. "I know that the nurses who went with that Florence Nightingale woman to the Crimean were seen as heroes, but here in Bristol, I most certainly am not regarded as any sort of hero."

Ellen put a friendly arm on Amelia's shoulder. "Listen, my dear, I have an idea for you. Why not become a baby farmer?"

"Adopt the unwanted babies of young women – prostitutes and the like – and bring them up in my house for money?"

"Exactly. That way you'll be doing everyone a favour. You'll make more money than you are making now and those who give you their babies will be happy to pay you to be rid of them. Rich women don't want too many kids and the poor ones can't afford to keep them."

"But what about the men, or the husbands? Don't they have to pay their women?"

Ellen smiled. "Oh, Amelia, you don't know much, do you? No, the men don't have to pay their women."

"Why not? That's not fair."

"I know, but since they passed that Poor Law thirty years ago, the men don't have to pay. So – what say you?"

Amelia said it was a good idea, and soon she was taking in babies to look after together with her own three small children, Ellen, Mary and William. Sometimes if a rich woman or couple wanted to secretly give away their baby, they would pay her up to eighty pounds (nearly nine-and-a-half thousand today); poor prostitutes and the like would pay only about five pounds.

And so Amelia Dyer, the country's most famous, or rather infamous baby farmer, began her grim and soon to be murderous career. It did not take her long to see that she could save money by diluting the babies' milk with water, or by just simply by cutting down how much she fed them.

Some of the toddlers, especially the noisy ones, would be given 'Godfrey's Cordial', a syrup containing opium which became known as 'Mother's Friend' instead of milk. When one baby died, Amelia immediately took in another. More babies meant more cash. Nobody investigated the deaths of these unfortunate infants and the cause of their demise was usually listed by the authorities as 'lack of breast milk', 'starvation', or 'debility from birth'.

Soon, Amelia was making her baby farming services known through advertisements like this in the local papers:

> *'Highly respectable woman, mother of three small children, wishes to adopt another child. Good home in Bristol. Premium required – very small. Apply to…'*

And so, Amelia Dyer continued with her new baby farming career. She quickly realised that she was supplying a service which met a necessary demand, and that as soon as a baby died, whether at first from natural causes, or later from deliberate malnutrition or strangulation, there would be another to take its place. The money flowed in and no questions were asked. However, if anyone did enquire, a sympathetic look of sadness from the respectable Mrs Dyer and a muttered, "Well, you know how it is. These little mites often succumb. Especially those from poor houses. There's not much you can do about it, is there?" would get her out of a potentially awkward situation.

But one day someone did ask a few pointed questions. In 1879, when she had been running her baby farm for ten years, a local doctor who had been asked to sign the death certificates in connection with Amelia Dyer's dead babies became very suspicious. He realised that he was signing too many. He contacted the local police and the baby farmer was arrested. Although she claimed that her wee charges had died naturally through illness, she was accused of criminal neglect.

"By rights I should charge you with murder or manslaughter," the judge decreed, "but I am going to sentence you to six months' hard labour. And that is for neglect."

These six months and the harsh conditions nearly broke Amelia, but she survived and, on her release, resumed her former nursing career. This was equally hard on her and as a result she spent some time recovering in mental hospitals. There, using her past experience as a nurse, she 'worked the system' and succeeded in obtaining opium-based drugs and alcohol.

After her release, she took in the illegitimate child of a lady to look after. One day the lady came to see her baby and became suspicious of Amelia.

"Mrs Dyer," she said, hands on her hips, "I've just looked at my baby, at least the child you say is mine, and I cannot find the birthmark which is on one of its hips. How do you account for this?"

Amelia could not and two officials came to see her. To escape from her predicament, for after all, she had already been accused and convicted of criminal negligence against babies in the past, she feigned a breakdown and swallowed two bottles of laudanum – an opium-based medicine – and so managed to wriggle out of this latest accusation.

However, none of this stopped her from going back to her baby farming days. It was easy money and there were always unwanted babies to be looked after. But now she operated in a different way – instead of involving doctors and the law with the disposal of the dead babies, she got rid of them herself. Taking care to escape the attention of the authorities, she moved house and changed her name. In 1895, during her last year in operation, Amelia Dyer was living in Caversham, Berkshire before moving to her final address in Reading, some two miles to the south. There she recruited Jane 'Granny' Smith to help her. This woman being older than Amelia, was called 'Mother' in front of the mothers who gave their unwanted babies to Amelia. It was all an outward show of 'mother-daughter' respectability.

30 March 1896 was the day that Amelia Dyer's murderous career began to unravel. A bargeman found a package floating in the river Thames near Reading and opened it. To his horror he found the body of a baby, Helena Fry, inside. He took the body to the local police station, where the police examined it and the package very carefully.

Despite the fact that the package had been submersed in the Thames for some time, the police were able to make out the name Mrs Thomas – Amelia's married name - on the outside. They were also able to decipher an address from Bristol which they discovered to be their suspect's former address.

From this evidence, the police began checking into Amelia Dyer, and from reading between the lines of her testimony, together with other people's evidence, Detective Constable Anderson and a Sergeant James decided to trap the ex-Bristol, now Reading, baby farmer. They asked a young woman to act as a decoy by presenting herself as a potential future client for Amelia. The new customer would arrange a meeting to discuss the details of handing over her unwanted baby to Mrs Dyer.

Four days after the package containing the baby girl was found in the Thames, the police raided Amelia's house. It was Good Friday 1896. It may have been a good Friday for the future of the nation's unwanted babies, but it certainly was not for Amelia Dyer. The police were shocked by the stench in the house, and although they did not find any bodies, they did discover much useful evidence. This included pawn tickets for children's clothes, advertisements and telegram receipts from women asking about their babies, as well as the white edging tape similar to that which had been used on the package fished out of the Thames. As a result, Amelia Dyer, now going under the name of Mrs Thomas, was arrested and charged with murder.

The police had just got to her in time. Among other items, they discovered that the baby farmer was making plans to leave Reading in order to set up shop in Somerset. Unfortunately for Amelia, the police did not stop there. They arrested her son-in-law, Alfred Palmer, as an accomplice, and they also began dredging the rivers Thames and Kennett as well as local ponds. They found six more bodies, weighted down with bricks, and on completing their investigation, they discovered that each of these babies had been strangled to death with white tape. While carrying out their investigation the police, going through some extremely gruesome files and statistics, estimated that the squat baby farmer they had arrested had murdered over four hundred hapless infants.

Later, Alfred Palmer and Amelia's daughter, Mary Ann, were released from police custody as there was no evidence that they had been involved in this gruesome business. As Amelia wrote two weeks after her arrest:

> *'...but I do feel it is an awful thing drawing innocent people into trouble. I do know that I shall have to answer before my Maker in Heaven for the awful crimes I have committed. But as God Almighty is my judge in Heaven and on earth, neither my daughter, Mary Ann Palmer, nor her husband, Alfred Ernest Palmer, I do most solemnly declare neither of them had anything at all to do with it. They never knew I*

contemplated doing such a wicked thing until it was too late. I am speaking the truth and nothing but the truth as I hope to be forgiven. I myself and I alone must stand before my Maker in Heaven to give an answer for it all.'
(Spelling and punctuation corrected)

Amelia Dyer was taken to the Old Bailey and charged with the murder of at least one baby and possibly more on 22 May 1896. She pleaded insanity and supported this claim by referring to her previous commitments to various mental asylums. None of this helped her case and it took the jury less than five minutes to find her guilty.

Between the time of her trial and execution she filled five notebooks with her final confession. She was hanged at Newgate Prison on Wednesday 10 June 1896 after eventually pleading guilty. Her final words were, "I have nothing to say."

A ballad soon appeared about the 'Ogress from Reading':

The old baby farmer, the wretched Miss Dyer
At the Old Bailey her wages is paid.
In times long ago, we'd 'a' made a big fy-er

> *And roasted so nicely that wicked old jade.*

Another more serious result of this sensational case was that the laws concerning adoption were revised and were more strictly reinforced. Local authorities were given the right to examine baby farms, but the wicked inhuman side of this business did not immediately cease as a result. A Mrs Stewart was arrested two years later for having dumped a baby on a train. Mrs Stewart said that a widow, Jane Hill had given her the baby to look after for twelve pounds. During the investigation it was claimed that Mrs Stewart was Polly, the daughter of Amelia Dyer!

Chapter 16

Adam Worth: 'The Napoleon of the Criminal World'
(1844-1902)

What do Kitty Flynn, an Irish barmaid, the Pinkerton Detective Agency, Georgiana Cavendish, Duchess of Devonshire and Sherlock Holmes have in common? The

answer is they are all part of the Adam Worth story – the story of an international criminal.

Of all the villains mentioned in this book, Worth was probably the most international. He was born in Germany and operated in New York and Portsmouth, London and Liverpool, Paris and Istanbul, Cape Town and Liège. At the end of his long and often very successful career, this dapper and bearded criminal, who among his many activities had served in the American army, stolen a famous painting and run a Parisian brothel, ended his days in a North London cemetery. Another reason why Adam Worth should be included in this book is that Sir Arthur Conan Doyle (among other writers) used this usually successful and non-violent criminal Worth as a model for James Moriarty - the underworld mastermind who caused so many problems for Sherlock Holmes.

*

"What's your name, kid?" the tall official from the Massachusetts Board of Education asked the small scruffy boy.

"Adam, sir."

"Adam, what?"

"Adam Worth or Wirtz, sir."

"What d'you mean, Worth or Wirtz? Which is it to be?"

"*Ich*, er, I don't know, sir. I've heard, er, *meine Eltern*, my parents, use both."

"Well, in that case it will be Worth from now on. And what's with the funny accent? Weren't you born here? Are you one of those immigrants?"

"No, sir. I wasn't born here. I was born in Germany. I came here when I was *fünf*, er, five, sir."

"Right, so will you start in Miss Bacon's class and make sure you will be a worthy pupil. Get it? Worthy pupil, Adam Worth?" And the official half-smiled at his own weak joke as he sent the small boy on his way.

But Adam Worth did not grow up to be a worthy pupil. He did not like school, and he did not like living with his poor parents in Cambridge, Massachusetts. His father was a tailor and life in the small town of fifteen thousand residents was boring. One day in 1854 when he was ten years old, he ran away to Boston. Somehow, he survived there for five years, living off of his wits and learning how to cope on his own. However, Boston was not enough for him and so six years later he moved to New York, an exciting city with a population of over one million.

Here he worked as a clerk in a department store, though he only lasted for a month – serving picky customers in a department store was not his definition of an exciting life – and it was to be the only time in his life that he had an honest job. In any case, his move to New York had not improved his financial situation.

Shop work was poorly paid, and it was the American Civil War that saved him from both boredom and low pay.

Although he was underage, he told the Union army recruiting officer that he was old enough to serve. He signed up and received $1000 bounty ($28,000 today). As an intelligent soldier and artilleryman in his New York regiment he was soon promoted first to corporal and then to sergeant. At last he had found some adventure and purpose to his life. He was made responsible for a cannon and he led his men in several attacks upon the Confederate forces.

This all came to an end in 1862. On 28 August, Confederate General 'Stonewall' Jackson led his troops against the Union army at the Second battle of Bull Run, where Worth was injured by shrapnel. He was shipped from the battlefield to Georgetown Hospital near Washington D.C. One day while lying in bed he overheard that he had been reported as killed in action. He took that as his signal for him to leave the hospital – and perhaps the army as well.

"Joe," he whispered one night to the soldier in the bed next to his. "Did you hear? They listed me as killed in action."

"So that means you can go home, no? No-one will be looking for you."

"Yes, I thought of that," Worth said, "but I've got a better idea. The Union's not doing well at the moment and men are deserting in droves. How about I change my name – I mean I'm officially dead now – and re-enlist under a new name."

"Why do you want to do that for? You might get killed this time."

"So that I'll get another bounty. I could easily use another thousand dollars."

And that is what he did. For the next two years, Worth became a 'bounty jumper' – a soldier who enlisted in a new regiment, fought and collected his bounty before deserting again to re-enlist in yet another regiment and receive another bounty.

In 1863, the Union passed the draft laws which put a stop to Worth's bounty jumping career. He left the army and returned to New York. At first, he worked on his own as a pickpocket, but later he organised and led his own gang of pickpockets. All went well for a while until he was caught and arrested while trying the steal the cash box of an Adams Express stagecoach, for which he was sentenced to three years in Sing Sing prison. If he thought that life in the slums of Boston and New York, or even in the Union army, was tough, he was soon to learn how hard life could really be.

The prison had been in operation for nearly forty years when Worth began his sentence. Prison Governor Lynds believed in running this correctional facility in a puritanical way. The criminal's rehabilitation could best be brought about, so he thought, through hard work in a completely silent atmosphere. The prisoners were not allowed to communicate with each other, whistle, dance, run or jump.

Nothing was allowed to 'disturb the harmony' of this grim institution. Convicts were issued with a Bible and rationed to two eggs per year. They were not allowed to receive visitors and any infraction was instantly punished by whipping and solitary confinement. Some of the inmates worked in the local marble quarries in ten-hour shifts, the marble being used for civic and church buildings. Those who did not work in the quarries produced household goods and boots.

Adam Worth was assigned to the quarries. His job was to warm up the cold explosive chemicals needed to blast the marble. Of this period of his life he said later, "I never questioned the guard and I always wondered why he left when I put the brittle chunks [of frozen nitro-glycerine] in the stove. When one of the older inmates told me I could be blown to bits, I decided I'd had enough of prison."

One day during a changeover of the guards, he managed to escape, hiding out on a tugboat in a nearby dock. He returned to New York, and to make himself unrecognisable, grew a pair of prominent mutton chops and a large moustache. It was this iconic image of him that was to appear in many books about him in the future. Meanwhile he changed his name from Adam Worth to Henry Judson Raymond, the same as the founder of the *New York Times* and a man who he happened to resemble.

He also decided to change his *modus operandi*. He moved from operating as a freelancer and began to work for Fredericka 'Marm' Mandelbaum, one of the city's most well-known dealers in stolen goods. It was during this period that Worth exploited his new-found knowledge of explosives, using them to break into a safe and net $30,000. Another benefit from working for Fredericka Mandelbaum was that she introduced Worth to Max 'The Baron' Shinburn, who worked with Worth to spring another robber, 'Piano' Charles Bullard, out of the White Plains jail.

This last-mentioned criminal had been born to wealth but had squandered his inheritance and, as a result, had tried to become rich again through criminal means. He had partly succeeded in doing so by bribing a Hudson River Railroad Express guard to pretend he had knocked him out so that he could then steal $100,000. Unfortunately for Bullard, the guard's injuries were considered too light for the authorities to be convinced they were genuine, and after being questioned he admitted that Bullard had conned everyone. Bullard was then arrested and held in custody pending his trial. Fortunately for him, Marm Mandelbaum was his friend. She got Shinburn and Worth to dig a tunnel under the jailhouse walls, bribe a few guards and rescue the man.

This was the beginning of a beautiful friendship. Although Worth and Shinburn became bitter rivals, each trying to outdo each other, Worth and Bullard became good friends and partners in crime.

"Charlie," Worth said to his friend one day over a meal. "I think the time has come for us to make some more money."

Bullard nodded in agreement. "Yes, but how, and where?"

"Well, banks are the best source for money, aren't they? I suggest that we rob the Boylston National Bank in Boston. It's not so far from here."

"Any ideas how?"

Worth took out a piece of paper which included a sketch-map of the bank and its surroundings. "What I suggest is this," he continued. "We buy up the shop next door to the bank and then break in through the side wall."

"That's a good idea, Adam, but people are always coming into a shop. You can't be digging holes when people are watching."

"That's true. But if the shop sells things that people don't often buy or we hang up a notice saying closed for family illness, then that shouldn't be a problem."

And that is what they did. The set up a fake health-tonic shop next door to the bank, dug their hole and one night soon after broke in. Again exploiting his knowledge of explosives, Adam blew off the door of the bank's strong room and the pair of them escaped with over $450,000 ($8,240,000 today).

Suspecting that the bank would employ the Pinkerton Detective Agency – the agency who had caught Bullard a year earlier, Worth and Bullard - now 'Henry Judson Raymond' and 'Charles H. Wells' – fled America for Europe.

Their first port of call was Liverpool, and this is where Kitty Flynn entered the story. She was a barmaid in the city and both men fell in love with her. Eventually she married Bullard but Worth did not hold a grudge about this. While the newly married couple went away for their honeymoon, Worth, perhaps because he could not let an opportunity slip through his fingers, robbed a few pawnshops and then shared the loot with the other two. Soon after this, in 1871, all three moved to Paris, where they continued their criminal ways.

They bought an old three-storey building near the Paris Opera House and turned it into an 'American Bar'. The restaurant and bar were on the ground floor, and there was a gambling den on an upper floor. Since gambling was illegal, the gaming tables were so designed that they could easily be hidden if the police ever raided the place.

This business flourished for two years, until Worth suspected that the Pinkerton Agency were onto them, so they decided to close the operation. However, on the last night they robbed one of their customers, a jewellery salesman, of a bag of diamonds worth several thousand dollars. In accordance to Worth's usual way of operating, this was done quietly without resorting to any violence.

Paris had now become too 'hot' for them and so the three of them fenced off all their stolen jewels and moved to London to try their luck there. Here, the Bullards bought the Western Lodge, a Georgian mansion house in Clapham Common, while Worth rented a flat in fashionable Mayfair. From here Worth, still calling himself Henry J. Raymond, became the *eminence grise* – the hidden mastermind of a vast criminal syndicate. He ran this empire of larceny and swindling, safecracking and robbery through several trusted intermediaries, none of them knowing the identity of the man at the top. What was common to all these activities was that the use of violence was forbidden.

However, despite his successes, all did not go well. His long-time partnership with Bullard began to unravel as the latter, as a consequence of an increasing dependence on alcohol, became evermore violent. This was too much for Kitty, who took her two daughters and moved to the United States.

At the same time Worth's brother, John, who had been working with Worth for a while, was sent to cash a forged cheque in Paris. However, he used a bank Worth had told him not to use. He was caught, arrested and extradited to England. The detective responsible for bringing John Worth to justice was John Shore. This persistent man was to prove a problem for Adam

Worth's future career. Fortunately for John Worth, his big brother was able to supply him with a good lawyer, who succeeded in getting him off the hook. John then left England and sailed to the United States.

Another problem that arose during this period was that four of Worth's most trusted men were arrested in Istanbul. They had happily been using forged credit notes all over Europe, a trail of crimes which now had come to light. Like John Worth, they were arrested and convicted, and then sentenced to seven years hard labour. Again, Worth proved himself to be a loyal employer – he bribed the relevant officials and had the men released before the Pinkerton Agency could have them extradited to America.

While all this was going on Worth himself was not just sitting behind a desk pulling the strings. He also took a hand in several heists. To recoup some of the money he had lost in Istanbul he went with several of his men to South Africa. There, in Cape Town Worth and his partner, Charley King, set out to rob a horse-drawn wagon carrying a load of uncut diamonds. Unfortunately for Worth, the guards fought back, and King fled the scene.

Worth was determined to try again, but this time he used a new tactic. He pretended he was a feather merchant and became very friendly with the local postmaster at whose post-office the diamonds were to be stored if they missed the ship to England.

Worth managed to forge a key to the post office, and when the next shipment was due to be sent to England, he robbed the transport ferry and ended up with half-a-million dollars' worth of diamonds. He took them back to London and, through a new fence called Ned Wynert, opened a shop where he sold off his loot at bargain prices.

It was also during this period, in 1876, that Worth pulled off one of his most spectacular robberies, stealing Thomas Gainsborough's famous portrait of Georgina Cavendish, Duchess of Devonshire.

"Listen, you two," Worth said to Jack 'Junka' Phillips and 'Little Joe' Eliot one night. "We're going to try something new."

"What? Like giving all of our money to the poor, like it says in the Bible?" Eliot asked.

"No," Worth replied. "We're going to steal a painting – a famous portrait of Lady Georgina Cavendish by Thomas Gainsborough."

"How much is it worth?" the two crooks asked.

"Well, it recently sold for $50,000."

"What, fifty thou just for a painting?"

Worth nodded and continued. "It's in Thomas Agnew's gallery in Bond Street and this is what we're going to do. We'll visit the gallery, cut it out of its frame where it's on display before we leave and then sell it again in a few months' time after all the noise has died down. That way we should be able to come away with a goodly profit."

The accomplices agreed as they knew Worth was almost always successful and that they would get a good cut from the sale. The robbery went according to plan and soon afterwards Adam Worth was the proud owner of Gainsborough's masterpiece.

But then there was a problem. Worth really liked the paining and decided not to sell it. Phillips and Eliot were not pleased with this at all; they became impatient, wanting their percentage. In fact, Phillips became so angry that one evening he set up a situation that he and an undercover policeman who Worth did not know began talking about the portrait with Worth in a bar. Somehow, possibly through his past experience or his well-honed instincts, Worth caught on to what his henchman was doing and promptly stopped the conversation by tipping the table over onto Phillips.

Seeing that Eliot was also impatient, Worth bought him off. He bought him a ticket to America, where he was later arrested for robbing the Union Trust Company.

While Eliot was in prison, he thought he would curry favour with the Pinkerton Agency by telling them about Worth's art theft. They in turn informed Scotland Yard. However, since Eliot could not tell where the painting was hidden there was nothing that the Yard could do. In fact, the painting was kept in a specially designed case which Worth used when he was travelling, or lay beneath his mattress between two boards when he was sleeping at home.

It was also during this period that Worth, now almost forty, married Louise Margaret Boljahn. The couple had two children, Harry and Constance, but it is not known if the new Mrs Worth knew about her husband's criminal activities.

In 1892 Worth heard that his past accomplices, Bullard and Shinburn, were in jail in Liège, Belgium. They had been working together, and then caught, arrested and imprisoned by the Belgian police. However, before Worth could do anything to save Bullard, the latter died. Never one to waste an opportunity, while in Belgium Worth took on two new partners, including a small-time Dutch crook, Alonzo Henne, and an American bank-robber, Johnny Curtin. Neither of these two was very professional. They tried to rob a money delivery cart in Liège but of the three of them, it was Worth who was caught.

He refused to identify himself, but the Belgian police learned the truth through their contacts with Scotland Yard and the New York Police Department. In addition, Shinburn, who held a long-time grudge against Worth, also informed the Belgian police what he knew.

Worth was tried on 20 March 1893 and although he denied all the charges against him, he was sentenced to seven years to be served in Leuven prison. While incarcerated, although he never heard from his family he did, surprisingly, receive a letter from Kitty Flynn. She sent him some money and also offered to pay his defence costs.

This term in prison may have been the worst period of Worth's life. Shinburn paid other prisoners to beat him up, while Johnny Curtin, who Worth had asked to look after his wife, seduced and raped her. She had a nervous breakdown and was committed to an asylum. Their children were sent to America where Worth's brother, John, cared for them. In addition, Kitty meanwhile died. The only positive aspect of this grim period was that Worth was released from prison three years early for good behaviour.

He returned to England and went to visit his wife in the asylum. It was a disastrous meeting as she hardly recognised or reacted to him. He decided to visit his children in America and one story says that he robbed a diamond store to finance the journey.

While there, Worth arranged a meeting with his old enemy, the Pinkerton Detective Agency.

"Ah, I see they let you out," William Pinkerton said.

"Yeah, and what are you planning to do here in the States?" his younger brother, Robert asked.

"Nothing," Worth replied quietly. "I've come to make a deal with you."

"A deal," William scoffed. "Pinkertons don't make deals with bank robbers. We put them away."

"Well, you won't put me away after you hear what I have to say," Worth replied. "So pour me a bourbon and I'll tell you what I have in mind."

The result of this meeting was that Worth returned the portrait of the Duchess of Devonshire back to Thomas Agnew and Sons. The exchange happened in Chicago, where the ageing criminal received $25,000 ($700,000 today), before returning to England with his children.

Unlike many of the villains who appear in this book, Adam Worth died of natural causes, passing away on 8 January 1902 aged 58. He was buried in Highgate Cemetery, north London, his grave being not too far from that of Karl Marx – another individual who had worked hard on how to redistribute the world's wealth.

Worth's gravestone reads:

ADAM WORTH
a.k.a Henry J. Raymond
"The Napoleon of Crime"
b. 1844 – d.1902

It was Robert Anderson, the Assistant Commissioner of the Metropolitan Police who gave Adam Worth the epithet, 'The Napoleon of Crime'. However, the final irony of Adam Worth's life is that his son, Harry, went on to become a detective working for the Pinkerton Agency.

It has been suggested that the story of Adam Worth was used by the writer Sir Arthur Conan Doyle as the basis for Sherlock Holmes' arch enemy, Professor Moriarty. However, several other English villains, including the Victorian barrister and forger, James Townsend Saward, also have the dubious honour of being a possible inspiration for the fictional criminal mastermind.

And as for the painting of the Duchess of Devonshire, after Worth handed it over, the American financier, J. P. Morgan bought it for $150,000. It remained with his family until 1994 when it was auctioned off by Sotheby's and bought by the eleventh Duke of Devonshire. He paid $408,870 to ensure that after 118 years the painting of his beautiful ancestor returned to Chatsworth House, his country estate in rural Derbyshire.

Chapter 17

The Forty Elephants

In all the other chapters of this book, the focus has been on a particular villain: male, female, thief, pickpocket, highwayman or imposter. In this final chapter, I will use a different approach. I will look not at a specific individual, but rather at a gang of villains as a whole. And this was not just any gang. It was a very well organised gang of shoplifters and pickpockets which consisted of allegedly high-class women only!

Therefore, the 'Forty Elephants' gang is the 'star' of this chapter, and not just its charismatic leaders who organised their long-lasting and successful criminal exploits.

Picking pockets and stealing from shops and markets are some of the oldest crimes in the game. It may be said that of all of the thousands of male pickpockets who ever lived, only a select few ever achieved any sort of fame, such as the Elizabethan, 'Cutting' Ball and the 18th century 'Gentleman' George Barrington and James Filewood, alias 'Vilet'. However, picking pockets was not a crime for men only. Several women, a few of them appearing earlier in this book, also achieved a dubious sort of fame. They included: Mary Frith, alias Moll Cutpurse, Moll King and Maria Carleton. Sarah Bibby, a female style Fagin, as well as Mary Morgan and Sarah McCabe also succeeded in making a name for themselves. Indeed, this last-named villain even used four aliases, worked with two or three others and had a twenty-five year 'professional' career.

However, what these all these men and women did, either as individuals or in small groups, pales in comparison, both in terms of the number of people involved and the duration of their activities, when considered against the criminal actions of 'The Forty Elephants' gang.

Everyone knows the story of Ali Baba and the Forty Thieves. *Far fewer people know the story of 'Diamond Annie and the Forty Elephants'. Those who would have known were probably shop-owners, policemen and judges, especially if they lived between the 1850s and the 1950s. This gang of thieves operated mainly in London and existed for about one hundred years (some historians say even longer), stole many thousands of pounds worth of goods from shops and ran their own reign of terror. The gang's exploits only came to an end when women's fashions changed, shops and department stores learned to improve their security systems and many of the leading members had been imprisoned or had moved out to the suburbs.*

Perhaps the most fascinating fact about the 'Forty Elephants' is that this was a female-only gang. It was run by women for women and all the gang's beneficiaries were women.

*

The name of the gang, 'The Forty Elephants' was in fact an inside joke made by the gang about themselves. One of the places where they operated, especially from the mid-19th century, was around the Elephant and Castle area in south London, where one of the important male-run gangs terrorising this area was called the Elephant and Castle Mob. They were also known as the Elephant Boys or just simply, the Elephants. In order to show that the women's gang was on par with their male counterparts, the women adopted the men's gang-name. The first time the gang was mentioned in the press was in 1873, but some historians claim that an all-female gang like this had existed since the 1700s.

These 'Hoodlums in Bloomers', as the *Daily Mail* called them, ran a very sophisticated organisation. One of their favourite shoplifting methods was for a whole group of gang members to swarm into a jeweller's shop and surround the counter. They would then all ask questions at the same time about the price and quality of certain items, for example, a brooch or necklace. In this way they would cause the poor shop assistant to become completely muddled up and confused. In the confusion, one or more of the gang would then slip a piece of jewellery into their large pockets and then the whole gang, like a flock of locusts, would move on and disappear.

Another technique they used was called 'the ringer'. One of the gang would enter a shop and ask to see an expensive piece of jewellery. In the meanwhile, they would have made a cheap copy of the item, and in the resulting discussion with the shop assistant, the expensive item would be switched for the cheap copy.

Perhaps a more brazen technique the Forty Elephants used was a method called 'the decoy'. In the same way the later Mafia leaders were not shy about showing themselves in public, this female gang would also deliberately show off their infamous leaders, who they called 'queens' in public. The queen would enter a shop or department store that knew of her reputation and deliberately cause the assistants and other staff to keep an eye on her. While they were being so distracted, another member or two of the gang would be busy shoplifting elsewhere in the store without being noticed.

"What have you got there?" Jennie asked Susan when they were half-a-mile away from the big store on St. George's Road. "Anything good?"

"Well, look at this bracelet," Susan replied as she delved into her specially made deep pocket and pulled out a sparkling piece of jewellery. "Just look at those little diamonds. See how they catch the sun."

Jenny inspected the silver bracelet set with diamonds and emeralds. "It must be worth a fortune," she said, "I'm glad you weren't caught lifting it."

"Yes, so am I. And yes, I also pinched this string of pearls while I was at it. Here, look. They're beautiful, and they'll go well with this brooch I took. What d'you think? How much d'you think it's worth?"

Susan shrugged. "I don't know. Show it to Mary when we get back and see what she says. I'm sure that she'll have a good idea."

'Mary' was Mary Carr, the first 'queen' of the Forty Elephants gang. She was born into a criminal family and very early in her criminal career became well-known for her successful light fingered activities and ability to 'fence' the goods she and others had stolen. Later she changed her name from Mary to Polly, and also used the name Molly Mayne. After spending several periods in prison and serving as the gang's first queen it is alleged that she died in 1924. She was succeeded by Anne Diamond, alias 'Diamond Annie', who was probably the gang's most well-known leader.

She was born in 1896 in Southwark, south London, the daughter of a well-known criminal. By the time she was seventeen she had been caught stealing a hat in Oxford Street. Three years later, she was running the gang with an iron fist. She used to divide the members up into groups and individuals, and then with military precision, organise their next robbery. Rules of this 'robbers' code' included: going to bed early and no partying before a raid, no drinking before a raid, and making sure that the women were able to provide an alibi for fellow 'Elephants' if they were arrested.

Annie also made smaller gangs pay her a certain percentage of what they stole, especially if they had stolen from shops which she considered to be her 'turf'. In other words, this woman ran a regular reign of terror in both the worlds of crime and commercial shopping. She was nicknamed 'Diamond Annie' both because of her real name and because of her habit of wearing several diamond rings on her fingers; rings that could be, and were, used as knuckle-dusters if necessary. Crime historian, Brian Macdonald, has written that she 'had a punch to be aware of' and that the police considered her to be 'the cleverest of thieves'.

The operations that she organised and controlled included the wholesale plundering of thousands of pounds worth of expensive clothes, jewels and furs. The women would wear large knickers and specially tailored clothes, muffs and cummerbunds that contained hidden pockets, always appearing in good clothes and giving off an air of respectability. They would demand to be allowed to try on clothes in complete privacy, and in that way could hide any stolen watch or piece of jewellery they had taken, or easily switch a pre-made cheap copy for the real thing.

As well as using the 'decoy' and 'ringer' techniques, they would sometimes fool shop assistants and managers, asking them with fine manners if they could possibly take a dress (or fur or watch) to the door of the shop so that they could see it in natural daylight. Of course this request would be granted, and while one of the gang was standing by the doorway examining the item in question, other members of the gang would be busy distracting the salesperson, leaving the would-be purchaser free to disappear with the stolen goods.

The gang members usually did not wear what they stole. They stole to make money, not to be dressed in the high fashion of the day. They got rid of their 'hot' property through a very well-organised chain of fences – pawnbrokers received the watches and jewellery, clothes were passed onto shops which would change the labels, while less expensive items were transferred to street market traders for a price.

As for the fences they worked with, they were similarly smart. One of them, Ada Macdonald from Walworth, was raided by the police in 1910. She was suspected for fencing for five different gangs, but she managed to fool the authorities by showing them ledgers of goods that she had apparently purchased legally. Another female fence who cooperated with the Forty Elephants was Jane Durrell. She managed to fool the police for a long time before she was arrested and sent down after the police found hundreds of pounds worth of stolen goods in her house.

As the gang with their cooperative fences prospered under the leadership of Queen Diamond Annie, so the 'turf' in which they operated also grew. From south London they expanded their reign of shoplifting terror to include the West End, where the pickings were even better. But success also brought problems.

"Y'know, Annie," a member of the gang said one evening as they were sorting out a pile of jewels which they planned to fence, 'I've been thinking about what we were doing in the West End this afternoon."

"What? You're not thinking of quitting, are you?"

"No, no, Annie. Of course not. No, what I was thinking was that we've become so well-known in south London and the West End, that it's becoming harder to nick stuff and…"

"So?"

"I was thinking, how about we leave London for a while and try our luck elsewhere? Say, Birmingham, or towns not too far from London where the rich knobs go."

"Like Brighton or Cheltenham?"

"Yes, that's it. We can go by train in the morning, do our bit and then come back on the afternoon or evening train. All in a day's work. No staying overnight, no hanging about, no hotels. Just a quick in and out."

And that is what they did. A group of them would arrive at a certain destination – a party of respectable ladies carrying their posh bags and suitcases. They would drop these off at the station's left luggage office and then later fill them up with the goods that they had stolen during the day. After all, it was far more comfortable to sit in the carriage when all of their 'shopping' was stashed away in their suitcases and not in their specially designed capacious knickers.

Sometimes they used fast cars as an alternative to trains. However, there was the possibility that doing so would arouse suspicion as this was a period when few women drove – especially sporty, fast cars.

Another problem was that, due to the scope of their activities, every so often one or more of the women was caught red-handed. When this happened and the 'Elephant' in question was brought to the court for her trial, she would usually turn on the sex appeal and hope that she could charm her way out of prison or a hefty fine.

When it was Alice Turner's turn to face the magistrate because she was found with a 'hot' fur coat in her possession, she burst out into tears, saying, "I don't know what made me do it." This plea seemed to work until the officer of the law heard about twenty-five other stolen items that were also found in her bag. Her tears failed to melt the judge's stubborn heart and she was sentenced to three months in prison.

Annie also introduced another aspect of robbery into the gang's list of crimes.

"Now, ladies, I want to start varying our activities," she told several of the leading members one day. "We have become so good at nicking stuff that many of the big shops are becoming very suspicious. So I suggest we try something new."

"What, like returning the stuff for money?" a well-dressed young lady asked.

"No, Peggy, we are going to start cleaning houses."

"D'you mean cleaning them out of their silver and cash and stuff?" the same Peggy asked.

"Yes and no," Annie smiled. "On the one hand, if you see something worthwhile pinching, don't waste the opportunity, but if you can't pinch it, then tell another one of us and she'll arrange to pinch it instead. That's one new idea. Now here's another. I want the best-looking ones of you to not only try and pinch stuff from these posh houses, but also to seduce the husbands there."

"Why, what will that give us apart from a nice time?" a buxom lass from north London asked as she thrust out her chest.

"Money," Annie replied. "And without the risk of the police interfering."

"How?"

"Because after you have seduced Mr So-and-so, you'll be able to blackmail him into not telling his wife."

"Yes, and perhaps paying you for services rendered as well," another woman smiled.

"And if he doesn't want to pay up?" another young woman asked.

"Then you tell him that you'll tell his missus," Annie smiled, clicking her fingers. "It'll be as easy as that. I guarantee you, he'll pay quietly as he won't want his wife to know…"

"And as you've just said, the police won't be involved."

Another member of the gang who fell foul of the law was Maggie Hughes. Because she was less than five-feet tall, she was called 'Baby-face' by the gang. In contrast, Annie was nearly six-foot. Despite Maggie being known as a clever and experienced thief, she was caught committing one of the most basic mistakes in the world of shoplifting. One day in 1923 she stole a tray of thirty-four diamond rings. While she was running out of the store, she ran straight into the arms of a policeman, who promptly arrested her.

Two years later, two other women in the gang, Maria Jackson and Bertha Teppenden, came unstuck when they were caught for inciting a riot against a former member of the gang. This took place at the

Canterbury Arms pub in Waterloo, south London. Both women had drunk too much and had begun to insult each other. Words led to blows and Jackson attacked Teppenden with a broken wineglass. It was at this point that Jackson's father, Bill Britten, hit Teppenden, and then all hell broke loose in the pub. Everyone, male and female, joined in and the brawl only came to an end when Britten dragged his daughter outside.

However, that was not the end of the story. Later that night, at least a dozen inebriated drinkers made their way to Lambeth in order to beat up Bill Britten. This mob was led by Diamond Annie. When she knocked on Britten's door, she was greeted with a jug of water poured all over her. As a result, some of Annie's mob, armed with knives and iron bars, broke down Britten's front door, swarmed into the house and smashed everything up and attacked Britten and his fifteen-year-old son. The disappointed members of the mob who found themselves left outside on the pavement had to satisfy themselves by hurling bricks and bottles through the windows instead.

The police arrived quickly and most of the people involved, both men and women, received sentences ranging from several months to five years. Diamond Alice 'went down' for eighteen months and Maggie Hughes received a five-year sentence. Perhaps because she was the leader of the gang and did not want to cause them any unwanted publicity, Annie did not make any fuss when she was convicted. Maggie was the opposite. When she heard the judge sentence her, she screamed and shouted abuse at him, which of course did not help.

By the time Annie was released, she found that her 'queenly' position had been taken over by Lillian Rose Kendall, the 'Bobbed Hair Bandit', famous for her short fringe and side-curls. She was also well-known because of her habit of using her car to smash shop windows before she robbed them. One store that suffered this dramatic treatment was the West End branch of Cartier's on Bond Street.

And as for Diamond Annie, she did not fight her usurper to become queen again. She left the gang quietly and set up a brothel in Lambeth, south London, where she taught future shoplifters how to operate. She died in 1952 aged 55 after having contracted multiple sclerosis.

And so the gang grew from strength to strength as they shoplifted, seduced and robbed their way all over England. They used fast cars, trains and most of all, female cunning and the exploitation of the feeling that 'posh' ladies could not be responsible for what went missing in high-class shops.

Finally, the record reign of the 'Forty Elephants' came to a quiet end. Ironically, one of the reasons for this was the question of women's fashions in respectable society. After the First World War, women's high-class fashion changed dramatically. Gone were the voluminous skirts and dresses, puffy leg-o-mutton sleeves and large coats and capes of the turn of the century. Instead, the affluent post-war woman wore looser and straighter clothes that needed much less material. This meant that there were fewer places for hidden pockets and all the other ways of concealing stolen goods that the 'Elephants' had used in the past. In addition, the fashion and jewellery shops had finally learned from past experience and now had improved their security systems.

In the end, the passing of time was also a relevant factor. First of all, after thousands of women had worked in munitions factories and as agricultural labourers on farms, or driven ambulances and acted as nurses on the Western Front, attitudes towards women had changed. Women had proved themselves capable of doing most anything a man could do, so just because you looked like a respectable lady did not mean that you were now above suspicion if something went missing in a shop. Also, many of the members of the gang 'retired' and moved over to the life of middle-class respectability.

And so, the 'Forty Elephants', the longest surviving gang of villains and thieves, disappeared. Perhaps because they were women, they never achieved the infamous reputation of other gangs, but in many ways they succeeded in stealing and fencing much more successfully, and certainly less violently, than the all-male gangs working in the Elephant and Castle area of south London.

About the Author

D. Lawrence-Young was an English teacher and lecturer in schools and universities for over forty years until he retired in 2013. He is happiest when he is researching Shakespeare, English and military history or quirky aspects of British social history. In addition to rewriting *Communicating in English,* a best-selling textbook, he has written one crime and twenty historical novels which have been published in the UK, USA and Israel.

He has been a frequent contributor to *Forum,* a magazine for English language teachers and also to *Skirmish,* a military history journal. He is a member of the local historical club and from 2008-2014 was the Chairman of the Jerusalem Shakespeare Club. He is also a published (USA) and exhibited photographer (UK & Jerusalem). He loves travelling, plays the clarinet (badly) and is married and has two children.

Bibliography

1811 Dictionary of the Vulgar Tongue, Macmillan Publishers, London, 1981.

Wilbur Cortez Abbott, *Colonel Thomas Blood: Crown –Stealer, 1618-1680*, Cedric Chivers Ltd., Bath, Somerset, UK, 1970.

Jake Arnott, *The Fatal Tree*, Sceptre, London, 2017.

Derek Barlow, *Dick Turpin and the Gregory Gang,* Phillimore, London & Chichester, 1973.

David Brandon, *Stand and Deliver! A History of Highway Robbery*, Sutton Publishing Ltd., Stroud, Glos., UK, 2001.

Alan Brooke & David Brandon, *Tyburn: London's Fatal Tree,* Sutton Publishing Ltd., Stroud, Glos., UK, 2004.

Alan Doherty, *The Great Crown Jewels Robbery of 1303: The Extraordinary Story of the First Big Bank Robbery in History*, Constable, London, 2005.

Owen Dudley Edwards, *The True Story of the Infamous Burke & Hare*, Birlinn Ltd., Edinburgh, 2014.

Antonia Fraser, *King Charles II*, Weidenfeld & Nicolson, London, 1979.

David C. Hanrahan, *Colonel Blood: The Man who Stole the Crown Jewels*, Sutton Publishing Ltd., Stroud, Glos., UK, 2003.

Alan Haynes, *Sex in Elizabethan England*, Sutton Publishing Ltd., Stroud, Glos., UK, 2006.

Charlotte Hodgman (ed.) *The Story of Crime & Punishment*, BBC History Magazine Publications, 2018.

David Hutchinson, *Deacon Brodie: A Double Life*, CreateSpace Independent Publishing, USA, 2015.

Robert Hutchinson, *The Audacious Crimes of Colonel Blood,* Weidenfeld & Nicolson, London, 2015.

Brian McDonald, *Alice Diamond and the Forty Elephants: Britain's First Female Crime Syndicate,* Milo Books, Wrea Green, Lancs., UK, 2015.

James McDonald, *A Dictionary of Obscenity, Taboo and Euphemism*, Sphere Books Ltd., London, 1988.

Ben Macintyre, *The Napoleon of Crime: The Life and Times of Adam Worth – The Real Moriarty*, Harper Press, London, 2012.

Philip Rawlings, *Drunks, Whores and Idle Apprentices: Criminal Biographies of the Eighteenth Century*, Routledge, London, 1992.

James Sharpe, *The Myth of the English Highwayman*, Profile Books, London, 2005.

Mihoko Suzuki, 'The Case of Mary Carleton: Representing the Female Subject, 1663-1673', *Tulsa Studies in Women's Literature*, Vol.12 No.1, University of Tulsa, USA, 1993

J. J. Tobias, *Prince of Fences: The Life and Crimes of Ikey Solomons,* Vallentine, Mitchell, London, 1974.

Janet Todd & Elizabeth Spearing, *Counterfeit Ladies: The Life and Death of Mary Frith. The Case of Mary Carleton,* New York University Press, 1995.

Alison Vale & Alison Rattle, *Amelia Dyer: Angel Maker*, Andre Deutsch, London, 2007.

Rick Wilson, *The Man Who Was Jekyll & Hyde: The Lives and Crimes of Deacon Brodie*, The History Press, London, 2015.

David L. Young, *Of Plots & Passions: A Thousand Years of Devious Deeds,* Librario Publishing, Kinloss, Moray, Scotland, 2008.

www.ingramcontent.com/pod-product-compliance
Lightning Source LLC
Chambersburg PA
CBHW071724080526
44588CB00013B/1891